MARIN'S OLD DAYS

As published in the *Marin Journal* 1922-1923

Edited by Brian K. Crawford

The Crawford Press
San Anselmo, California

Copyright 2016 by
The Crawford Press
TheCrawfordPress@gmail.com
All rights reserved
Printed in the United States of America

Introduction

The *Marin Journal*, the oldest newspaper in Marin County and the forerunner of today's *Marin Independent-Journal*, was first published on March 23, 1861 by Ai Jerome Barney (1804-1866) and his son, Jerome August Barney (1834-1876). When Ai died five years later, Jerome carried on the paper by himself. The paper remained a weekly, appearing on Thursdays.

In 1921, after several changes of ownership, the paper was purchased by E. L. Kynoch. A year later, a series began to appear called Marin's Old Days, recounting the early history of Marin County. The author chose to remain anonymous, promising to reveal his name at the conclusion of the series. With a few intervening lapses, the series continued each week for a total of fifty-eight articles. The last appeared on May 10, 1923, and ends with the usual "Continued next week", but it never did, and the author remains anonymous. Much of the early history, especially of the Indian and Mission eras, reflects the attitudes still prevalent in the days it was written – and some of it is inaccurate. Nevertheless, the series provides a fascinating insight into how Marin County viewed itself in the 1920's and the state of the knowledge of its own history.

I have added numerous footnotes with additional information on people, places, and events mentioned in the text. Notes in parentheses are in the original; those in square brackets are mine.

Brian K. Crawford
San Anselmo CA

CONTENTS

Marin's Old Days 1
The Early Indians 18
Mission Days— (Foreword) 25
The Marin Mission Period 28
Novato Township 55
The Marin Mission Period (Cont. from March 23) 60
Marin's Land Grant Days 74
Fremont in Marin 88
Early Marin Industries 96
Lumbering In Marin 102
Marin's Organization Period 106
Marin's Mining Days 117
San Rafeal Township 125
Sausalito 147
Bolinas 155
Nicasio 163
San Quentin 169
Olema 171
Point Reyes 178
Marin's Educational Development 186

Marin's Old Days

19 January 1922

(ANONYMOUS)

(Note — The writer will welcome any notes or reference on any tradition or fact omitted in the following, and comment will follow thereon.)

Out here in California we are a comparatively new commonwealth and not even yet at all conversant with the personal value of its tradition, the true significance of the romance of its early days, the pioneer struggles and sacrifices for permanence of home loving peoples, and in particular the apparent guidance of this great state from out of the hands of at least three continually warring nations of Europe. Imagine if you can, how the lives of our school boys and school girls would be quickened and their loyalty to their state and nation be everlastingly strengthened, if properly proportioned and interesting accounts of these early times could be available.

It might be a venturesome body indeed which would properly edit a straightforward history of California for public school use in view of the plain censure due on various political, religious, national and foreign practices which for centuries embroiled the West; —yet there will someday arise a writer who will present the stimulative phases of these early times in a way to meet the needs in view. But here in Marin County we have no such issues to avoid, and without any attempts to write a history of Marin's early days, we believe some general notes will afford a beginning for further material, and will make better citizens of all who may read something of Marin's Old Days.

This attempt is offered after a perusal of a list of immediately available sources thereon. While there is a fairly complete record of the basic facts of early Marin County History, yet we woefully lack any proper fund of incident, anecdote and tradition of those old days. Some such review as present plans outline may bring forth most valuable additions from some of the few old settlers still with us.

Much of that portion of early Marin County History published in 1880[1] which discusses outside historical matters is decidedly in error, perhaps because of the manner of its collection; and mainly because versions from previous writers were unwisely included as facts without checking against basic authorities thereon. In consequence our versions from any source, concerning these outside matters have been verified in many ways and finally checked against the earlier Bancroft articles and the quite recent Eldridge[2] translations from the original. At the same time we have attempted to treat them in a fairly narrative form with the hope of more directly interesting the younger readers.

There is an irreplaceable fascination and interest in checking up the oldest records available, and from time to time discovering items which promptly settle or at least record traditions and arguments of long standing. Various translators have given us widely divergent accounts of the early foreign language records and we must in all cases allow for such unintentional errors. Almost overnight, some of these versions are radically changed by a newly discovered record. For example, in 1888 the great historian, Hubert Bancroft, whose life work was a search amongst documents all over the world for the history of our Western Coast, prophesied that particularly vital accounts of General Fremont's activities in Central California would someday be found in the lost twelve chapters of the General's diary, always missing in his published memoirs. In recent months these manuscripts were found in New York City among some old books and papers, and an invaluable and long missing portion of the record of his north of the bay early days will now be forthcoming. So also, it is quite possible that in the possession of relatives of our own pioneers there are many facts and anecdotes filed away and perhaps in decaying records, which would immeasurably add to our present store and could be looked

---

[1] "History of Marin County, California: Including Its Geography, Geology, Topography and Climatography: Together with a ... Record of the Mexican Grants ... Names of ... Pioneers ... a Complete Political History ... and Biographical Sketches of Its Early ... Settlers and Representative Men: Also an Historical Sketch of the State of California, in which is Embodied the Raising of the Bear Flag", by J. P. Munro-Fraser, 1880.

[2] Zoeth Skinner Eldridge (1846-1915), a banker and amateur historian.

over for additions to present attempts. In particular there is need of further record of the pastoral period of Marin County, since as above noted, only its main historical facts are of record.

There are innumerable questions which we should like to have answered. For example, why was San Rafael's post office closed and all southern Marin mail sent to Tomales for distribution and return? Was this a part of the evidently strenuous fight for the County Seat? Just why were the Nicasio people flying the County flag on a high pole for a while, and yet San Rafael obtained the prize? Why did Northern Marin develop first and for years maintain the leadership of the County? Why does not Marin repeat the phenomenal crops which in early days astounded the entire West and were the means of attracting such earnest agriculturists from the East and South as first located here? And again, why indeed were the large and flourishing shipyards and factories, and the gold, copper, magnesite, lime, granite and other workings fairly well started and then abandoned? As our story proceeds, perhaps some of these questions may be answered by old settlers or be cleared up by submitted data. We earnestly invite the assistance of anyone interested.

Marin County is next to the smallest in area of any in the state. Yet in spite of its diminutive size in comparison, in the early days of the West it held perhaps the most important part of any other territory in Northern California if the temporary gold section excitement matters be disregarded. Since California is undeniably a child of Spain, so also the early annals of Marin are filled with Spanish names and tales of Spanish pioneers and home-seekers, and direct descendants of many of these early families still reside here.

The territory now called Marin County was first of record in 1542 when Juan Rodrigues Cabrillo[3], a Portuguese navigator under the Viceroy of New Spain, arrived on its western coast. Cabrillo was the first representative of the white race to visit California, arriving at San Diego Bay while exploring the coast for the Northwest Passage. Came a time when he proceeded north, sailing into Monterey Bay but was unable to land there on account of storms and consequent rough waters. Continuing north, he sailed for Cape Mendocino, passing the as yet undiscovered great Bay of San Francisco while far off shore in a heavy wind storm. This finally drove him in to a safe

---

[3] Portuguese name João Rodrigues Cabrilho (1499-1543).

haven and he anchored in or close to our Drake's Bay, which he called the Puerte de San Francisco. A recent historian claims that Cermenon[4] gave it this name fifty years afterward. It is claimed also that Cabrillo named the Farallone Islands in honor of his navigator, Captain Ferrelo, but the absurdity of such statement is seen in the fact that the Spanish word "farallones" means "rocky, sharp pointed islands in the middle of the sea;" and that when the Portola party arrived on the ridges back of San Francisco nearly two centuries afterward, they at once recognized these outposts of Cabrillo's Puerte de San Francisco of 1542. A map is stated to have been issued in Spain in 1545 which notes Cabrillo's new port and these islands, but it was nearly two centuries before the real San Francisco Bay was discovered and named.

While no record remains, or tradition of Cabrillo's landing existed among the coast Indians when Drake visited Marin thirty years later, it is possible that he did so; unless he arrived in a typically dense Pt. Reyes fog, the greatly attractive Drake's Bay would have assuredly caused him to further investigate. In any case every Portuguese child in Marin County and the West should know that to Portugal belongs the honors for the first navigator reaching the western coast, though to Spain belongs the credit of the expedition.

Though as previously noted, a Spanish map was issued within three years of Cabrillo's visit, a period of nearly two hundred years elapsed before any attempt was made to learn about the lands beyond Marin's shore. It is also possible that Drake may have had this Spanish chart of the Puerte de San Francisco, because he is said to have returned directly to it and not as so often claimed, missed the real San Francisco Bay either by reason of thick weather or accident. Royce claims that Drake could not have known of this map but it is quite possible that he seized it in his raids on the Spaniards at and about Panama just before coming north.

Next comes the supposed landing of Sir Francis Drake on Marin soil in 1579. Fleeing from the wrath of the Spaniards after his piratical raid at Panama, he sailed up the coast in search of the Northwester Passage for a

---

[4] Sebastián Rodríguez Cermeño, Portuguese name Sebastião Rodrigues Soromenho (ca. 1560-1602), Portuguese navigator and pilot in the service of Phillip II of Spain. He was given command in the Philippines of the 200-ton Manila galleon *San Agustin* and explored Oregon and California. The ship was driven ashore in Drake's Bay in November, 1595.

quick return home to England. But the rigors of the Oregon coast climate forced him to turn back as it had Cabrillo so long before; and Drake had to find a sheltered bay where his leaking ship could be beached and repaired. He "arrived at a convenient and fit harbor" where, after a stay of thirty-six days he hurried away for the Cape of Good Hope and thence to England. Many years afterward, when leading historians agreed that he had visited Marin's most important ocean bay and not one of several others nearby, his name was given to the Pt. Reyes inlet in honor of his having been the first man to circle the globe[5]. It has puzzled historians of all ages to account for his not sending parties to any one of several points only a few miles away, from which could have been seen evidence of the great inland sea which is now recognized as the world's greatest harbor. Nor is it explained why, since his secretary gives such extended accounts of interviewing the Indians there, he did not learn from them of the great body of inland water to the south. Yet it must be remembered that in the month of June, the Pt. Reyes region can exhibit its densest fog curtains. Moreover, and perhaps of greater moment, he was in desperate fear of pursuit and discovery by enraged Spaniards from the south, and consequent loss of the party and its rich Panama plunder. Therefore it is reasonable to believe that his crew must have worked night and day to complete repairs and get away, rather than to indulge in outside excursions of any kind. In particular, the plain exaggerations and misstatements in all of Secretary Fletcher's[6] log of his voyages makes the accounts extremely unreliable. Drake personally classes him as a prize knave[7] in such writings.

Equally good claims can be made of Bodega Bay for Drake's landing and in fact the Spaniards insist upon its being the location of this early visit. Yet again, an otherwise responsible Padre shows that it was at the mouth of the Carmel River. Hence why dispute in the matter. Though repeatedly asked to clear up inaccuracies in his log, Drake consistently declined to do so, possibly in an intent not to render any assistance to Spain which at that time was at war with England.

---

[5] Drake was the first expedition commander to circle the globe, but the eighteen survivors of Magellan's crew under Juan Sebastián Elcano were the first men to accomplish the deed, on September 6, 1522.

[6] Francis Fletcher (ca. 1555- ca. 1619) was an Anglican clergyman and kept a journal of Drake's voyage.

[7] Drake actually called him "The falsest knave that liveth."

For many years in a more modern period, it was not an uncommon thing for some enterprising Pt. Reyesan to "discover" an ancient anchor chain or ring bolt and profit handsomely thereby; and once or twice an "authenticated" Spanish helmet of sixteenth century period has been "found" in some landslide or excavation on the Point. Anyone who has ever seen the old time iron work carried by the early whalers, will agree that since all of them for a period of a hundred years or more, anchored at times in Drake's Bay to escape coast storms, its bottom has a generous supply of well incrusted and rusty iron "Drake Souvenirs" for all future generations.[8]

If one wants to really enjoy these accounts of the old explorations and expeditions of pre-California days on this coast, let him study the lives of these men and the logs of their journeys and then mentally place himself in the position of and under the intention of the particular leader concerned. For example. Cabrillo was not a colonizer nor yet even a collector of new world products or possibilities. His whole effort was based on a quick discovery of the Northwest Passage and not on exploring new territory. While these old leaders had an indomitable spirit, it must be remembered that their crews were made up of the ordinary people usually steeped in the superstition attending any unusual portent or incident. The New World was considered to be the Devil's Mystery, hence to be delved into with extreme caution. So with other leaders and their plans, the discovery of the great Bay of San Francisco and its inland empire of far more wealth and resource than even the fabled India of that time was left to the close of the 18th century.

Next came the Cortez[9] regime in the West. New Spain became organized; and a flourishing trade route was developed between Manila and Acapulco. From there goods were transferred to the Caribbean and thence to Spain. But the voyage was extremely long. Many attempts were made to have Spain establish a calling port on the upper coast for refitting, watering and especially relief from sickness (usually scurvy) of the ships' crews.

Failing in this, the distressed vessels would call at some of the Mission ports of Lower California for relief, and thereafter take up the long trip to Acapulco. Spanish vessels took the northern route across the Pacific in those days so as to gain advantage of the currents flowing toward the coast, hence

---

[8] Several authentic Spanish relics and Chinese porcelain have been found at Drake's Bay, but these could as well be from the 1595 wreck of Cermeño's *San Agustin*, which is known to have occurred there.

[9] Hernán Cortés de Monroy y Pizarro Altamirano (1485-1547), conqueror of Mexico.

Spanish merchantmen must have frequently passed within sight of our land. In 1594 Francisco Gali, sailing from Macao, mentioned having passed down the coast from Cape Mendocino within sight of the land, and accurately described it. In 1595. Sebastian Cermenon, also tentatively investigating the coast on a voyage from Manila, was driven from his course and his ship ran ashore in or near the Puerte de San Francisco as marked on Cabrillo's map of fifty years before. Either a consort accompanied his vessel, or his ship was itself floated again, because the incident was fully reported at Acapulco and thence to Spain, and no tradition or remains of any "wreck" existed among the coast Indians.[10]

Hence there is a reasonable doubt of Marin County having the dubious honor of "the first shipwreck in the western world." If Cermenon had not himself reported the event at Acapulco later and made no mention of loss of his crew, there might be some connection between his castaways and the fabled Spanish descent of Chief Marin of the inland tribe of Lacatuit Indians and other chiefs of similar date in the north of the bay region.

A fourth trip to our coast followed in 1602, when New Spain sent Sebastian Viscaino[11] to carefully explore the north coast. Just sixty years after Cabrillo, he "rediscovered" San Diego Bay, Monterey Bay, and the same "Port of San Francisco" of his predecessors. His log shows a visit thereto to locate Cermenon's cargo of "boxed silks and wax" left there seven years before. The certainty of his Marin visit lies in his record of arrival "at the Port of San Francisco," wherein was a wreck." (Cermenon's). His "was a wreck" is also translated "had been a wreck," hence perhaps showing that Cermenon had beached his cargo and proceeded on after floating his ship. A later translation states that Cermenon reported the loss of his ship, the *San Augustin* at the Puerte de San Francisco, but it is almost certain that if it had been wrecked there, the Indians would have had some relic of the vessel or tradition of its cargo.

To Viscaino we owe the name "Pt. Reyes." It is said that from a certain angle of approach from the sea, a fanciful picture of a gigantic chair with its kingly occupant, is plainly seen on the granite bluffs of Pt. Reyes. It may be that from this Viscaino named the Punta de los Reyes (Point of the King). Yet it is equally possible that having successively passed countless numbers

---

[10] Cermeño's crew assembled a launch they had brought with them and sailed to Mexico.

[11] Sebastián Vizcaíno (1548-1624).

of low headlands all the way up the coast from Mexico, our gigantic cliff in comparison appealed to him as deserving a king's attention or note as Punta de los Reyes (King of all Points). A third and the most probable suggestion is that whenever an unusual event occurred, the Spaniards always recognized the religious significance of that day. Therefore, since January 6th was the day of Los Santos Reyes (The Three Wise Men: Psalm. 72:10) and the day after Los Reyes Viscaino found shelter there from dangerous winds, —he named it La Punta de los Reyes (the Point of the Kings).[12]

Once more it is an age old puzzle how such an experienced and painstaking map maker and explorer as Viscaino was, failed to note the evidence of an inland sea on the trip up the coast; or having missed it, failed to make inquiry of the natives at the "Port of San Francisco" concerning the inland territory. More than likely since his vessel was a hastily constructed affair from materials of western Mexico, he kept well away from the coast and its treacherous currents in stormy weather and so missed the tidal currents outside the Golden Gate which in after years and in fact in other then known bays were plain indications of a great inland sea.

And so Marin County had Cabrillo, Drake, Cermenon, and Viscaino, all arriving at the same point on its coast in a period of sixty years, and each by a providential guidance being denied the discovery of the finest and largest of all world harbors only a few miles away, in fact well within sight of the Golden Gate in clear weather. How the history of the world might have been changed and what different peoples might have been in possession of California today had more opportune fortune attended these early voyagers! Undoubtedly fair California would have been war-torn for centuries had either of the belligerent countries or several of their envious neighbors gained even a hint of our great empire. But for a hundred and fifty years more the afterward Golden State was left undisturbed as "a place of lowering skies, fierce native peoples, and forbidding coast storms." As well have a southern neighbor describe it!

26 January 1922

Meanwhile the Spanish occupation of Lower California was completed, and exploring with its resulting subjugation of native Indians pushed

---

[12] The author's third guess is correct – the point was named for the Three Kings.

steadily up the coast. The journey was a trail of the early California Missions when Church and State marched hand in hand for nearly five hundred miles, in a period of two hundred years or more, establishing a joint religious and military post at intervals of a day's journey throughout. It makes a story which every child should know and every western school should study, since by it California was developed and saved for its present inhabitants. No story in the history of the modern world can in any way compare to it in fascinating interest, if the reader or student is sufficiently well-balanced to be without prejudice and intent only on tracing out the romance and the far-planned results of the old Mission Padres' work. It becomes more and more marvelous as one finds that it was not a European or a general church plan, but evolved in the minds of but three of those old leaders who had in the years of mission work in Mexico, been inspired to carve out new empires solely for the humanity's good. Since neither the church, under the Cortez rule, nor the members of the Franciscan Order by their own rule, could possess any property, the self-sacrificing work of those old Padres and their just resentment of the ultimate disposal of the Indian property they accumulated for the natives under prearranged Government rules, is now better understood by the impartial reviewer. The story is of absorbing interest and recorded fact and hence properly material for school use.

In 1769 Gaspar de Portola[13], the then governor of the Californias, was ordered to extend the then frontier line to the northern-most limits of Spanish discovery. (Note —this "limits," for it meant the Marin county "Port of San Francisco" as the base, and the unknown mouth to the 42nd parallel as the frontier; thence the strenuous later attempts to reach the present Drake's Bay). Then only did the Marin history period of real development begin and settlement matters to rapidly develop, hastened by European causes, not local desires.

To this "Port of San Francisco" (Drake's Bay), belongs the real cause leading up to the discovery of San Francisco Bay by the Portola party. But when they found the great inland sea and it was viewed by them for the first time from the peninsula hills, it was to them of significance only as a last remaining obstacle in their path to the "Port of San Francisco" of Cabrillo. Drake, Cermenon, and Viscaino. From those ridges they could plainly see

---

[13] Gaspar de Portolá i Rovira (1716-1786), born in Catalan, Spain, a soldier and first Governor of Alta California.

the Farallones off the fabled port, easily recognized from the typical appearance and previous note. Then followed strenuous and repeated attempts to march around San Francisco bay to reach the Marin coast, which expeditions time after time failed to do since it would have taken years to skirt the bay, the San Joaquin, the Sacramento, and the multitude of inlets and smaller streams enroute. Hence report was made that until boats were provided, the frontier post must be at San Francisco, and thereby the Presidio and Mission of San Francisco was established, later changed to the Mission Dolores site and the present military location being retained.

It was not until ships arrived from Monterey long afterward, and detailed exploration of the Bay proceeded, that the Spaniards at all understood what a prize they had attained. Thereafter all interest in the goal of the "Puerte de San Francisco" was lost as vessels reported its small area in comparison, and its inaccessible land approach beyond the Spanish frontier of San Francisco Bay.

The discovery of San Francisco Bay was brought about wholly by the eagerness of the Spanish to reach the Puerte de San Francisco of Cabrillo's record, Viscaino's description and the impetus given by Drake's claim to its discovery later. They wished to establish a presidio and mission there at the earliest moment so as to insure that locality as part of the Spanish possessions. It would be silly for us to claim for Marin county the honors of all discoveries and settlements north of Monterey; yet history shows that all of the territory from Monterey north and east up to the north shore line of San Francisco Bay, was traversed and mapped as merely incidental to attaining the goal of the fabled Puerte de San Francisco. Thereby we would be entitled to claim the discovery of San Francisco Bay, Palo Alto, Alameda, (there was no Oakland for many years), the Berkeley hills, Martinez, and on up the Bay to Antioch: also the Sacramento and San Joaquin rivers,—all as a part of the early history of Marin county. But such claims, even though made elsewhere under similar conditions, only serve to make the claimants ridiculous to later generations. Marin County has quite enough early history to spare any such items for neighboring counties to which they more directly belong.

There were so many of these special expeditions from Monterey, from San Diego and from Sonora, all directed to survey the Puerte de San Francisco in our territory, that a reader of these notes urges a brief account of them as of direct interest to our story. Perhaps there are few Marinites who have kept pace with the several volumes issued in recent years as translated directly from the original diaries of these Spanish travelers. In Eldridge's "Beginnings of San Francisco"[14] they will find most interesting accounts thereof in detail, and it is from that authority previously collected notes and reference have been checked and compared for a brief mention here.

Every Marin child should be afforded a chance to read the absorbingly interesting accounts of the many land expeditions sent north in the next few years following the discovery of San Francisco Bay. While to some extent they are outside matters, they belong to Marin's early history for they were all organized for, and aimed to, Marin territory.

In 1769 Governor Don Gaspar Portola came north with a party to survey the Puerte de San Francisco and from a high ridge below San Pedro on the peninsula, recognized the sharp outlines of the Farallones and the Pt. Reyes entrance to the fabled port. Establishing a camp in the valley below, he sent out two parties, —one to hunt deer on the eastern ridges, and the other to follow the coast line to the before visible Puerte de San Francisco. The hunters returned with note of a wide and endless estero to the east; and later the other party reported that a greatest of all great bays lay to the north and effectually blocked further advance toward Pt. Reyes, which they said appeared to lie just behind a high sierra (Mt Tamalpais) on the opposite shore.

Thereupon the great inland sea was named in honor of St. Francis, the patron saint of the Franciscans, and the Portola party returned to make report on the northern territory and this great Bay of San Francisco.

Eldridge, in a careful comparison of the journeys of these two parties from Portola's camp and of the probable difficulties and delays encountered by each, considers that the honor of the discovery of San Francisco Bay belongs to the northern party under Sergeant Jose Francisco Ortega, whose view of the bay on November 2, 1769 probably preceded that of the deer hunters by many hours. Be that as it may, it was many years before it was at all prized or considered as anything more than the last obstacle to surmount before attaining the Puerte de San Francisco. Party after party came to the bay, only to be blocked by the wide expanse of its waters.

---

[14] "*The Beginnings of San Francisco, from the Expedition of Anza, 1774, to the City Charter of April, 1850,*" by Zoeth Skinner Eldredge, 1912.

The first of these was under Don Pedro Fages[15], Commandant of California, who in 1773 took the right bank path of the estero north of Monterey and after several days arrived in "the Alameda," wherein was a great grove of oak trees. Therefore Fages named its stream the Arroyo del Bosque (Creek of the Oaks). At this point the party had its first glimpse of the Golden Gate, which from then on was called the La Bocana de la Ensenada de los Farallones (the entrance to the gulf of the Farallones). This shows the still existing ideas of the surrounding topography. Next day found him on the Berkeley hills, from which the party could look far out on the Pacific through the Golden Gate.

Proceeding on up the bay and pausing on the high hills near Martinez, they studied the surrounding country. From here they saw the Southern Marin territory to best advantage and named our mountain the La Siere de Nuestro Padra San Francisco (the high ridges of our Father San Francisco). But disappointment of reaching Pt. Reyes and after going up as far as the present Antioch, they completed the circle and returned to Monterey across country. But few names of this trip remained for our territory. Suisun Bay was called the Bahia Redondo as the round basin into which the junction of the three great inland streams, the Rio San Francisco, poured its fresh waters to sweeten the bitter depths of San Francisco Bay. It was on this journey, that the famous palo alto (high tree) was viewed for many leagues before reaching it, and thereby originated the name of the present University City.

Next came Rivera[16], successor to Fages, who started up the coast with a party determined to reach the Puerte de San Francisco, but on reaching Pt. Lobos he encountered bad weather and returned to Monterey. A fourth expedition, this time by water and from faraway San Blas in Mexico, effected the long hoped for detailed survey of the Bay region. There were three vessels. The *Santiago*, a frigate under Don Bruno de Heceta[17], proceeded up the coast and discovered the Columbia River. A second, the schooner *Sonora* in charge of Don Juan Francisco de la Bodega y Cuadra[18],

---

[15] Pere Fages i Beleta (1734-1794), Catalan soldier, explorer, first Lieutenant Governor of Ata California, and second and fifth Governor of Alta California.

[16] Fernando Rivera y Moncada (1725-1781), Mexican soldier and third Governor of Alta California.

[17] Bruno de Heceta y Dudagoitia (1743-1807), Spanish Basque explorer.

[18] Juan Francisco de la Bodega y Cuadra (1744-1794), born in Lima, a Spanish Naval officer.

sailed north and discovered the bay of his name. He also surveying [sic] the back country thereof. The third, a small packet boat called the *San Carlos*, was in charge of Don Manuel de Ayala[19]. The story of his struggles to beat up the coast in so small a ship, of the sickness and distress of his crew and their rescue in Lower California, and of the long trip to Monterey,—should be read by all for an understanding of the Providence which must have guided him safely to the end. He was assigned the survey of San Francisco Bay.

We are mainly indebted to the Eldridge volumes for intimate details of this work along our own shores, since only short references have been found elsewhere. From Monterey, the *San Carlos* took 73 days to reach our Bay, a distance of only 85 miles. Approaching the Heads the mate, Don Jose Canizares, departed with a party in the ships boat to survey the unknown entrance and select a proper place for anchorage. Meantime the *San Carlos* was swept far out to sea by the strong tidal currents, and in late afternoon managed to return on the inflow again. But the ship's boat was seen making an attempt to come out but had to finally turn back on account of the swift currents flowing in. Then Ayala was forced to find his own anchorage and in spite of the forbidding rocks and frowning cliffs to risk an entrance before night. Committing all hands to Divine guidance the little vessel kept close to the north shore and slipped through unharmed, casting anchor in twenty-two fathoms of water off Sausalito Point. Next day Canizares joined them. In this diary Ayala notes that all the way in great weights of lead on sixty fathom line failed to find bottom, and that at half past ten o'clock on the evening of August 5th, 1775, his ship dropped anchor inside the Bay entrance.

This little *San Carlos* was the first hint of the many vessels which followed in early days: of the great fleet which filled the harbor from end to end in the mining days; of the navies of the world which have called here; and of the continually increasing shipping interests which place San Francisco Bay as among the finest of the world's harbors.

Now comes an account of the first visit of white men to Marin County in modern times, and several months prior to the Olompali visit of the 1880 Marin County History version. Ayala's detailed surveys of the bay proceeded, Canizares making these in the ship's boat and with an armed

---

[19] Juan Manuel de Ayala y Aranza (1745-1797), born in Andalusia.

crew. First came Richardson's Bay, which he declared unsafe from southeast winds and as having an improper bottom for anchorage. Numerous Indians appeared on its shores as the boat proceeded in its work but no landing was made. Commander Ayala named the Bay the Ensenada del Carmelita, ("because of a rock in it which resembled a Friar of that Order"—Eldridge). While circling Belvedere Point they saw many more Indians who made every effort to have them come ashore. Then the *San Carlos* moved to an anchorage off Tiburon Point where both anchors failed to hold in fifteen fathoms of water (probably in the Raccoon Straits).

The Indians continued to entreat a landing and on August 9th Fray Vicento Santa Maria, with Mate Canizares and an armed crew, took beads and other gifts and landed near a large rancherio (probably at Tiburon Cove). They were most hospitably received. The diary states that "pinole" a parched acorn-meal bread was given them, also "tomales" of seeds, etc. Hence our "tamales" were not of southern origin. They found that the Indians could easily repeat certain Spanish words after hearing them, which perhaps establishes the "teaching" in the Bay Region.

Commander Ayala continued his surveys and explorations, finally inspecting and selecting the Isla de los Angeles for a permanent base because of its good and safe anchorage, wood and water and complete protection from winds. This was probably the cove on the Straits or possibly where the Quarantine wharf is now. There he securely anchored and tied his vessel, also dropping the sails, and proceeded in his surveys of the entire Bay. He mentions the barren and rocky island nearby which he named Alcatraces on account of so many albatrosses[20] there. The name has since been shortened to the singular of the Spanish name.

The *San Carlos* remained in San Francisco Bay for forty-four days and then returned to Monterey. While Ayala named and mapped all the Bay points, only Angel and Alcatraz islands still bear his titles. Two parties were sent up the Bay at different times and a direct inference of another landing on Marin shores is made in the fact that he named our San Pedro Point the Punta de Langosta (Locust Point[21]). In fact on these trips of several days each, the ship's boat party must have several times camped on Marin territory because the surveys were made of all inlets of the Bay, which must have taken several days in Marin territory alone.

---

[20] Pelicans.
[21] Lobster Point.

Then a fifth expedition, while immediately coming from Monterey, started from far away Sonora in northern Mexico, also having the Puerte de San Francisco in view and making every effort to reach that territory. If any one wishes to read the elements of a real epic of the West, then the Eldridge translation from no less than four diaries of this trip from Sonora and return will satisfy the most particular taste.

In 1774 Juan Bautista de Anza[22] made the trip from northern Mexico to bring the first quota of Spanish families for settlement in California. The fact that several of the heads of these families were afterward Marin County pioneers properly makes this journey a part of our story. In fact it deserves a first place in all western annals on account of its purpose and ultimate effect on early California matters.

Pushing up the coast from Monterey, he arrived at Fort Point, and verified the earlier story of Ortega. Then circling the entire peninsula, he passed around the Bay and practically followed the previous east shore travels of Fages some years before. He also shared in the disappointments of not reaching Pt. Reyes. One incident of this trip caused our Olompali visit a year later. While on the opposite shore Padre Font, who accompanied Anza on the trip, expressed the belief that a distant estero (Napa River) was the strait between San Francisco and Bodega Bays (the latter having been discovered a short time before). This led to Moraga's[23] expedition through southern Marin County in the following year.

Upon Anza's return to Monterey, plans were at once made for the *San Carlos* to bring men and materials to establish the presidio and mission at San Francisco, which was done in 1776. Almost as soon as this was accomplished, exploring parties took up the search for Padre Font's inland strait to Bodega Bay, which resulted in the first penetration of our territory by men of the white race. In 1776 a land and water expedition started up the Bay. A ship's boat party, with provisions for eight days investigated the bay shore and passed up Petaluma Creek until compelled to return home on account of not meeting the land party for further supplies. The second party was in charge of Lieutenant Moraga, Commandant of the Presidio, and doubtless landed at the nearest Marin beach, probably Lime Point or Sausalito, and followed around the Bay Shore line.

---

[22] Juan Bautista de Anza Bezerra Nieto (1736-1788), of Basque heritage, born in Sonora, Mexico.

[23] Gabriel Moraga (1765-1823), born in Sonora, Mexico.

Here the careless reader has a problem to solve in the reason why the land party took weeks to advance to Petaluma Creek instead of a few days planned. But it must be remembered that in those days there were no bay marshes or mud flats, since deforestation, destructive farming, and deposits of mining silt were unknown and all the bay inlets were "blue water" and had sandy shores. Take a Marin shore map and trace out such a journey and be mindful of the fact that the land was heavily wooded to the shore, and the explorers fearful of probably hostile natives and other supposedly hidden dangers of the new lands. Such a journey would come from Sausalito, go far inland toward Tennessee Cove, well up to Mill Valley, on to the head of Alta Station Valley, thence back to Hilarita Point, around to Corte Madera and up to Kentfield, then to Greenbrae around to the head of Richardson's Bay, down to Belvedere, around to California City and a legion of new inlets back to San Quentin and up to central San Rafael. Can any one wonder that this wearisome trip ceased at San Rafael, and the party determined to go north and over the eastern sierra (high ridges) in an attempt to dodge further bay inlets? It finally arrived at Olompali, a rancheria known as Burdell's[24] Rancho, and located a few miles above Novato. There it was hospitably received by the Indian residents and remained for some time, probably being told that there was no "Bodega Strait." The Spaniards taught the Indians how to make adobe bricks and to erect houses thereof, with thatched roofs. In consequence Marin County had the first building erected in Northern California and the first "settlement" also. Long afterward the Olompali chief's son built a second house, a portion of which still remains at Burdell's, and which Doctor Burdell considerably added to in early days. It is said that the fire-blackened adobe bricks of the original Indian house, when exposed to moisture and sunshine immediately sprout the "wild oats" now all over Marin county, giving rise to the tale that the seed was carried by this Spanish party thereto and became mixed into the adobe clay in the housebuilding preparation.

So Moraga's party was the first of the white race to visit Marin County other than the shore visits of Drake and Ayala. It may well be added that the Olompali Rancho has ever since been a nourishing and successful home, because early in 1800 it was found almost exactly as described in this visit of 1776, and in the Mission times was operated in succession by two of the

---

[24] Dr. Galen Burdell (1828-1906), early Marin dentist.

few enterprising and successful Christian neophytes of the Mission San Rafael Archangel, —one Santasimo Rosaria[25] and later Camilo Ynitia[26]. A tradition of a possible reason for naming Marin territory arises about this time, in the note of officers and men of the *Santa Marina*, a vessel in San Francisco Bay, visiting a hospitable rancho several times on the shore towards Pt. Reyes. This may have been Tennessee Cove, Big Lagoon, or Bolinas Bay since there are few possible points elsewhere. Perhaps this land was then spoken of as the Marina's land, whence came the term Marin. But the word is said to be of Indian origin, hence the "'Chief Marin" origin is generally accepted.

Next comes the establishment of the Mission San Rafael Archangel in 1817, and the period of its development of all Marin County as part of its lands except the peninsulas of Tiburon, Sausalito and the Bolinas-Pt. Reyes territory.—all of which the Government refused to part with.

This coming account of the Mission's activities and of its rise and fall through a period of thirty-eight years makes an interesting story of early Marin History. It is usually called the early history of San Rafael, but as the story proceeds it is seen that it is from beginning to end the story of Marin county and not San Rafael, which could not make a beginning until the Mission was sold in 1845. Hence the Mission San Rafael Archangel is a county memory and not one of merely local account.

In the foregoing review of the pre-Mission period of Marin territory, we have not been able to locate any account of a Spanish landing party at the old Puerte de San Francisco, after the real San Francisco Bay port was established. There must have been several and note thereof was probably of no interest to the translator or it would be a valued item to add hereto. This general review may alone be of sufficient worth to our reader as showing how important a part Marin territory played in the exploration and development of the entire West Coast. But the real interest comes in the story to follow, of how after the explorer Portola, Fages, Rivera and finally the great Anza suffered such disappointment in being blocked from entering this territory: and after Ayala had thoroughly explored its bays shores and no doubt also reported on its fertile, open lands. —the Mission penetration and development made it one of the most widely known on the coast, and immeasurably aided in its later solid development.

---

[25] Santísimo Rosario, baptismal name of a Miwok leader.
[26] Ynitia was the only Mission Indian to receive and retain a grant of Mission lands.

2 February 1922

CHAPTER III

THE EARLY INDIANS

    Before reviewing the Mission days in Marin County a short sketch of the western aborigines may provide a better understanding of the Mission activities. A period of nearly forty years elapsed from the visit of Spanish soldiers to the Olompali Rancheria in 1776, and the beginnings of Mission Days here in 1817, yet during all of this period our County was thickly settled with Indians, grouped in various localities in practically independent tribes.

    No record of the Ancients gave any note of the Americas, nor do the most ancient Mexican and Aztec traditions throw proper light on the origin of the Western Indian, a decidedly inferior race and comparable in many respects to the present Tierra del Fuegan people. They more nearly resembled Asiatics than any others, but were said to be plainly mixed with negroid stock. Some ethnologists claim they were descended from the lost tribes of Israel of Biblical times. For our purposes it is sufficient to know that in California, Pacific Coast Indians were grouped as in Northern, Central and Southern District. The Northern Indians formed large tribes and covered great areas of territory. Central California Indians, and especially those south of the Bay, formed almost innumerable small tribes and seldom traveled away from their base. The Southern Group were a polyglot mixture, plainly evidencing lack of good qualities of some others, and at times arousing to a fierce, cruel nature for short periods. All of the level country types seem to have been extremely lazy, with filthy habits, were non-roving, and either eating, sleeping or dancing all of the time. In our north of the Bay section, however, the natives had none of the Apache raiding tendencies or rancho attacking spirit, no absolute loss of civilized life, were hospitable at first, and interfered very little between the Christianized (neophyte) Indian and the native (gentile) type. They were much more numerous than the Southern Indians, and many were brave, warlike, and very hostile when imposed upon. No doubt General Vallejo's[27] iron hand in the north as military governor and his consistently continued protection of the Indians' rights, together with his wise alliance with the leading northern chiefs, had much to do with peace on the northern frontier of Spanish and later the Mexican possessions. Yet when the white man's maladies appeared, the unsanitary sleeping halls of the Missions, and especially the Indian habits of living, proved perfect mediums for epidemics causing such enormous death rates among them in 1834, 1836 and 1838. Authorities estimate that seventy thousand perished in that period from the Sacramento Valley to the Bay. One third died in infancy, one third in adolescent age, and the remaining third, weakened in health and broken in spirit, thought the land of their fathers was accursed, and in despair fled to the mountain region. From these old Indian tribes we have retained many names such as Tehama, Pomp (people), Yokio (Ukiah), Gualala, Yoloy (Yolo), Colusa, Sonoma (Valley of the Moon), Petaluma, Napa, Suisun, Bollanos (Bolinas), Tamale (Tomales), Karquinez (Carquinez), and many others.

In general, our early Indians were far from the fabled noble red men of the Eastern States. They had flat, unmeaning features, coarse and straight black hair, big mouths and fine though irregular teeth, strongly negro profiles and black skins. While short in stature, they were very muscular, yet almost bestially lazy and non-hunting types. Perhaps the ease of subsistence here and the universal northern Indian superstition against killing any large animal, prevented such development. In all cases they treated their women like animals.

Yet there were exceptions. Chief Marin, of the Tamale tribe on the Western Coast, was many times mentioned as an able leader, a good campaigner, an organizer and a great traveler. His fighting men were rated as the fiercest Indians in California and were a terror to the Spanish and Mexican authorities, except General Vallejo in whom they had implicit confidence. He and Quintin, a sub chief, were worthy types of the proverbial chieftains. One version states that a tradition persisted that Chief Marin was of Spanish-Indian descent from an early day sailor deserting or being cast upon the western coast, who was cared for by the Tamale tribe and became one of them. He, with several of the nearby chiefs had many characteristics of Spanish features and ways, and may have gained their unusual leadership

---

[27] Mariano Guadalupe Vallejo (1807-1890), born in Monterey, rancher, politician, and military commander of northern California.

qualities thereby. He was finally baptized a Christian at the Mission San Rafael. Chief Marin had been a thorn in the flesh of the military authorities and had again and again evaded their expeditions against him. He was captured once but escaped and resumed his operations. Finally he was again apprehended and sentenced to death but the San Rafael Padre so earnestly interceded for him that he was pardoned and was then baptized at the Mission and died there some years later.

Bancroft failed to find any Spanish accounts of him at all, or any trace of the exploits either of him or Quintin except Vallejo's general comment. The name "Marin" should be accented on the first syllable as an Indian word, and it is said our pronunciation comes as a contraction of "Marine" in indication of the territory having such extended shore lines.

The Marin County History of 1880[28] has a story about Chief Marin which while interesting will not bear analysis as a probability, when correlated dates are compared. It is to the effect that Chief Marin was known far and wide as the bravest of all Indians, who considered him to be a superman in many respects. At that time Indians shunned the vicinity of Tamalpais and under no circumstances would they travel on its slopes or approach its top, because of their superstitions regarding its being the dwelling place of certain gods. But an Irishman who was a surveyor, desired to use the top as a base point and wished to have some one place a location thereon. Having asked Chief Marin, it was shown that anyone going there would perish at once, under no conditions could he persuade the Indians to accompany him. Thereupon he decided to go himself, and on reaching the top succeeded in placing a timber up in a tree in the shape of a cross. The story states that the Indians assembled in great numbers awaiting the return of the surveyor. When he finally appeared, Chief Marin determined to uphold his reputation for bravery and against the wishes of his people set out for the top of the mountain. Arriving there he was puzzled to know how he could prove that he had been there at all. His most prized possession was a red shirt and though loath to part with it, he did so and placed it on the cross so that all might see it from the surrounding country. Thereafter his reputation was greatly enhanced since he had not only braved the terrors of Tamalpais but had also in defiance flown his personal flag from its top. In Vallejo's papers note is made of his being so hard pressed by the military

---

[28] *The History of California*, seven volumes, 1880, by Hubert Howe Bancroft (1832-1918).

authorities that he took refuge on the Marin Islands, whereupon a sub chief, Quintin, surrounded the islands with boats filled with armed Indians, which demonstration discouraged any further attack of his position. So the tradition comes down to us that "Chief Marin's land" came to be known as Marin County.

It must be understood that the early Indians were distinct from the Spanish and Mexican peoples arriving later, and of whom many descendants are still with us under the original family names. It was unfortunate that Mexico saw fit to send its convicts to California to colonize the territory, and that many soldiers sent here later by the Mexican authorities were of a turbulent class at home, and on deserting or being discharged here were often confused in their outrages, with the Spanish and Mexican settlers of proper repute called the gente de razon (aristocrats).

Jean de la Perouse[29], French scientist, was one of the keenest of many European visitors here, and as early as 1786 foretold the failure of the missionizing plans for the natives, and said, "The neophyte is too much a child, too much a slave, and too little a man." Father Boscana[30], in his admirable treaties describes the Indians as constantly enjoying themselves. "When," he says, "they were not eating, sleeping or gambling, they were dancing,—sometimes for weeks at a time. At a birth, a marriage or a burial they danced to propitiate the divinity, and then danced to thank the divinity for being propitiated by dancing." Father Junipero Serra[31] found no opposition from the natives toward his work. They had no word for god, or devil or angel, nor conception of any kind as to heretofore or hereafter. Yet it is possible that a great part of their zeal for Christianity lay in the quick knowledge that under its care they were compelled to have still less responsibility for subsistence by their own efforts. The historian, Hubert Bancroft, tells of some of the Bay Indians protecting themselves from chilly winds by wearing a thick coat of mud, probably the sticky adobe of our time, and calls attention of less fortunate brethren to this matter, describing it as "a convenient dress; cost nothing; is easily put on; and no encumbrance to the wearer."

---

[29] Jean François de Galaup, comte de La Pérouse (1741-1788), French explorer, circumnavigator, and scientist.

[30] Gerónimo Boscana (1776-1831), born in Mallorca, Spanish priest and historian.

[31] Junípero Serra y Ferrer (1713-1784), Franciscan friar who established many of the California missions.

Their houses, later responsible for the frightful mortality from the white man's epidemics of measles, smallpox, intermittent fever and more lasting troubles, were merely the bush or tree shade in summer, and in winter a conical brush hut.

Usually a group would make an excavation sometimes thirty feet square, and bend saplings over this to ward off storms, then place a fire in the middle and pack all blood and marriage relatives into this habitat—the closer the better—and dwell there until forced to move and build another.

A collection of huts was termed a Rancheria, from the word rancho, meaning a food distribution place in Cuba in early Spanish times. Extreme laziness prevented hunting. Bows and arrows for an occasional small deer, snares for small animals and water fowl, primitive nets for fish, and fleet footed boys were food gathering appliance. For food, any possible living thing which they could lay their hands upon was welcome. Acorns, seeds, (mainly clover) and berries were eaten raw or prepared.

Worms, ants and all insects, reptiles, shell fish, and especially grasshoppers were not passed by. Acorn flour was pounded out by the women, and resulting bread was a coarse preparation resembling a black, clayey substance, so filthy were the preparers before the Padres came. Properly made, acorn meal bread was not unpalatable. The clover seed made a dish much like our mush. Grasshoppers chrysalides were considered the greatest delicacies, eaten raw or prepared, and dried in large quantities for the winter months as were also ants. Meat as we know it was not used. In fact it was a common epithet or expression of deep contempt for one tribe to speak of another, saying "They eat venison." Yet seal and sea lions were avidly devoured and it was feast indeed for the countryside when a stranded whale arrived on the coast or in the Bay.

In connection with the matter of feasts, there is no evidence of any kind as to when the various shell mounds about the bay were formed by probably tremendous gathering of Indians from the interiors. Yet in far previous times there must have been veritable pilgrimages of tribes from even east of the Rockies to account for such great residues of shellfish and accompanying debris of the feasts. It is now known that these great shell heaps were mainly discards in drying shellfish by inland tribes. In early battles they carried arrows poisoned by a commonly growing shady place plant found hereabout. These "engagements" were frequent though hardly for serious purposes. Each side always desired a quick finish, so that first blood usually decided the issue. Sometimes they chose heralds from each side to decide matters for the enjoyment of the others. "In these disputes," says Bancroft, "they formed long lines of men at intervals, and 'fought' the first stages by wildly shouting and gesticulating in order to overawe or intimidate the other side." Then they would discharge volleys of arrows at each other, (presumably shooting high), after which a halt was called until children from either side could enter the ranks of the opposite warriors and collect the arrows for another trial!

9 February 1922

One of the strangest things about the Bay Indians was that they had no boats, in fact moved about so little that there was no need of any. Its nearest approach was a "bolsa" made of tules, a kind of float probably used to spear fish from, or to cross narrow streams with. This was several feet thick and of buoyancy enough to keep the paddler out of water as long as it was dry; yet when wet through; he was submerged to the waist by his own weight.

Since they had nothing to steal, murder resulting from gambling bout quarrels, was the occasional serious crime. For this the blood relatives exacted an "eye for an eye," or were bought off by a gambling bet or other issue. In favor of the early Indians it should be said that they were of a free and loving nature, tractable, without guile or treachery, were not cruel or vicious until learning the habits of the white man, and held infinite sorrow for their dead. In fact no Padre in the west, succeeded in having them change their practices in deeply reverencing the departed. In this connection also, the Bodega Indians would not under any inducements, affiliate in any way with Mission work. Just why all of these native westerners were of such a low scale in intelligence, initiative and ordinary progressiveness is a complete puzzle to ethnologists. They inhabited a land of plenty, of fine climate, good water and abundant game: and had everything a people might want. Yet from Alaska to Central America, while they were living as men, a majority were closely akin to brutes in their habits and activities. Their "calendar" is interesting, being one of sensation and not of time. Beginning in our December there were periods each noted as of cold, of rain, of the first grass, of the rise of waters, of the roots, of salmon fishing, of heat, of wild fruits, of bulbous roots, of acorns and nuts, and of hunting.

In Marin territory the Lacatuits occupied Central Marin and the north side of the Tomales Bay region and were closely related to the Tamales. The Tamales, also termed Tamallos and Tamalanos, occupied the sea coast from Bodega Bay south; while the Bollanos dwelt along the coast from San Francisco Bay north, probably to Bolinas. While the Spaniards called the tribe in San Rafael territory the Tulares, this body of Indians were on the east shore and far into the back country thereof. The proper name was the Lohuas. The Patalumas fringed our northern border around the present Petaluma region, and the Cainimeros (also noted as Kamimares) dwelt on the Sonoma shores with some of the Suisunes whose proper base was on the east bay shore.' A note states that in 1821 there were ten thousand natives in the Canimeros tribe. Numerous smaller tribes were scattered here and there. The Nicasios was a name applied in later times apparently to dwellers in that valley. So also the Olompalis at the Burdell Rancho was probably a name given to some Cainimeros who lived there. The Huchinnes occupied Angel Island.

Hence we have a number of Marin county names derived from the early Indian tribes, mentioned in another article. It is interesting to note that even in these earliest periods, Marin territory began its five geographical centers of community life, each having little or no relation to the others. Since those aboriginal days succeeding residents have done little or nothing to change the handicap of difficult road communication between these groupings,— the vital necessity before having a unified territory. Our present disunited position is the result of it.

So passed the early residents, children of nature happy in their way until the white man came. A last sad remnant moved to Nicasio for a time but rapidly died away, and a few more remained about Tomales Bay for a period. The records show that Timothy Murphy, who was major domo at the Mission San Rafael, made a fight for a permanent land grant for the Nicasio Indians but failed in the attempt. For many years the Tomales Bay Indians were undisturbed in their fish and shellfish grounds but little by little were dispossessed and now only a few families of intermarriage descent remain there on sufferance.

IV
MISSION DAYS— (Foreword)

It is an exceedingly difficult matter for one to read of particular Mission development and view its work with any proper understanding unless one has a proper background knowledge of the history of the Mission work in western Mexico, then in Lower California, and finally from San Diego to Sonoma in our own great state. Otherwise it must be considered as the work of one or more old Padres, isolated far from home connections, struggling to gain further aid from church and state which was again and again refused them, and bit by bit being overcome by the rising tide of totally unforeseen difficulties in the development of original plans.

Popularly understood, the Missions movement in California had its origin and support from Spain and from continental church Orders. To a limited extent this was at first true, but from the student's point of view it was most decidedly not so. Its inception, at least for the Californias, arose in the failure of Cortez and others to conquer the north coast after losing eight expeditions thereto from 1526 to 1683. So he decided that the Californias might be attacked in another way and offered the Jesuit Order a chance to try other methods, he pledging the necessary expenses therefor. That the Californias should have defied his efforts after all of Mexico and the south coast territory bowed down to him with little opposition, seems to have been another of the seemingly foreordained matters for future generations.

Thereupon the Jesuits, the wise men of that age, offered to supply men for spiritual work though unwilling to be responsible for the temporal force needed. Yet at the same time their General disapproved of the matter, considering the plan to be impracticable in any case.

But to every crisis there arises a man or men to meet it. So also with the Jesuits. In their New World ranks were three men of inexhaustible energy and exceptional ability, who considered that the opportunity was a Divine inspiration and proceeded to surmount every difficulty in attaining result.

Fathers Knio[32], Juan Ugarte[33], and Salvia Tierra[34] were the real instigators and antecedents of the Mission plans to follow, and were time after time refused permission to undertake the work. Yet they persisted in an almost person to person solicitation for funds and equipment and in 1697 were given permission to launch the movement. Father Ugarte remained in Mexico as the agent for further supplies and materials and Father Kino accompanied by an assistant, Father Piccolo[35], sailed up the coast with an escort of ten soldiers. Landing on the Lower California Coast, they built a barracks and chapel. Then an image of Our Lady of Loreta, patroness of the new movement, was brought from the ship and with due ceremony the real work was started.

Then came the crushing news of refusal of pledged support from a jealous Government and of praise from Spain, —but without support therefrom. Father Ugarte, still undismayed, gathered up all he could collect in Mexico and straightway threw his life effort into the movement. Father Kino determined to take the interior development, and proceeded far up Lower California Bay when he established the Mission of San Marcalo. Father, now Padre, Ugarte journeyed into the mountains and established the famous Mission of St. Xavier. He of all the Missioners, committed himself to Providence and dismissed the Spanish soldiers, building his way step by step through his own efforts.

This St. Xavier Mission was the Utopian dream of all the later Padres, for Father Ugarte taught religious truths as he understood them: taught the Indians to be self-supporting; to restrain their senseless ferocity: to change their manner of life; to cultivate gentleness and humility as well as energy; and to fill the choicest land with all manner of fruits, harvests, horses and cattle; —to the end that before long he was able to assist the hard pressed Mission at Loreta. He was a Padre peculiarly fitted for the work, who had been a Professor of Philosophy at Mexico City. Then in his work he became a farmer, bricklayer, carpenter and priest, an example to all of a kindly, scholarly, and accomplished artisan of the true Padre-mechanic-citizen building type. The Father Tierra passed away at Loreta, having exhausted

---

[32] Eusebio Francisco Kino (1645-1711), Italian-born missionary, explorer, cartographer, and astronomer. He established 24 missions.

[33] Juan de Ugarte (1662-1730), born in Tegucigalpa, was Procurator of Baja California.

[34] Juan Maria de Salvatierra (1648-1717), born in Milan, was Provincial Superior.

[35] Francisco Maria Piccolo (1654-1729), born in Palermo.

himself with strenuous explorations and his labors in the First Mission field. But the work went on, Mission after Mission being placed in the links of a chain pushing north to the Upper California border.

Then Padre Ugarte died in 1730 and though he was the strong right hand of the entire work, his real tribute came in its permanence after his passing.

Government stepped in and demanded future aims of this growing religious power, and some hidden force encouraged unscrupulous tricksters and vicious natives to foment trouble and make attacks on the Missions. But those on the coast continued to afford aid and care to the Manila ships pausing on the long journey to Acapulco, and thereby gained a stiff home support in spite of Government opposition. So those old Jesuit Missioners remained until for many years, "unsuspicious, undisturbed, and increasing the wealth and influence of their circles," until the jealousy of Government prevailed and in a single night every Mission was seized and the Padres deported. Then the Franciscan and Dominican Orders shared the Lower California Missions until in 1767 the Dominicans assumed full charge and the Franciscan Order under Father Junipero Serra embarked for the spiritual and temporal conquest of Upper California.

So there came a time when church and state came marching up the California coast, a Padre or two representing the spiritual zeal and two or three Spanish soldiers the temporal power behind it. In 1770 the San Diego Mission was founded: in 1771 at Monterey: in 1776 at San Francisco, with numbers of others spreading out from the mother stations, each being placed a day's journey from the last one, and annexing as Presidio and Mission lands all of the intervening territory from the coastal line as far inland as they cared to claim it.

In turn the Government, this time as Mexico, displaced the Franciscans, at least banished all the Padres who declined to take the oath of allegiance to the new control, and virtually substituted its own friars from the Zacatecan college for the old Missioners from San Fernando College.

This action, and the confiscation of the so-called Pious Fund of some $900,000.00 painstakingly gathered through the years of Mission efforts for further extensions, began the decline of the California Missions, for the Zacatecans were in no sense the equal of their predecessors, and wholly inexperienced in control and direction as had been developed by the Franciscans. Very soon also, Government supplanted the Zacatecan Friars in all temporal powers by appointing "Administradores," and the confusion and disaster became worse confounded. Shortly before California revolted from Mexico, in about 1836, the Mission Rule was ended and only a cherished Indian memory.

No one claims that the Padres were perfect, for they were but men. They were engaged in an earnest spiritual and temporal endeavor to break the barbarian line further and further north, and to uplift and protect the Indian from the coming onslaught of the white race certain to otherwise bring disaster to the aborigine. Their stay was but an incident in the country's history, yet a solid, constructive means of a later development in the West. Their help to the Indian was the only assistance rendered him, and who shall say but that it was not better for him to have perished with them and in the spiritual uplift of their work, than to be with us today as typified in the remnant of his race to be seen here and there amongst us! Those old Padres governed by the power of love and of inspiration, and at times if more violent measures were used, we must not misjudge the acts any more than the present day child does his home discipline:—for they directed happy, simple children, almost Nature's spiritualists in many ways. The unpleasant memories of Mission Days arose from the impressions of foreigners in the period of the Mission decline: and when the work of the old Franciscan friars from San Fernando had been supplanted by less inspired successors.

16 February 1922

THE MARIN MISSION PERIOD
CHAPTER V

A much better understanding of the so-called Marin Mission Period is possible after the foregoing brief review of the progress in and development of the Mission movement in the West extending through a period of more than three hundred and fifty years. This work on the northern frontier of the early Spanish possessions was therefore the closing chapter of the famous plan which succeeded in a religious way, backed by a semblance of military control. A half century of attempts to effect it by violence and force of the military alone under the Cortez plan had utterly failed.

In the inception and subsequent success of the Mission Plan on this northern frontier of the early Spanish possessions, there were elements of definitely constructive aims for the civilization of the Indians and their ultimate possession of the lands of the new territory. The conditions under which it was established and afterward operated might well be considered as warranting a separately considered treatment from that of any part of the general California Missions development. The Indians were of a far more intelligent, teachably receptive and progressive type than their south of the Bay brothers, and decidedly more spirited, independent and better charactered individuals than early Indians of any section from Alaska to the Isthmus. But the unseen hands of the successors to the Cortez regime, aided by the decided lack of any proper territorial government system in California virtually cancelled the carefully laid plans of the old Mission Padres.

As dispassionately viewed in the light of history however, the extended Mission control of our territory at that time probably resulted in a lasting benefit to our afterwards county. By the delay a decidedly more progressive and energetic type of home builders located here later, as judged by the conditions resulting in some other counties where the secularization plan was more promptly effected.

Many newspaper and other general accounts of this period have been written, for the most part based on a few facts and enlarged with the average details occurring all over the coast in that period. The present account does not attempt to present other than a more abundant offering of authenticated and recorded facts directly applying to our territory. A few of the more interesting traditions are noted as such. There is unquestionably a wealth of similar material somewhere available, and it is with the hope that much of it will be located and brought into this series of "Marin's Old Days" reviews that a general account based on the definite facts is presented at this time.

Only recently we have been able to locate an authentic copy of a map of the entire lands of the Mission San Rafael Archangel, and it clears up many heretofore puzzling questions concerning the complete isolation of San Rafael for so many years. In consequence we have been able to much more clearly and completely piece together a fairly accurate account with this knowledge before us and in fact this map provides the basis heretofore needed for such a review. With its aid the many references to places and descriptions of localities under long forgotten names are now clear and decidedly interpretative of otherwise isolated allusions. Necessarily an account of the Mission period has to more or less overlap later accounts planned for the early days of the county and of San Rafael, but each item included has a direct reference to the distinctly Mission Period and its activities.

From this map it is shown that all of the present county was Mission lands territory except the peninsulas of Tiburon and Sausalito, and west of a line from about Corte Madera to the point at the head of Tomales Bay. All of this excepted territory came under the Spanish Government exceptions for possible future coast defense purposes. Since the Government at all times reserved such sections in new territories, and plans for strong fortification of the northern frontier were constantly looming as necessities in this locality, the reason is very plain why the wise old Missioners omitted these locations as either uncultivatable, too difficult of easy communication, or to be later taken by the Government forces. On the latter, no travelers of any kind were allowed to loiter.

Hence San Rafael and its environs were totally isolated from any approach except by water, and even then open only to Mission and Government travelers and expeditions. No roads led to it and none away from it. No vehicle transportation was that time available and only pack animals or strong backed natives were then used. Hence trails were for many years the only land routes of the period. By [a] carefully maintained system of lookouts the approach of any party either by land or water was known at once, and if apparently of a hostile nature the Mission forces were promptly organized and all surrounding Indians brought in for emergencies long before any possible surprise attack could develop.

Of the twenty-one Missions founded in California, only the record books of the San Rafael Archangel Mission seem to have been utterly lost, —a fact that is wholly unaccountable in view of the careful, methodically prepared data first recorded there by the old Franciscan Friars. Yet after 1833 the Zacatecan control of the Missions and the frequent criticisms and complaints thereof may indicate the employment of much less efficient methods in the declining period of the San Rafael Mission.

But such handicaps only serve to make the research efforts of the historians all the keener, and do not materially block them except in the loss of an irreplaceable rich store of local incident and detail not put down in the formal official reports of the period. So a number of these trained research men and women have found a sufficient store of official Government reports, personal letters, individual and official diaries, military and church accounts and reports to and by other California Missions concerning San Rafael Archangel, —to enable us to piece out a fairly consecutive story. There would be a different account indeed, if one depended on the fantastic tales and interpretations of wholly misunderstood incidents and acts as reported by early official and unofficial European visitors to the Coast.

It is certain that there are still many sources of such local incident accounts, which if all sent in for review, would materially add to the human interest of reviews of the period, and little by little enable us to prepare a complete and imperishable record of those old days. No Mission in California could have had a more interesting day by day record than was unquestionably prepared by old Padre Amoros[36] for the San Rafael Archangel and was similarly noted by every one of the other California Padres for their own posts. Yet the best we can now do is to substitute a pieced together remembrance instead.

Two books were all that remained as original data of our Mission, and unfortunately these were of the vital statistics only. One, a Book of Marriages dating from 1840 was found at our St. Vincent's Orphan Asylum; the other, of Baptisms, Marriages, and Deaths came to light at the San Francisco Mission Dolores. This later volume had a note which confirmed several accounts of San Rafael Archangel as having at first been only an "asistencia" or branch mission of the San Francisco post.

The San Rafael Archangel Mission was founded on December 4th, 1817, at a place called by Indians "Managuanui.[37]" Curiously enough there are several accounts giving the date all the way up to 1824, in direct contradiction to the recorded facts and subsequent dates of activities elsewhere. Prefect Padre Sarria[38] from San Francisco officiated, and in the presence of Fathers Duran[39], Abella[40], and Gil[41] installed the then youngest Mission with all the ceremony attending the foundation of the older and

---

[36] Juan Amorós (?-1832), formerly chaplain at Monterey.

[37] Usually now transliterated as 'Anaguanui or Nanaguani.

[38] Vicente Francisco de Sarría (1767-1835), of Basque heritage, also founded the asistencia at Santa Ysabel. He baptized the first Anglo citizen of California, John Gilroy, in 1814.

[39] Narcisco Durán (1776-1846), of Catalan birth, served as Father-President of the California Missions.

[40] Ramón Abella, (?-1842).

[41] Luis Gil y Taboada (?-1833), was in charge of the mission at San Luis Obispo from 1830 till his death.

larger institutions of similar nature; doubtless inferring that in its development in such a favorable territory it would soon take rank as a regular Mission in the long chain of them from Mexico up the California Coast. Padre Gil remained in charge for two years, and was succeeded by Padre Juan Amoros, who had already spent fifteen years at the San Carlos Mission down the peninsula. To him is due almost the entire credit for the great good accomplished at San Rafael Archangel and for its rapid development to the standard and gravity equal to any Mission in the western territory. He labored here for thirteen years and was enabled to practically develop his own plans in the work. As matters followed it was indeed a mercy that he passed away at the height of the success of San Rafael Archangel, rather than to have remained to see himself displaced by less competent wholly different leadership and plans which resulted in the loss of all that had been gained.

In consequence of the apparent loss of its records, few of the intimate facts of the early history of San Rafael Archangel can be noted. Yet for years there was a persistent idea that the records were not destroyed or lost, but retained by someone having an ulterior purpose in hiding them away. However that may be, the Mission was at first an "asistencia," and consequently its own constant reports to the parent post and those of inspectors frequently visiting it were regularly forwarded and filed away in the Spanish and later the Mexican State Archives. It is this data which affords some idea of the Mission's activities and progress. For example in the height of their prosperity and while the San Rafael Archangel was only getting a start, the property of the California Missions totaled $435,000 and included that of San Rafael at $5000: while in later year ours was rated at $18.000, the others declined so that that average was about half of this sum elsewhere.

One has to study accounts of all of the Missions in order to gain a fair idea of the methods followed at any one of them and of the general plan governing all, both in their period and as projected for their future. Father Gleason affords this view in his excellent "History of the Catholic Church in California"[42] but it is too exhaustive an ecclesiastical treatise to supply extracts for any general account for a particular locality. A short statement of the average plan it presented at this point in our narrative, may however,

---

[42] *History of the Catholic Church in California* (1872), by William Gleeson (1822-1903).

provide a needed substitute for the missing data concerning the probable system of the Mission San Rafael Archangel.

In founding a Mission it was placed about a day's journey from the one last established. A site was chosen, usually after previous careful exploration from the nearest post, and consecrated with all due observances of church and military ceremony. Then rough shelters were provided, to be later amplified by Indian labor under the Padre's instruction and the supervision of the escolta[43], which was composed of a few soldiers and often only one for the immediate Mission guard. Usually two priests and two or three soldiers made up the entire party and the more intelligent natives were quickly trained to assist in the simpler directive work.

The Presidio (soldier quarters) was at least two leagues distant from the Mission buildings and at the port or water approach, amply distant to prevent any contact with the Mission life. Nearby Indians were either induced to come in or were brought in to live at or near the Mission for instruction in the work of erecting the Mission buildings and homes for themselves. Later they were instructed in the faith and expected to till soil for the Mission and State (soldiers) subsistence.

This may seem to have been a one sided affair, unless we consider that it was wholly for their instruction so that later the natives could become independent of direction in the new manner of life and that the fruits of their labor could at first be held in trust for them and ultimately be divided amongst them.

23 February 1922

The average daily routine at any California Mission was about as follows: at sunrise all attended church service for morning prayers and other ceremonies. After the morning meal the neophytes were assigned to daily work much as a foreman now assigns his men. From about noon to two o'clock was the dinner and "siesta" period after which work proceeded until the evening Angeles called all in for service about an hour after sunset. All attended evening services after a sufficient recreation period following the third meal of the day. In the play period, the time was given up to games,

---

[43] "Escort."

dancing, and amusements of various kinds, just as now with our own children.

Settlers were not allowed anywhere near the Mission properties, and since the Mission lands joined at each post, all the sea coast territory and fertile land extending back to the mountains was denied to any settlement, all the way from Mexico to Sonoma on the north of us. Later, discharged soldiers were allowed to live near the Presidios and direct small "nationales" (government) ranchos for subsistence of the soldiers. As the Indians became Christianized, the "Haciendo" ranchos were organized on Mission lands whereon a qualified gente de razon (aristocrat) supervised and directed work of the natives for Mission crops and cattle. The revenues therefrom were also placed in a common fund and eventually given to Christianized, properly trained Indians (usually considered so after twelve years of instruction.) In fact, before the secularization orders went into effect, this was accomplished at some of the older Missions.

When a Mission had sufficiently developed, permission was given to establish a pueblo (village) about the Presidio, and when this developed to proper size and quality it was granted the status of a "town" with comparative self-government. It was altogether an ideal system, founded on perfection itself as to proper development and retention of the lands for the Indians and their colonization thereon after the race had been properly raised to the standard of what was then considered to be the proper degree of civilization. But inevitably the greed and rapacity of politicians and other outsiders, of roving disturbers, discharged soldiers, shady citizens and convict colonists sent from Mexico, —and in particular the constantly increasing pressure of settlers desiring to locate in the new territory,— resulted in constant dissension and turmoil. These idle folk, since they could not settle, had to live in the few pueblos established or reside on sufferance elsewhere; and the term "gente de razon" came to include many of them not at all intended in a proper meaning of the word. We would now call the Haciendo supervisors "Farm Managers." Later the term "pablodores" was applied to free men not connected with the Missions but belonging to the pueblos and towns.

Then too, the Franciscan Order, by its own rules, could not possess any property. Hence the question as to its right to hold such a vast empire in trust was vigorously disputed and many seizures followed, partly or wholly connived at or assisted by the soldiers and certain friends of government officials looking for what we would in these days term the "inside chance" in a new country. So the shell of organization, which in strong hands or if properly supported by Government would have withstood any ordinary attacks,—weakened, crumbled and eventually broke down completely.

Also, and most vitally affecting the entire Mission plans, continuing raids of Government on the so called "Pious Fund" brought chaos indeed. This had been painstakingly and persistently gathered by the California Missions for support of the weaker institutions for further expansion plans, and for the promised distribution to all neophytes.—-amounting to some $90,000. Upon its relinquishment by the Church a mad scramble followed for the Mission properties. Then the old Friars plainly saw that their institutions could not stand alone without such a reserve. Again, aside from the lack of Government co-operation probably the most vital defect in the whole Mission plan was the annexation of all coast lands from the shore line back as far as the Missioners cared to claim it: and the consequent denial of settlement by any free man whether church or non-church, — proved to be an impossible position in such a rapidly advancing and growingly republican territory.

Besides the church at a Mission, which was, usually a most pretentious affair, the Mission buildings included dwellings for the Padres and their attendants; barracks for the scolta; storehouses, outhouses and corral sheds. Then came the huts of the natives, of all descriptions but mainly of adobe and intended for the Christianized Indians only. Married folks had houses of their own; but those of single persons were divided as to sex, who were counted each night before being locked into sheds. All children over five years of age had to live in the Mission. One must not deride these rules without knowing the stern necessity therefor and the carefully planned future for the young people and children of these and defective simple older natives.

San Rafael seems to have had no Presidio as such though a somewhat similar post was established somewhere along the San Rafael Creek or its estero, far enough away to note the approach of visitors from any point. In fact the numerous references show that whenever hostile parties, Fremont's men, exploring expeditions, or other travelers approached — the Mission was always aware of it long before they arrived. One version describes the landing place as we infer it to have been, at about the present Cijos and Third street. There was no marsh then. Hence the Mission territory having no Presidio as such, could not be granted the pueblo or village rights and therefore could not start a settlement until after the Mission ceased activities and even in the ensuing period up to 1845. In fact it was not until that year that any house was built in San Rafael outside of the Mission grounds.

Various accounts are given concerning the reasons for establishing the Mission San Rafael Archangel. If the Russians are to be believed, it was purely a subterfuge of the Padres to be able to trade with the Fort Ross depot since Monterey was the only port open to trade on the coast and particularly forbidden to the Russians at all. It is extremely unlikely however that such plans were made in defiance of Government rules. If the military records of the Spaniards are authoritative it was solely to establish an outpost within easy reach of the San Francisco Presidio so that plans of the Russians in the north could be watched through the aid of friendly natives and by reconnoitering parties constantly in the field for that purpose. Naturally the constant friction between the temporal and spiritual forces at these Missions would color such reports if from the Spanish military folk. So they state that the Friars seized the chance of accompanying the soldiers to San Rafael in order that they might use it as a base for further investigation of an opportunity for additional Missions to the north. But like all versions from various sources in that period each one seems to be made up to prove a certain case.

Careful examination of the Mission and Church records of the period, from up and down the Coast and in Mexico and Spain, convinced the historian Bancroft that it was purely a case of the Padres' initiative in taking advantage of both the long discussed military desire to start a post across the Bay and the continuing discussion of transferring the San Francisco Mission elsewhere. This had been advocated as far back as 1786, since its location allowed of no farming or activity other than stock raising and little of that: and the rigorous climate was no place for naked Indians brought from warmer climates. Therefore the following account is perhaps a true one, and verified by various notes and reference from various sources in State, Church, Mission, and the General Vallejo reports and records. Many official reports of the period show that while other reasons for such a move had been for a long time under consideration, the vital distress of the natives at San Francisco was the immediate and hastening cause of the final action: and that the attractive climate and continuous sunshine advantages of the San Rafael territory as reported on again and again by exploring parties for years past, finally established the Mission San Rafael Archangel in Marin territory.

The neophytes of the San Francisco Mission, mainly brought from distant warm valleys south and east of the peninsula, were dying in such numbers on the fog swept and chilly winds section of Mission Dolores and its Presidio as to bring on a near panic to them all. Captain Sola[44], the Commandant, suggested transfer of some of the sick and ailing neophytes across the Bay to San Rafael; and on trying the experiment found that they were at once greatly benefited. But Prefect Padre Sarria[45] while agreeing with the plan, found himself without a Friar to take charge of the proposed post and hesitated also on account of the difficulty of easy communication therewith. Yet after several more neophytes had died at the Presidio without religious rites. "Padre Luis Gil y Taboada, late of San Jose, volunteered to be an extra assistant at San Francisco and to take charge of its branch to be located at San Rafael." Thereupon Prefect Sarria ordered that (Spanish punctuation) "a kind of rancho, with its chapel, baptistry and cemetery be founded across the Bay with the title of 'San Rafael Archangel,' in order that this most glorious prince, who in his name expresses the 'healing of God,' may care for bodies as well as souls."

So our Mission began as a Sanatorium instead of a regular Mission or a military post, which however was attached to it and in 1825 received orders to build a strong fort here. Happily it was never started. The Mission site was undoubtedly advised by Captain Moraga, who forty years before had made the Olompali visit previously mentioned; had thereafter surveyed the Bay and Petaluma Creek; and had often passed through San Rafael on survey and exploration trips to and from Bodega and the north territory.

2 March 1922

San Rafael Archangel was founded with all the ceremonial observances in dedication of the larger Missions, but as previously noted was first considered an "asistencia" to the San Francisco Mission Dolores with chapel instead of church. Yet the only later difference in comparison with any other Mission in California was in its unpretentious buildings. This

---

[44] Pablo Vicente de Solá, (1761–1826), was the twelfth and last Spanish colonial governor of Alta California, 1815-1822.

[45] Father Vicente Francisco de Sarría (1767–1835) was a Basque Spanish missionary.

removal of the sick and ailing neophytes from the exposed San Francisco side to the sheltering hills and welcome sunshine across the Bay, became known all the way down to Mexico and back to Spain; and later many aged and invalid Padres and Christianized Indians came from distant points for these far famed health restoring, peaceful days in Marin.

Two hundred and thirty neophytes were first transferred from San Francisco; and we can well imagine their joy at the change into sunshine and warm surroundings again. Three years afterwards the Mission had five hundred and ninety neophytes, increasing later to nine hundred and seventy and at its peak of success in 1828-30, there were eleven hundred and forty.

Old records do not seem to agree with the long after painted views of the Mission San Rafael. Bancroft quotes from the State Papers in the Mexican Archives: "In 1818 an adobe building, eighty-seven feet long, forty-two feet wide and eighteen feet high had been erected; divided by partitions into chapel, Padre's house and all other apartments required; and furnished besides with a corridor of tules." This was probably the official inspection report of the President Padre's visit referred to below. But the Marin County History of 1880 (without quoting authority) tells of its being in the shape of an "L," roofed with tiles made on the grounds, and the old altar having been upon the same spot where the present one now stands. Since it notes the front of the building being about twenty-five [feet] from the present Fifth Avenue line, the following description in the history would hardly correspond. "The main church wing was eighty feet long, and at right angles the building went back one hundred feet, being divided into a kitchen next to the church; then the Juzardo (Justice Room) of forty by twenty feet, and finally the apartments of the Padres and their attendants. The garret of this rear portion was used as a storehouse for grain and other products."

Since the official description was in 1818, only a year after the foundation, it is quite possible that both accounts are correct and that the "L" part was subsequently added in the particularly active years following. The reference last quoted also states that there was an adobe building above the Mission where the old William T. Coleman[46] home still remains, then

---

[46] William Tell Coleman (1824-1893), born in Kentucky, ran a steamship line, started the twenty-mule team borax mining in the Mojave, and founded the Vigilance Committee in San Francisco that lynched several men. He was also active in persecuting the Chinese. He founded the Marin County Water Company, forerunner of the Marin Municipal Water District.

used by the Indians; and that a second large adobe building was on the present Court House grounds. This was later the residence of Mrs. Merriner, whose sons, J. O. B. and Jacob Short[47] had much to do with early San Rafael developments.

A third mention of the old Mission building is a report of its inspection in 1849, when it was found to be somewhat in ruins, and "one wing was used as the church, the other as Court and Jury Rooms, and other apartments occupied by Mexican families with their dogs, hogs, children and cattle." This might indicate that the structure was still as originally described in 1818.

But what wonderful energy must have been displayed by Padre Gil in his first year here, to have erected his buildings and arranged the Mission in such shape as to be ready for President Prefect Payeros visit a year later! This was in May, 1918, when with Commandante Arguello[48], afterward Governor, the party made a trip to San Rafael by water and conducted a careful survey and exhaustive inspection of the surrounding country. It must be remembered that at this time both Padres and the Spaniards were deeply concerned at reports of Russian plans and possibilities of other nations joining in efforts to block the Mission movement to the north. In consequence, this visit and the careful reports made thereon seem to indicate a planned policy of making a strongly fortified northern frontier. Sometime thereafter, as will later appear, General Vallejo, the Military Governor of all California, received orders to establish such a stronghold near Santa Rosa, afterward changed to Sonoma where he resided. But the overthrow of the Spanish rule in 1821 and that of Mexico following in 1848 prevented the full plans being carried out.

One can imagine the pleasure of this visit in the time of year when vegetation, sunshine and clear atmosphere for views from high points, —in fact every condition was at its best in this territory. And the rapid convalescence of the San Francisco neophytes had effectually removed the

---

[47] Jane Merriner (ca 1809-1893), her sons John Orey Baptiste Short (1828-1902) and Jacob Short (1834-1895), and her daughters Elizabeth Merriner Upton (1840-1891) and Catherine Mary Merriner Partee (1843-1897), came over the Donner Pass from Missouri in 1846, lived for a time in the ruined San Rafael Mission, and went into the dairy business. They developed the southern half of San Rafael and the northern portion of San Anselmo.

[48] Luis Antonio Arguello (1784-1830), first California-born governor of Alta California and the first under Mexican rule.

growing concern of the mortality records on the peninsula, accounts of which had furnished sharp criticism from enemies up and down the coast who seized every chance to deride the Missions Plan.

A report states that "the party climbed to the top of the hill near the Mission" (undoubtedly our Boyd Park summit and later known as San Rafael, and North Hill), "and looked upon the Canada de los Olompalis and the Llanos de los Petalumas." President Payeros disapproved of the site of the San Rafael Mission as any proper place for the northern frontier stronghold and doubtless this view from Mission Hill had much to do with the establishment of the Mission Solano at Sonoma five years later. Since Captain Moraga had made such careful military surveys and corresponding government reports on this country again and again, he had doubtless pointed out the disadvantages of our location for such purpose, as indeed any modern officer would now do.

Pretty as this setting is of President Prefect Payeros climbing our Mission Hill, the extract given did not satisfy the writer because from this point no hint of the Olompali Valley or the Petaluma Plains can be gained. But Chapman's "A History of California"[49] (just published) gives a complete translation of the Payeros original report which clears up the matter. It is another evidence of how easily successive translators give differing versions from the same text. "Passing through San Rafael," the account read, "in an investigation for a Mission site, they (the party) went to a tract of land back of Point San Pedro, which Payeros called Gallints. Climbing the highest hill to the east (doubtless the "Cat" Ranch there) they looked out on the Petaluma Plain on the one hand and the great river and mountain range to the east on the other." Anyone who has taken this not difficult tramp will find as wonderful a view as can be found anywhere in Northern California, and will instantly recognize the description of the view therefrom as noted by Prefect Payeros in 1818.

One Romas Lasso de la Vegas died at San Rafael in 1821. Since the records show that he was a schoolmaster, (salary was $25 a year) at San Jose in 1795, it is possible that he came here with Padre Gil or Amoros and assisted in the instruction of the natives. He was an expert clerk and accountant and may have been attached as Recorder and Accountant in those years. Perhaps then, he was Marin County's first school master.

---

[49] Charles Edward Chapman (1880-1941), *A History of California: The Spanish Period* (1923).

Frequent and detailed surveys of this territory continued, showing an increasing concern of both Mission and Spanish authorities as to foreign plans and activities at Bodega and in the north. In 1821 Captain Arguello led a survey expedition up the Sacramento River as far as Red Bluff, returning across the Coast Mountains to San Rafael and including another survey of Marin territory on the trip here. Returning the next year with President Prefect Payeros, he completed the local inquiry and passed on to Bodega and the north again. These many expeditions clearly showed the growing concern of the authorities as to the northern frontier situation, and indirectly distributed a knowledge of San Rafael and its environs throughout the whole western territory.

In 1822 the Oath of Allegiance to the Mexican National Congress was taken by Padre Amoros and his neophytes at San Rafael Archangel, a rather unusual matter since it was the only instance of its kind in the entire California Missions History. The old Padres had almost to a man declined to do so, claiming immunity therefrom yet pledging themselves from engaging in any political matters. One cannot but admire the dignified yet sternly expressive letters to the Mexican authorities by such old Missioners as Padre Sarria and Padre Duran on this matter, but space does not allow of such context here.

It is a curious fact that even as late as 1820 the Spaniards knew little about the country joining the Bay territory and its streams, but still relied on the Indian versions of three great rivers of which Upper San Francisco Bay was said to be the combined Great Estero. The first, the Jesus Maria, began beyond Cape Mendocino, passed back of Bodega and proceeded on south to the Bay; the second, the Sacramento or as it was first called the Rio San Francisco, had its source far up in the Rocky Mountains near where the Columbia began and entered the east end of the Bay; the third, the San Joachim, started far south in the Bolbones' country and flowed north to just above the Sacramento entrance to the Bay. In consequence the early Spanish geographers gave most inaccurate accounts of the Central and northern California interior country.

9 March 1922

From this point on to the close of Marin's Mission Period, the story of San Rafael Archangel must be made up from fragments of notes, references, extracts from reports and letters, and from accounts found in many reviews of the period,—all being arranged in such chronological order as to afford a reasonably consecutive account. Such items as are tradition only are so noted, the remainder being of record.

Padre Amoros' direction of Mission San Rafael Archangel was exceptionally successful and prosperous for the decade and from such a small beginning. There were twice as many baptisms as deaths and the population, not counting ninety-two neophytes sent to Sonoma, nearly doubled in the period, reaching the greatest total of eleven hundred and forty in 1828-30. The worthy Padre had extended his journeys and work even up to the Santa Rosa country. In fact that name first appears in an account of one of his trips with a single companion, when he baptized an Indian girl there and according to the Spanish custom, probably gave the territory a Saint's Day name connected with that date.

On July 23rd, 1823, Padre Altimera[50] came to San Rafael from San Francisco and took possession of such Mission property as was needed to establish the Mission San Francisco Solano at Sonoma. A sufficient number of neophytes was included for the labor thereon and an escort for proper protection. There he at once began to erect buildings under the plan of moving both San Francisco and San Rafael Mission activities to the new frontier. But his Prefect vigorously opposed such a plan and after much correspondence San Francisco and San Rafael were not suppressed, but one half of the San Francisco neophytes were transferred to Sonoma. Thereafter any neophyte was allowed to transfer from the peninsula post to San Rafael if agreeing to return after one year's absence.

This compromise seemed to meet all objections and the work proceeded. Padre Estenaga[51], from San Francisco, began the direction and later Padre Fortuni[52], a lifelong friend of our Padre Amoros, continued in charge of the new Mission.

In consequence of the start with so many transferred neophytes there was a great lack of women there for Indian wives,—and incidentally workers for the husbands to be. Padre Estenaga was forced to keep the peace by allowing the single men to go south in a lancha (boat) on a hunt for wives,

---

[50] José Altimira (1787-after 1828), a native of Barcelona, founded the mission at Sonoma.

[51] Tomas Elluterio Estenaga.

[52] Buenaventura Fortuny (1774-1840).

and supplied the party with numerous gifts to assist in winning them. The expedition evidently succeeded by other means, for it started back with a boatload of captured femininity. But a complaint reaching Padre Amoros at San Rafael of the wholesale kidnapping, he pursued the party and caught it near Angel Island: rescued the girls and gave the daring Lotharios fifty lashes each for their action! One can imagine the jeers of their friends when they returned to Sonoma sans both gifts and maidens.

An interesting description of the Mission lands and a Register of Brands report in 1828 reads as follows: "In the west beyond the range of hills is an Estero from the port of Bodega, called Tamales. The range extends north nine leagues, then the Plains of Livantonome (Santa Rosa to Petaluma country). Mission lands from the rancherias of Annamus, called San Pedro Alcantara, in the Corte de Madera, and the Rincanada del Tiburon. The grain lands de temporal (of the State) begin in the Canada of Arongues or San Pedro Regalado. Livestock feeds northward to the rancheria of Olompali, of Santisimo Rosario, the chief being a Christian and a farmer. Cattle graze in the Canadas of Las Gallinas, Arroyo San Jose, Novato, Colomache, Echatamal and Olompali. The horses go farther to Olemochoe, or San Antonio, where the stream, dry in summer, rising in the laguna Ocolom, or San Antonio; the lands of which join those of Novato, Colomache, and Echatamal, going round the hill. The Laguna of Ocolom[53] seems to belong to the Mission, but the natives are warlike."

In the same year the famous Indian bandit, Pompanio[54], was captured at the Canada de Novato. He was a refugee neophyte from San Francisco, and a native of the San Rafael region. For several years a notorious outlaw and criminal, his depredations extended from San Rafael to Santa Cruz and even further south, though he was continually and vigorously pursued. His outrages and murders were confined to Indian victims but when a Spanish soldier was included his day was soon over. After the capture as noted he was court martialed at Monterey and shot a few days later. Another version states that after his Mission experience he was determined to lead the Indians toward a revolution against the foreigners but failed to have them turn against the Padres who had brought such betterments to all.

---

[53] An extinct lake at the headwaters of San Antonio Creek on the northern border of Marin.
[54] Pomponio, native name Lupugeyun (1799-1824) was a Coast Miwok from Bolinas.

In the statistical records of San Rafael Archangel reports the final account of Padre Amoros' tenure, including a following year and dating from 1817 to 1834, reads as follows and gives a fairly accurate idea of the great establishment one of these old Padres could build up in so short a time against obstacles few present day men would care to encounter: "Total baptisms, 1873, of which 1096 were Indian adults, 768 Indian children, and seven de razon; an average of 103 annually. There were 543 marriages, of whom eight were de razon. During seventeen years the deaths numbered 458 adult Indians, 239 Indian children, and one de razon. The largest population was 1140 in 1828. The largest number of cattle was 2120 in 1832; of horses, 450 in 1831; of mules, 4; of sheep, 4000 in 1823; of swine, 30 in 1823; and of all kinds of animals, 5508 in 1832. The total products were wheat, 17,905 bushels, yielding eight fold; of barley, 12,339 yielding nine fold; of corn 3657, yielding forty fold; of beans, 1360, yielding thirteen fold; of miscellaneous grains, 412, yielding eight fold. The crop of 1829 was very poor and badly damaged by rats, locusts and 'other causes.' Shipments to the Presidio from 1826 to 1830 amounted to $1134." From this it is seen that Mission San Rafael was not only self-supporting and supplying a very large population, but for several years had assisted with Presidio supplies also. It would be interesting indeed if present day farmers would give us present day averages of increases of grain crops and compared them to the results of primitive methods and from the first tilled fields of those days.

In 1825 there was a widespread epidemic of measles all through the Indian country, carrying away thousands of children and some adults as well. San Rafael somewhat escaped this scourge,—another testimony to its climatic advantages and probably also largely due to the careful oversight of the competent Padre Amoros.

On August 25th, 1826, a courier passed through San Rafael with the welcome news that our Mission and that at Sonoma was excepted from the Secularization Order of Governor Escheandia[55], which affected all the others. This was probably done because of the still disturbed and threatening conditions on the northern frontier, as well as the comparative immaturity of the Missions in this northern territory. One can picture the venerable

---

[55] José María de Echeandía (?-1871) was twice Mexican governor of Alta California from 1825 to 1831 and again from 1832 to 1833. He was the only governor of California that lived in San Diego.

Padre Amoros summoning all of his Mission forces from the uttermost bounds of his territory, and telling them the glad news as well as having them all join in giving thanks to the Providence which had so rewarded his efforts. The first rules for territorial land Grants were issued in Mexico in 1828 and then began the first hint of Marin County's permanent development. Before this, under the Mission rule all lands were held in trust for the Indian neophytes. Those conducted by the soldiers were not open to location except under definite restriction as to retention of title, by the State, and agreement to graze the ranges and till the soil for state subsistence. The sea coast lands and peninsulas were not yet available. Then followed a General Order for all land owners to appear in 1827, and again in 1830 to give information about their holdings and facts as to the titles thereon. Those failing to do so lost their possessions at once.

On January 31, 1831, Padre Amoros sent his President an account in his concise way "of a tour he has made from San Rafael among the pagans," showing that almost up to his death this faithful old Padre allowed nothing to interfere with his work. The laconic reference to this "tour" meant a trip with a single companion up as far as Mendocino. He, like the beloved Padre Ugarte of Jesuit fame, scorned the escort of soldiers and would commit himself and his companion to Providence and trustfully penetrate to any territory, even if occupied by hostile natives.

This was about the time that the incident is supposed to have happened as so often told by Rafael Garcia, then a Spanish Corporal of the Mission guard and afterwards a pioneer rancher in the Olema Valley. No account of such occurrence has been located in any record, and only one simple reference is noted of such an attack on the Mission, but the story is interesting and even inspiring. What a wealth of such stories we have been denied by the loss of the Mission records. Garcia stated that a band of hostile Indians was threatening an attack upon the Mission and as a last chance to save his children, his wife, Loreta and the old Padre, they were all placed on a tule 'balsa' (a frail yet floatable raft of tules) and set [a]drift on the tide so to be out of reach of the attackers. But the party finally arrived safely on the Presidio shores without mishap. Meanwhile the capable soldier, mindful of his responsibility and freed from concern in protection of his charges, returned to the fight and by strenuous endeavor organized the Mission forces and drove off the raiders with heavy losses.

This supplies a fine picture of the venerable old Padre, committing Garcia's family and himself to the mercy of the tidal currents of San Francisco Bay and his beloved Mission to the protection of his redoubtable Corporal, the implicitly trusting in Providence and his Patron Saint to carry them through safely! It is worthy of the best talent of our land to reproduce this picture of Padre Amoros and his companions astride of an awkward tule balsa, utterly oblivious of the dangers of the unexpected journey and proceeding with implicit confidence that a Divine Providence would properly care for them all.

16 March 1922

In 1832 came an irreparable loss, in fact the beginning of the end of San Rafael Archangel's history, in the death of its beloved Padre Amoros. In a decade or more he had raised it from an "assistencia" not only to a regular Mission, but by his keen administrative direction had from a small beginning made it one of the most prosperous and successful in California. Doubtless the efforts of Padre Gil in its first two years had been largely applied to erecting proper buildings and on the original purpose of caring for the sick and afflicted neophytes from the San Francisco area. Doubtless also, Padre Amoros during his fifteen years at San Carlos, had shaped the plans for his future success in the north and had one of the fairest of all Mission territories upon which to develop his aims. He was buried in the church at San Rafael by Padre Fortuni from Sonoma, "who had known him from boyhood and declared him to be a Saint." In many ways Padre Amoros is to be compared with the early Jesuit Padre Ugarte, the "Father of Missions" in the West, or to Franciscan Padre Junipero Serra, the "Founder of Missions" in California. He indicated his attitude of broad tolerance by being one of the few Missioners who boldly urged fairer treatment to foreigners and a further extension of trade privileges. Fortunate it was that he passed away before any knowledge came to him of the way in which the later foreigners would have repaid his endeavors!

He was rated by his superiors as of unusual ability and well fitted for his pioneering work in the north. Especially was he noted for the zeal with which he undertook every task, whether of spiritual or temporal nature. A scholarly, kindly man; a successful business manager and organizer; a skillful mechanic; a Missioner who treated his neophytes as the simple children they were,—he was particularly loved by neophyte and gentile Indians alike. He strove to please all classes and to engage in no controversies, —a typical frontier Missionary having a natural instinct for uplifting primitive people. Would that the history of his Mission could have continued to its end in such way as he had developed and advanced it, and with the love and respect which all the Indians and his own people had for his institution and his unselfish effort thereon. The example of his tenure here should be the most valued heritage of San Rafael and its Mission memories.

Next came a period in the direction of the affairs of San Rafael Archangel, and of some of the California Missions as well, which is too often criticized without proper perspective of the conditions governing or of the changed type of direction resulting from the Mexican control of Mission affairs. The Government had prepared to substitute its own Friars from its Zacatecan College, for the Franciscan Padres on the California Coast and in 1833 sent ten of its first representatives. These demanded the surrender of all the Missions but as there were twenty-three Missions and ten Zacatecans available, only a partial substitution resulted. As they arrived in the period of rapid decline of the Mission Rule their tenure was very short, and ended before a second contingent was ready to join them here.

In no sense of criticism, but merely in comparison, they were not the equals of the Franciscan Padres of old, who had slowly, painstakingly and thoroughly built up a Missions system, and who planned years ahead for coming difficulties in their pioneering.

The Zacatecans appeared to have had a different training, and no such comprehensive education as those old Padres: nor were they men who had from the beginning consecrated their lives to such duties for humanity's sake. They were too inexperienced in a work which only the wisest and most tactful direction could hold together under the rapidly increasing difficulties. They were in a sense comparable to the immature young college graduate at once desiring to step into an old College President's chair to assume his multiplex duties; or of a novitiate suddenly being elevated to the responsibilities of the head of the church.

The Zacatecans were unwilling to take up assistant's work, whereby proper idea of responsibility could have been gained: and being suddenly placed on their own initiative after years of implicit adherence to direction of others. Only a few of the ten here and there properly succeeded in the difficult task accorded them. The impartial reader can view their errors with every allowance for the impossible duties thrust suddenly upon them.

Not mentioning the increasingly trying conditions of carrying on Mission work at all under the old plan, there were three main matters which tended to now antagonize and alienate neophytes and their supporters all up and down the coast and prevent the success of even reasonable direction of the Zacatecans. For one, Padre Mercado's action at San Rafael (noted below) thoroughly enraged and prejudiced both neophyte and gentle Indians everywhere and aroused a storm of comment among all foreigners. A second was their belief in the free use of the lash to enforce discipline of all kinds, while former Padres had reserved such penalties for only the most serious offenses. Thirdly, the remaining Franciscan Padres had little patience for the views or the immorality of a certain type of Mexican and Mexican Indians arriving in constantly increasing numbers in Mission territory and seriously interfering with Mission peoples. But the Zacatecan Friars would not countenance proper punishment therefor. To further complicate matters, the government soon cancelled all temporal powers of the Padres and substituted so called "Administradores" for civil control and direction. The usual result followed of incompetent, inexperienced and too often unscrupulous politicians being so assigned. Control of both temporal and spiritual matters, and perfect cooperation between two departments, was the vital keystone of the Mission system,—and when the house became divided quick disaster followed as an inevitable consequence.

Therefore we must consider the conditions and not unduly criticize the individuals, in viewing the work of the Zacatecan Friars at San Rafael Archangel following the earlier success of the Franciscan Padres. The old policy of leading the simple natives by love and affection, and of gaining full respect and implicit confidence in their direction, gave way to a rule by force and often the severest cruelty,—with the certain result of arousing all the latent resistance and objectionable tendencies of the primitive Indians as well as the more advanced neophytes.

Padre Jesus Maria Vasquez del Mercado, a Zacatecan, relieved Padre Estenaga at San Rafael in 1833 or 1834. He was described as a man of fine presence, engaging manners, a winning personality, and of more than average ability and education, but extremely intolerant and lacking the essential quality of patience and tact which Missioners had to exhibit at all times. In later years he continued an intriguer in constant trouble at several

Missions, and with his secular superiors. Finally he was peremptorily banished to Mexico by Governor Michtelorena[56] for intriguing in political matters.

In 1833 Padre Mercado complained to the Governor that the Russians were enticing his neophytes to the north and protecting those who had deserted. Further, that they were buying stolen cattle and in many ways invading the Mexican rights. This again indicates that the foreign difficulties were becoming more and more troublesome. About this time also, the Russians planted crops three leagues south of Bodega at a place called Talamanca, which may have been in present Marin territory and therefore on Mission lands. But on vigorous protest of the Commandant at the Presidio, they abandoned the territory after the first harvest. Nevertheless this action greatly increased the alarm of the authorities. Then Baron Wrangel[57] arrived at Fort Ross and planned to establish an inland post near Santa Rosa. His plans for colonization of Northern California were later so perfected that an offer was made to the Mexican government for purchase of all the Mission and government rights north of San Francisco Bay and payment for the settlements already there. But before the matter was up for decision, he received news from home that the Czar would not support his efforts.

This sounded the death knell of Russian hopes in the West, and gave a decided impetus for outsiders to colonize this territory beyond the Missions' furthest frontier claims. But before such matters became known Governor Figuero[58] had issued orders to General Vallejo to strongly fortify all the northern frontier posts. The work was never started, but the General while awaiting supplies and further directions therefor, maintained a strong garrison at Sonoma at his own expense for several years.

23 March 1922

---

[56] José Manuel Micheltorena (1802–1853) was a brigadier general of the Mexican Army, adjutant-general of the same, governor, commandant-general and inspector of the department of Alta California.

[57] Baron Ferdinand Friedrich Georg Ludwig von Wrangel (1797-1870), Russian explorer, founder of the Russian Geographic Society, and chief manager of the Russian-American Company, essentially Governor of Alaska.

[58] General José Figueroa (1792–1835), was a General and the Mexican territorial Governor of Alta California from 1833 to 1835.

(With Cabrillo's discovery of Marin territory in 1542 was a world event. It marked the beginning of civilization in the west, and of the initial history of California. Further desire to reach Marin's coast directly resulted in the establishment of the long chain of western Missions, and of the exploration, colonization and development of our great state. The story of Marin's History should indeed stimulate its children and its citizens to a better pride in its traditions. Our story began with Marin's Savagism and proceeds through the various periods of development to a review of each of its important sections. Our contributor's name appears with the final article—Editor.)

THE MARIN MISSION PERIOD

(Continued from last week)

Padre Mercado's trouble at San Rafael become almost a national matter. Let us consider that it was no doubt largely caused by his brooding over constant restraint and reproof from General Vallejo who would not allow any abuse of Indian rights and sternly remedied such cases as came to his attention, whether from Mission or any other source. The prompt action of Padre Mercado's superiors ended any reflection on the church for this act. Governor Figuero, through General Vallejo, had persuaded Chief Toribio[59] to visit the Mission San Rafael Archangel with his tribe and cultivate friendly relations therewith. Leaving the party near San Rafael, the Chief and several followers reported to the Mission but when the message was given the Padre he declined to see them until next day. During the night a robbery occurred at the Mission, for which the guests were at once blamed. Padre Mercado arrested the visitors and hurried them off to San Francisco, which action should have been taken by the guard and if necessary the trouble referred to General Vallejo. The next night, Mercado armed thirty-seven of his neophytes and ordered his major domo to disperse or capture the remaining Indians, who he said were about to attack the Mission to rescue their Chief and his men. It is not explained why the Padre had the arms or entrusted them to the neophytes, but at dawn the armed party

---

[59] Of the Pulia Rancheria.

surprised this tribe who were peacefully awaiting the return of Toribio. In the attack twenty-one gentile Indians and one neophyte were killed and a number of men, women and children, many of them badly wounded, were brought back as prisoners.[60] Strange to say, Padre Mercado then coolly reported the "attack" to the Governor, with request for reinforcements to aid in pacifying the rancherias.

In consequence, Governor Figueroa was exceedingly angry at this treachery to friendly Indians, and ordered General Vallejo to the scene at once. Vallejo sent Padre Mercado in arrest to his Prefect, who properly ordered him for trial before his College. Then Vallejo had Toribio and party released and brought back from San Francisco and discharged the San Rafael prisoners also. But the mischief was done, and as a result all the Indians in Northern California were inflamed and began preparations for immediate retaliation.

General Vallejo, fully recognizing the seriousness of the matter himself quickly visited every rancheria up as far as Mendocino, quieting the excited Indians, convincing them of the Governor's good intentions and no doubt showing them "that this wicked Padre had represented nothing more than himself in the matter." A number of state reports were made on the case and the facts seem to have been fully accepted. By his prompt and efficient action Governor Vallejo undoubtedly avoided a long and bloody Indian war in our north of the bay country, which would probably have at once brought the coalition of the Russians and perhaps the French with the Indians,— inevitably resulting in later foreign colonization of the territory.

Padre Mercado's unfortunate action must be viewed in all charity, and to have undoubtedly been caused by a mental lapse rather than arbitrary intention. But forever afterward, the Northern California Indian's confidence in Mission work was shattered, and indeed extended even to Lower California territory. It is noted here because it happened in Marin territory and because of its widespread and generally evil effect in all circles, and not as a criticism of the individual or of the organization he represented. Accounts of it are found in many foreign articles of the period and from that date further conversion of the Indians in the north was practically over.

---

[60] The massacre occurred November 20, 1833.

He was succeeded by Padre Jose Lorenzo de la Conception Quijos, also a Zacatecan Friar who thereafter had charge of both the San Rafael and Sonoma Missions until the close of their activities. But Government "administradores" were soon placed in charge of all temporal power at the Missions, and his position became one of a curate only. His residence at Sonoma for some time might indicate that the Mercado incident had completely disrupted the immediate spiritual relations at San Rafael Archangel. He later returned to San Rafael, having preferred charges of disrespect and refusal of beef by the Vallejos, and of immorality and disrespect by Major Domo Ortega at Sonoma, refusing to stay there unless the latter was discharged. This failing, he thereafter lived in San Rafael but spent most of his time at surrounding ranchos. Up to 1836 his name appears in many north of the Bay matters, but thereafter he was badly handicapped by unfortunate conditions and diversions in entertaining foreign visitors. About 1843 all activities ceased at San Rafael Archangel, when he then went to San Jose and in 1846 is noted as having assumed a proper place. In 1854 he was noted as being in religious work in the mountains of Mexico.

Padre Quijos was an Ecuadorean, a muleteer and trader who joined the Zacatecan College for religious training. He also was described as a man of large stature, fine looking and of good general ability. He was kind hearted and popular with everyone, made few enemies and yet was a man of strong convictions and arbitrary in his attitude at times.

It is to be regretted that the many foreign explorers and scientists, all men of note, should have visited San Francisco and the north of the Bay territory when its Missions were on the eve of disruption and especially when these Zacatecan Friars were in charge. For they judged the entire Mission work by several of these unfortunate impressions, and most unjustly commented on Missioners in general, never having met the truer type of the real "padre of the Missions."

If one may judge at all accurately, it is certain that to General Vallejo, residing at Sonoma, belongs the major credit for holding all of the north of the Bay territory intact and free, both from Indian troubles and Mission mistakes as well as blocking the many plans of Russians and the French attempts to territorial aggression. His great tact and firmness in opposing unwise *regulamentos* and *pronunciamentos* of the faraway Spanish and Mexican governments and of the constantly reversed policies of changing governors, showed him to have been greatly in advance of any official of his times and a sturdy and successful defender of the territory and peoples under his charge. Again and again his name appears in the early history of Marin territory matters, and in every instance on the side of right and justice to those concerned. If for nothing else his record of protection of the Indian rights in the era of the final distribution to them is a lasting monument to his integrity and kindly practices. He seemed to have an unusual sense of humor which can be traced in many of his acts both official and unofficial.

Padre Gutierrez[61] at Sonoma, learning that the General planned to have settlers locate at Petaluma and Santa Rosa to help occupy the northern frontier, rushed a few Indians to the Petaluma site to build some huts and graze a band of horses, so as to claim the locality as Mission lands But the General calmly established a few settlers there, had them sow their crops and, no doubt, to insure their stay, hired them to plant some for himself, — leaving the question of title to be otherwise settled. Next he applied for a Land Grant of the whole territory and received it in 1833, whereupon he courteously offered the worthy Padre the use of the territory for grazing. His first intention was to interpose a line of settlers on the frontier, but the Padre could not see the point at that time. One can infer something of the same nature in the Santa Rosa matter. Padre Gutierrez at once sent two neophytes and a few hogs there to build huts and establish a rancheria in order to be first on the ground in claim as to Mission lands. But Vallejo, under cover of a great amount of talk, effected a strong garrison and settlement at his own home. Sonoma, where it was probably planned all the time. Again, we can see the old General's point of view in deciding for Padre Mercado at San Rafael, when Corporal Pacheco of the Mission guard refused to deliver a prisoner arrested for a major offense, though exactly following the General's previous orders. Later, Pacheco had seized a Mission sheep for meat for his men, after the Padre curtly stated that "he had no meat for wolves." With reports from both parties before him, the General judicially wrote the Corporal "to act very carefully, avoid all disputes, and take no supplies without politely asking the Missionary first." Surely this was a tactful message which applied to everyone concerned and which the angry Padre could interpret both for and against him in future! So with every issue presented to him, General Vallejo was tactful, just, efficient, and prompt in his decisions. His excellent action in the unfortunate Indian affair at San

---

[61] Padre José de Jesus Maria Gutierrez, last padre at Sonoma Mission.

Rafael, and his success in pacifying the northern Indians regarding it, won him unstinted praise in many quarters. Without such instant action the history of the whole Northern section might have been vitally changed.

An American traders' caravan visited San Rafael at this period, bringing blankets and serapes and for the first time offering a change from the Mission stores. Doubtless the Mission profited thereby also, since it still had products for exchange. In the following year a terrible pestilence of smallpox and intermittent fever raged all through the Sacramento and San Joaquin territory but was delayed in the Bay counties and south of the peninsula for a year or more. Young[62] and Warner[63], on a trapping expedition that year, came over the mountains and down the Sacramento River, reporting a dense Indian population everywhere. But on the return trip the next year dead bodies were found at every point and they saw only five Indians from Sacramento to the headwaters ridge. In the territories where there were no Missions the Indians were helpless before the white man's maladies, particularly because their mode of housing and sleeping gave perfect ground for spreading any epidemic and their practice of chilling a fevered patient finished the matter.

30 March 1922

(Note: the Novato section of the series was advanced to this point to coincide with a project of the Novato schools to promote knowledge of local history. The main story continued the following week.)

To Novato belongs the credit of the first dwelling built in Northern California. The early history of Novato Township dates from about 1839, when Governor Alvarado granted the Novato Rancho to Ferdinando Felis[64], who constructed an adobe house 20 by 40 feet, with two rooms and having a wonderful old eight foot fireplace. The rancho then passed down through

---

[62] Ewing Young (1799-1841), Tennessee-born fur trapper and trader in New Mexico, California, and Oregon.

[63] Jonathan Trumbull Warner (1807-1890), known as Juan Jose Warner in California, was born in Connecticut, became a fur trader, and settled Warner's Ranch in Warner Springs, California, an important stop on the Butterfield Stage Line.

[64] Fernando De La Trinidad Feliz (1795-1859), born in Los Angeles, San Jose councilman, first grantee of Rancho Novato.

several owners to the Sweetzer[65] and DeLong[66] families. The names of the old Novato families are among the best known in the county's history.

The Marin County History of 1880 seems to be the only available general account of the various localities of the county prior to 1861, after which the "*Journal*" files are fairly representative of subsequent events. The following notes are largely based on the data listed in the history mentioned and supplemented by many notes collected from various sources. It is intended to present in a general way the beginning and development of the various earlier sections of the county. No doubt many of the relatives of some of the earlier Marin families could contribute more extensive and even more interesting data than here afforded. We should have every county school collect these items of early local history if for no other purpose than to have each school child take a more intimate interest in its particular surroundings. In his Admission Day address at Monterey in 1908, John F. Davis aptly states the matter of need for more local history in our schools. "It is indefensible," he said, "that in the face of incidents in our history such as these, sons and daughters of California should be ignorant of the lives and experiences of their fathers and of those who preceded them on this coast. The history of the nation, and the record of the achievements of the empire builders of this Coast is one that inspires civic pride and a reverence for their memories."

NOVATO TOWNSHIP

To Novato belongs first mention in Marin's sectional history, not for its immediate early development but because its territory was first of definite record of the entire Northern California territory in the matter of intimate comment and description by early Spanish exploring parties.

We have heretofore noted the visit of Spanish soldiers to the Olompali Rancheria in 1776, where they instructed the Indians in the mysteries of making adobe bricks and in the building of the first house in north of the Bay territory. This dwelling was on the site of the Burdell home, the present mansion retaining one of the old time adobe walls. The building was sixteen

---

[65] Joseph Bryant Sweetser (1813-1886) of Massachusetts, a Novato pioneer.
[66] Francis C. DeLong (1808-1885) of Vermont, opened a grocery store in San Francisco and formed a partnership with Sweetser.

by eight feet in extent, with walls three feet thick and the roof composed of thatched tules. A hole therein took the place of the chimney of later days. This first adobe house was probably erected by the grandfather or perhaps the father of the Camilo Ynitia[67] who was finally awarded the Olompali Rancho Land Grant after passing through the twelve years training at the Mission San Rafael Archangel. One of the visiting Padres notes that one Santisimo Rosaria was a Christian and a successful farmer at Olompali in the early Mission days, and it was either he or his father who so hospitably received the Spanish party in 1776. This first adobe house was located near the one existing there many years afterward, the first having crumbled away in the passing years. The second dwelling was a more pretentious affair, twenty-four by fifty-five feet, and having three rooms while the first had only one. If Camilo Ynitia constructed this it shows how the Mission training had stimulated him to better things, and if Rosario built it his initiative was probably derived from frequent visits to the Mission as well as his desire to properly provide for his son Camilo after the new training. The second house was used as a residence by Dr. Burdell for many years. With a portion of this old structure now protected in the walls of the Burdell home, the old and the new Olompali can assuredly take rank as the oldest continuous dwelling place in the entire West. Nowhere else do the consecutive Indian traditions of earliest aboriginal days so connect down through the ages to earliest Spanish period and thence in direct order on to the third generation of a present family. It is one hundred and forty-six years since the first visit of members of the white race to Olompali. But as an Indian dwelling place it must he dated back almost to the beginnings of man in the West. Various relics found in the enormous shell deposits nearby furnished the means of unending disputes among ethnologists, for they indicate eons of time concerning which we know nothing. These great shell deposits were of unknown depth, covering several acres and containing implements unknown to any archeologist as of earliest Indian origin. In addition to these, three distinctly different types of arrow heads were found at varying depths, which cannot be listed as belonging to any known Indian period checked up elsewhere.

---

[67] Camilo Ynitia (1803-1856), native name Hueñux, a leader of the Coast Miwok, was the son of Inutia and Minero (baptized as Aurelio and Aurelia). His father built the first house north of San Francisco at Olompali, which still stands.

The following may serve to illustrate just how extremely ancient such relics may be: Captain Moraga, who made all of the earliest Spanish explorations in Northern California, and to whom we are indebted for the selection of San Rafael as the first north of the bay Mission site, named the Calaveras River (river of skulls) on account of an immense heap of human skulls found there. These were on the surface, probably indicative of some great battle or the last gathering place of a people driven into the valley of volcanic outbursts and probably smothered there by poisonous gases. Years afterward a mine shaft was sunk nearby and a skull found at a depth of 130 feet below the surface. Above this there were seven successive strata of lava and gravel, thus plainly indicating that between each lava flow there were long periods of erosion. The California Academy of Sciences made an exhaustive investigation of the matter, showing the depth and probable age of each strata. Foster's "Prehistoric Races"[68] notes that "This skull (admitting its authenticity), goes back to the advent of man to the Pliocene Epoch; and is therefore older than the stone implements of the drift gravel of Abbeville and Amiens, or the relics furnished by the cave dust of Belgium and France." (These are the oldest known.)[69] Such data indicates how many successive geological changes must have occurred in our mountain regions and consequently on the coast sections afterward, in the formative periods of the west coast territory.

What a wonderful setting there is for the imaginative person lolling in the hospitable and beautiful grounds of the Burdell homestead and visualizing step by step these eons of time through which Olompali existed without change. It is now about eight miles distant from Petaluma Creek to the East. Professor George Davidson's[70] theory of the formation of San Francisco Bay reasonably shows that at one time the sparkling blue waters of California's great inland lake closely approached Olompali. One can therefore think of Olompali's establishment on this lake shore close to a stream rushing down from the hill in rear of it whose source was on the high wooded ridges about this point. Even as late as the Spanish visit in 1776 this fine stream was there. So the dwellers at this point undoubtedly saw the great lake rise for the central California river bed of Professor Davidson's

---

[68] "Pre-Historic Races of North America" (1887), by John Wells Foster (1815-1873).

[69] The Calaveras skull was later found to be only 1,000 years old, placed in the mine as a hoax by local shopkeeper John. C. Scribner.

[70] Professor George Davidson (1825-1911), geodesist, astronomer, and surveyor.

description, and reach higher and higher after the complete blocking of the Pajaro Valley outlet. Then they must have observed its gradual recedence when the wealth of waters broke through to the ocean and made our present Golden Gate. But when the Spanish party was at Olompali the Bay waters lay just below the Rancheria and none of the present marshes existed there. This accounts for the huge pile of shellfish refuse or so called shell-mound which accumulated there at a point naturally and thoroughly protected from attack, and where the permanence of a Rancheria was assured for ages and ages of time. One can climb the ridge in rear and trace out the source and the course of the stream from above, though it takes a true nature lover to visualize those bare ridges as a once heavily forested area which was necessary to protect such an all the year around stream as the Spanish party describes in several diary notes of its visit there in 1776.

In addition to this priceless tradition of age, Olompali was the rare occasion when the early soldiers returned Indian hospitality with kindly acts. Undoubtedly the Spaniards were vividly impressed by the then reigning Chief who was an Indian of rare ability, probably having qualities built up by his knowledge of and respect for the untold ages of his ancestry. All other California Indians knew nothing of earlier traditions and cared less. What a pity that those early explorers could not record the tradition of this Olompali tribe. Is it possible that our later Camilo Ynitia of the Olompali Rancho was the last of a race far antedating even the California Indians and concerning whom the inquisitive mind of man knoweth not? Can anyone supply a note as to the end of this Ynitia family? As before stated, to Novato territory belongs the credit of the first dwelling built in Northern California (Olompali). The early history of Novato Township dates from about 1839 when Governor Alvarado granted the Novato Rancho to Fernando Fells, who constructed an adobe house twenty by forty feet, with two rooms and having a wonderful old eight foot fireplace. The Rancho then passed down through several owners until Sweetzer and DeLong took charge. The carefully described two leagues of land proved on survey to contain three leagues, about 13,000 acres. Of the many names of earliest pioneers of the Novato territory, descendants of the Burdell, Scown, Pacheco and Sweetzer families still reside there. Thomas Schweisau, a pioneer of 1851, at present resides at Fairfax. With Stephen Richardson now living in San Francisco, these two are probably the earliest living pioneers of the county. The Mrs. Merriner family, better known from the names of Jacob and J. O. B. Short who were her sons, came to California on the overland trails, arriving at Sutter's Fort and thence proceeding to the Novato Rancho. It will be noted that this family later located in San Rafael yet the brothers carried on activities in many southern Marin sections.

The first industries of Novato territory were shipbuilding, woodcutting, grazing and small dairying and farming. A numbers of schooners were built at the Black Point estuary, and the oaken "ship 'knee'" for the *U. S. S. Saginaw* were cut there and sent to Mare Island in 1864. So perished the giant oaks of Black Point, referred to again and again in chronicles of early explorers and which if now growing there would make the place world famous. One of these old Marin patriarchs still stands at the entrance of Novato.

Black Point was then heavily wooded, and received its name from a darker appearance than any surrounding locality as viewed from across the Bay by the Fages and Anza parties marching up the East shore. A previous mention of the Post offices of Marin County now explains why Black Point took over the Novato territory post office and afterward lost it, for in those days the Point was the center of busy industries. —later given up as the time [tree?] supply was exhausted. The first hotel-store-saloon was the "Our House" at Black Point, and another called the "Half Way House" was some distance towards the present Novato. This town had the post office in 1856, it being the starting point for many interior valley Ranchos, —but lost it to Black Point in 1860. Its first school was in 1858 and a better one replaced it in 1878. Now Novato is erecting a modern concrete school building. From the earliest years a small vessel made regular trips from Black Point and Novato Creek to various Bay points.

There is a tradition that land grant matters were somewhat disturbed in the Novato-Black Point region and that many settlers were dispossessed after developing farms there under purchase from Fernando Felis. But no definite record thereof has been found and if this was the case it was probably due to the fact that there were no such determined and resolute leaders there at the time, as the twelve Tomales pioneers who sturdily and successfully fought their legal battles to a perfect title for the Bolsa de Tomales grant.

In 1840 Henry J. Pierce, a Honolulu merchant, visited San Rafael and considered the purchase of the Novato Rancho, which was then being offered for the sum of only fifteen hundred dollars. What a rush there would be for such land prices today! By 1862 the Novato land titles were finally settled and a United States patent obtained therefore. But though the patentee made plans so that residents thereon could purchase their properties at a fair price, many of them had spent their all in development over a period of years and were dispossessed for want of means to repeat the purchase. The remainder of the great Rancho was then subdivided into smaller portions. These are again being cut up into a small acreages and many of these small farms now afford more revenue than did the original extensive Rancho of 13,000 acres.

Undoubtedly Senator F. C. DeLong brought statewide attention to Novato and its possibilities, in fact his efforts and success in the Novato territory paved the way for much of the fruit and vine development of all Northern and Central California. This was at a later period. Novato then pioneered in the development of the grape and apple industry and the DeLong orchard was the largest in the United States. He planted apple trees, pear, apricot, cherry, peach and almond trees, and had a vineyard of 8000 vines. The grapes sold readily in the open market. He exported cargoes of apples to Australia, and had a storage house of 20,000 boxes of apples for the winter market about the bay. All of the poorer grades of apples were turned into bottled, barreled and champagne cider, also vinegar—all of which found a ready market at every offering. His vinegar vats held 56,000 gallons and his factory was for years the only source for vinegars of various strengths for the mines, shipping, export and local consumption. It may be of interest to add that in all early days vinegar was a valued medical agent and largely used in a wide variety of ways for all manner of ills and afflictions; and it still so employed by many of the older families.

6 April 1922

THE MARIN MISSION PERIOD (Cont'd from March 23)

We find an inventory of 1834, indicating a great gain in the prosperity of Mission San Rafael Archangel. In particular the inventory items are interesting, because they show the extent of the institution other than the farm products: church property: building $192; *Ornamentoes*, etc., $777; library of 75 volumes, $108; total $1,077. Mission buildings, $1123; garden and orchard, $968; boats, etc., $500; livestock, $4,339; Nicasio Rancho

$7,256; credits, $170; total $18,474; debts, $3,448; balance, $15,025. What a wonderful tribute to the generous management of Padre Amoros, since this was really the record of his development of the Mission. The library mentioned was the first in Marin County and was very likely brought in by Padre Amoros when he came here from San Jose after his fifteen years tenure there. If we could only know the character of these volumes, how much more valuable would his record of work appear to us, for since books were first possessed, it is well known that with a knowledge of the favorite books of a man one may know the sources of inspiration for his life work. They unquestionably contained the basic inspiration of his career, and no doubt included intimate accounts of the progress of such old Missioners as Father Ugarte and Father Junipero Serra, for his methods closely resembled those of the Padres named. These books must have been his studies in the long period at San Carlos, his mentors and comfort in his troubles in the north, his release from the trials of work, of recreation in his peaceful hours and the inspiration of his carefully planned aims for the Indians in his charge.

Note also the minimum total of credits, showing that the careful old Padre took no chances thereon. The debts were probably current accounts for invoices of supplies to be settled by exchanges after the harvest. Also note the inevitable salaries total of the Haciendo managers, major domos, *comisiandos* and proportion of the General Missions *Administradores* salaries, —a never ending list saddled on the Missions by Government which began piling up immediately after the old Padre's death.

In this year Ignacio Martinez[71] was appointed *comisiando* and directed to mark out the boundaries of the proposed San Rafael pueblo. In this the Mission properties were again but more briefly described (and as shown on the map previously mentioned) as follows: "From Arroyo de los Animas, down the Canada de los Baulinos to the shore, and on opposite or north side the Canada of the Arroyo de San Antonio to Los Tomales, and from Punta de Quintin to the mouth of San Antonio Creek along the bay shore." About the same time it was proposed to make San Rafael, Sonoma and San Jose

---

[71] Don Ignacio Martinez (1774-1848) was Commandante of the San Francisco Presidio. He was with Altimira on the early explorations of Marin and was present at the founding of the Mission San Rafael. His daughter married William Richardson of Sausalito.

Missions all into a parish of the first class and with one curate therefor, though it was never accomplished of record.

To better understand the swiftly moving breakup of the Mission here, with its great expanse of highly productive lands, a word as to general matters of the period may be of value. Beginning with 1834, the so-called Secularization (division of spiritual and temporal powers) of the Missions progressed, and major domos or *comisiandos* directed civil affairs and arranged for distribution of assets and assignment of lands to the neophytes of proper responsibility. To effect this change under proper *administradors* would have carried no harm to either church, or Padres or the Indians. In fact the secularization plan was entirely in line with the original license to the Mission forces, though long forgotten in the busy years following. Yet it would seem that even so long ago the anticipation of a rapidly developing territory was provided for, though the fatal difficulty of its becoming decidedly republican in its ideals was not then thought of. Therefore when the issue came after the weakness of territorial government through many decades had rendered almost any preconceived plan impossible, - the vital needs and marked absence of a strong directing hand, of honest and capable *administradores* and a helpful public spirit made it plain that absolute failure was inevitable. The humility, wise direction and stimulative personality of the earlier Friars, solely working for the development of a plan to uplift the simple Indians and strengthen them for the new era, gave way to greed, trickery, violence, and confusion of the political successors. They were inexperienced in such temporal work conducted from the Mission point of view; and when rival political factions constantly entered the game for a share of the rich prizes,—the end was certain.

Governor Alvarado's[72] rule from 1836 to 1842 effectually settled any hope of permanent good for early Mission endeavors, or allowed completion of a plan of Mission readjustment then proposed by the Friars. Another defect was the fact that the church had never had direct responsibility for the Missions, and had therefore failed to send any recruits as assistants to further assist the Missioners in their work. Therefore the old pioneer Friars, now for the most part aged and invalided, could not stem the tide of disaster as they might have done with proper assistance of trained younger men. But the church was not affected, and the old Padres were

---

[72] Juan Bautista Valentín Alvarado y Vallejo (1809–1882), a nephew and childhood friend of General Vallejo, was Governor of Alta California from 1836 to 1842.

honored and respected through all their troubles. Only the poor, simple Indian bore the brunt of painful results,—losing that which he had gained and vanishing from the land through withdrawal of the kindly Mission direction and through the pestilential diseases of the white man. Those who were spared very quickly reverted to their original degradation as soon as the white man gained his possessions.

No free citizen was allowed to settle where the Indians lived in any community, even after the principal Mission activities had ceased. Hence our own San Rafael could neither accept nor welcome new settlers toward the final closing period of the Mission Days. In consequence it was isolated long after other portions of Marin County began to develop.

In 1834 there were 500 neophytes at the Mission, just one half the number in 1830. During the year Ignacio Martinez was appointed *Comisiando* and directed to mark out the boundaries of the proposed pueblo of San Rafael. By the original Cortez *Pronunciamento* of 1513, the name of the Mission concerned was to be given to the pueblo formed thereat. Therefore the name "San Rafael" was originated here in this way, and not as often stated, merely a duplication of several towns of the same name in many former Spanish possessions. This settles beyond any doubt where we obtained the name of our county seat city, and in connection with the quotation previously noted from Prefect Padre Sarria's words in ordering the establishment of the Mission, — both from official records, —ought to be known by every child in our community.

It should be again stated that San Rafael Archangel was particularly fortunate in having had such [a] capable Military Governor as General Vallejo standing between the Indians in this jurisdiction and their possible abuse in the Mission's closing period. He it was who appointed the *comisiandos* of such sturdy types as became later well-known pioneers. Hence all of the *administradore* duties in this territory were in the hands of capable men such as Martinez, Reed[73], Pacheco[74] and "Don" Timoteo

---

[73] John Thomas Reed (1805-1843) was born in Dublin and came to Yerba Buena in 1826, the first English-speaking resident of California. He was granted the Rancho Corte Madera and built the first sawmill in Marin.

[74] Ignacio Pacheco (1808-1864) was born at Santa Clara Mission, both his parents having arrived with de Anza. He was granted Rancho San Jose in northern Marin (now the community of Ignacio), where his descendants still live.

Murphy[75]. At this time only 1250 Indians were listed on all the Mission lands which in reality meant the present county territory as shown before. The Mission had 3000 cattle, 500 horses, 4500 sheep, and 1500 bushels of grain.

As late as 1835 there were only three free towns in all Upper California which had advanced to the point where they were independent of Mission and Presidio control. They were Los Angeles with 1500, Monterey with 150, and San Jose with 600 inhabitants respectively. Some colonies were started, but very few were progressing, because the jealousy of the Missioners, or rather their necessity, naturally still controlled to a great extent. Only those settlers were admitted who were known to be firm adherents of the Mission Plan. In justice to the Friars it should be stated that they were compelled to deny the settlers in general because Mexico had decreed that California should be colonized by its convicts, who once here and released were a source of continual disruption to Mission communities in many ways. At this time there were not more than five thousand white and mixed caste people in all California. The later notes on Marin County will include other reasons why settlers declined to locate in the southern section of the county, especially in the region of San Rafael.

Governor Figueroa visited San Rafael at this time though there has been no record found as to his purpose in doing so. A note is found to the effect that between 1835 and 1840, the Mission at San Jose owed the San Rafael Mission money in the sum of $1235, and no statement of its settlement appears in the last checking up of the Missions by Hartnell[76].

General Vallejo transmitted orders to *Comisiando* Martinez "to place certain Indians in charge of the Nicasio Rancho of the Mission, which was to be given to them in full ownership and their rights must be protected." Note further on in the story and in the County Review to follow, how this "full ownership" was carried out under Governor Alvarado's rule and after General Vallejo had ceased to remain in office. On August 18th of this year

---

[75] Don Timoteo Murphy (1800-1853), born Timothy Murphy in Ireland, stood over six feet tall and weighed more than 300 pounds. He came to Monterey in 1828. In 1837 he was appointed administradore to liquidate the San Rafael Mission and made several land grants, including a large one to himself.

[76] William Edward Petty Hartnell, a.k.a. Don Guillermo Arnel (1798-1854), born in England, was a prominent early immigrant to Alta California. He ran a hide and tallow business, ranched, and opened a school that still exists. Two of his pupils were General Vallejo and Governor Alvarado.

the Governor urged Vallejo to care for the San Francisco Indians at San Rafael who were having difficulty in obtaining boats to move their property across the Bay. These two items indicate that the Mission organization was practically ended and broken up, and that General Vallejo was still keenly alert as to his responsibilities for the Indians and their rights. One wonders what had become of the Mission boats equipment, listed only a year before for $500, an amount which in those days must have included a considerable fleet of water craft used for transfer of the Mission Farms crops each year to an across the bay market. Another incident comes in April when two sons of a prominent trans-bay family went to Santa Rosa to get Indians to work on their San Pablo Rancho. The record reads that while there they took some property, and bought some Indian children from the Chief. Hearing of this, Vallejo had them arrested at San Rafael and released the children. Nothing could more clearly and painfully indicate how the earlier Mission control had lapsed than this particular episode does.

An inventory of the Mission San Rafael Archangel in November, 1836, shows how rapidly its values were shrinking: "Manufactures, etc., produce tools (and probably buildings) $1434; livestock, $1385; orchard, $891; rancho, $6644; credits, $464; total, $10,818; debts, $3,177; balance, $7,641. The population in 1838 was 365.

13 April 1922

Came 1837, when John Reed[77] resigned as *comisiando* and was succeeded by Timoteo Murphy. In that year Phillip J. Edwards[78] of the Willamette Cattle Company visited San Rafael and made a tour of the Mission territory. He mentions visiting the Reed and Martin Ranchos and speaks of how poorly the Indians were using the property distributed to them. Also that there were frequent complaints of vagabond foreigners in the vicinity. These were evidently some of the horde of outcasts banished from the Bay districts or other Mission vicinity, or deserters from the constantly arriving foreign ships. No doubt also they included many of the

---

[77] John Thomas Reed (1805-1843) was born in Dublin and in 1826 was the first Anglo settler in the Bay Area.

[78] Philip Leget Edwards (1812-1869), born in Kentucky, came to the Oregon Territory in 1834 and established a mission and became the territory's first teacher. He was later a California state assemblyman.

convicts which Mexico had sent to colonize California and who had become such a problem to the Mission communities. Later, a Vallejo record states:

"As the Nicasio Indians were not as a rule making good use of their liberty, and as the political and other troubles rendered proper supervision impossible, this property was collected under a common fund and under General Vallejo's solemn promise of a redistribution when circumstances would so warrant." What a story there is here between the lines of the previous several months, and which it is perhaps better to allow to remain in the forgotten past of the poor Indian's troubles. It is a story which had chapter after chapter at the Missions up and down the coast, where the old Padres' hands were tied, the political favorites were in power, and there was no General Vallejo to interfere!

In 1839 Chief James Jose Talis, surely an English-Spanish-Indian name, Captain of the Tamales, was permitted to leave San Rafael with those of his tribe "on condition of sending some men occasionally to hear mass if it was later conducted." One can well believe that this old Chief would have promised much more than that to be able to go back to former haunts and life habits, when viewing the rapidly occurring disillusions of his trustful people.

About this time the United States Navy sent a "scientific" expedition[79] out to the coast, as many foreign nations were doing under such pretenses, in order to make a survey of the wonderful Bay which was then being considered as any nation's greatest prize in this West.

Lieutenant Wilkes[80] and 600 men made up the party, who openly conducted a thorough survey of the entire Bay and its territory. The officer and his subordinates traveled over Marin county and mention having been entertained by Captain Richardson at Sausalito and Martinez at San Rafael.

Then came Hartnell, an Englishman and a previously successful trader and business man of San Francisco and thereabout. He was the Governor's representative to check up on all remaining Mission matters, and found the

---

[79] The United States Exploring Expedition (1838-1842), a thoroughly scientific around-the-world expedition in the spirit, if not the efficiency and effectiveness, of Cook and La Perouse.

[80] Charles Wilkes (1798–1877) was an American naval officer and explorer. He led the United States Exploring Expedition and commanded the ship in the *Trent* Affair during the American Civil War, where he attacked a Royal Mail Ship, almost leading to war between the U.S. and the U.K. His behavior led to two convictions by court-martial, one stemming from the massacre of almost 80 Fijians on Malolo in 1840.

accounts at San Rafael in bad shape. Timoteo Murphy had a better memory than he had clerical ability, which was not entirely satisfactory to an auditor. Hartnell's call for neophytes' complaints brought the whole Indian community upon him. They gave helplessly sad accounts of their dwindling hopes of any ultimate share in the Mission properties and especially the fast vanishing Mission lands which had been so often promised them, and upon which they had diligently and efficiently employed their efforts in labor and care of a long time with that end in view. This is practically the last record of their misfortunes:— "The old Christians desired their liberty and the distribution of the little land remaining for them. They needed San Anselmo, part of which the Saises[81] had, and part was asked for by Mr. Cooper[82]. Las Gallinas was desired by Berryessa[83]. The Arroya San Jose which was under cultivation last year by Murphy for the community was now possessed by Pacheco. Pt. Pedro, which Murphy wants; and San Geronimo was occupied by Rafael Cacho[84]. Neophyte Camilo Ynitia had occupied the Olompali Rancho since 1834, was industrious and successful, but now Mirandas[85] was encroaching and Camilo demanded regular title to the land. All complained that for two years no clothing had been distributed."

And so the story proceeded of group after group, patiently accepting the white man's training and heavily laboring during their twelve years period of qualification to return to the lands of their birth and forever possess and manage the farms which the old Padres had so long and so patiently trained them for. A few like Ynitia, Santisimo Rosario, Rafael Cacho and Mirandas, had been successful managers for the Mission Fathers on the Haciendo

---

[81] Domingo Sais (1806-1853) was a Mexican soldier at the Presidio. He was granted Rancho Cañada de Herrera, present day San Anselmo.

[82] John Rogers Cooper (1791-1872), Mexican name Juan Bautista Rogers Cooper, a native of Alderney, Channel Islands, came to Massachusetts as a child, and arrived in Monterey as master of the ship *Rover*. He became a Mexican citizen and married General Vallejo's sister Encarnacion Vallejo. He helped acquire a passport for Jedediah Smith, the first man to come to California overland from the United States. He acquired several land grants, including San Quentin.

[83] Probably Carlos Antonio Berryessa (1815-1881), who owned land in the Peninsula.

[84] Rafael Cacho, Mexican soldier, was given the land grant of Rancho San Geronimo. He later sold it to Lt. Joseph Warren Revere, USN, (grandson of Paul revere), who lowered the Bear Flag at Sonoma and replaced it with the American flag.

[85] The sons of Juan Miranda, Mexican soldier.

ranchos and in the breakup of the Mission had remained in possession, unaware that even then some of their directors had long before applied for the Grant titles of the farms these Indians had developed and considered as their own for all time. So must it be for the primitive peoples the world over when the stronger race arrives in their midst.

Practically no mention is made about the Mission Indians after this last plaintive appeal. The most terrible of the smallpox scourges followed a year later, which is said to have swept away seventy thousand Indians from north of the Bay territory and extending well up into the mountain regions. Nearly sixty per cent of all those residing in the Sacramento Valley perished in that year and in the preceding epidemic mentioned. The sickness raged from July to December in present Marin, Sonoma, Solano, and Napa sections, and General Vallejo sent out notices to all points of the State giving due warning of the widespread epidemic and resulting distress and urging the need of vaccination and all possible sanitary precautions. Naturally enough where there were no Missioners or Mission work the Indians died in great numbers, helpless in the path of the white man's malady and never knowing that their very manner of living was the chief cause of its ravages once the epidemic appeared amongst them. It was not long before they all knew that a soldier from Fort Ross had taken the disease to Sonoma, from whence it had spread everywhere. Is it any wonder then, that in ignorance of the few simple minded survivors, they thought that the very land was accursed by these foreigners and left it as fast as their weakened condition would allow?

In 1834 Sonoma formed a pueblo and several families were permitted to occupy the ranchos on the frontier, all with the object of checking further advance of the Russians and at one time the French, both of which even the San Rafael territory still considered a menace for the future.

It remained for Hartnell to run afoul of General Vallejo at San Rafael, and though Hartnell was backed by authority from Governor Alvarado, the old General as usual gained his point. Hartnell was now "visitador" to all Mission towns. Nevertheless Vallejo refused to allow him to take possession of any Mission property at San Rafael or to inspect its accounts. Hartnell was arrested and sent to San Francisco by the General, who claimed that since there was no longer a Mission at San Rafael, he was a prisoner for attempting to interfere with frontier matters. The Indian property had been partially recollected after the secularization order was carried out as mentioned before under Vallejo's solemn promise to redistribute it when the Indians could properly care for it. Hartnell had come to San Rafael, appointed Gregorio Briones[86] as major domo and ordered the Indians to return to live at the Mission under this plan. Finally Hartnell accepted Vallejo's idea of distributing the property after paying all of the debts of the Mission. Vallejo thereupon ordered his own administradore, Timoteo Murphy, to at once distribute three head of cattle and one horse to each Indian, which was done.

Hartnell's inventory of September 18, 1839, reads: "population 195 at the Mission; 475 horses, 26 yoke of oxen, 3 mules, (cattle and sheep memoranda torn off); 417 fanegas of grain; 42 hides; 72 deer skins; 60 arras of tallow; debts to Spear, Celis, Aguirre, Scott, Shaw, John Reed, Tim Murphy and Rotscheff, $1967."

In 1840 another report reads: "Indians in the community 190 and 150 scattered elsewhere." In the same year Murphy carried out Vallejo's orders and distributed 1291 sheep and 439 horses to 343 Indians, (probably representing heads of families or about 500 people).

A reminder to all that although the orders of the Mission were over those of the Military Governor were not, may be inferred from a note which reads, "Timoteo Murphy and Padre Quijos went to Fort Ross to buy bullocks or something, and were at once jailed by Vallejo." Naturally there were none but official parties allowed to either visit or trade with the Russian post at Ross and thereafter these gentlemen also knew it. Padre Quijos was supposed to attend to the religious instruction of the San Rafael and all of the northern frontier. But after about 1838 there was no resident curate at all though he was still here.

20 April 1922

In 1849 the Mission buildings were in ruins, especially the outbuildings. Murphy was *administradore* for but 20 Indians. There was no religious community and some 200 ex-neophytes were ordered to report to live at the Mission or else it would be sold. But they declined, in fact could do little else if reports as to the buildings were correct for that time.

---

[86] Gregorio Briones (1797-1863), Mexican soldier and Bolinas pioneer.

Governor Pico[87] then ordered that an inventory of the property be taken and all sold at public auction for which sufficient notice was to be given. From this order he excepted the immediate gardens, orchard, buildings, land, and livestock of the Mission and confirmed their award for the perpetual use of the church ministers. It is also shown that prior to this he made a private sale to his brother and a friend which the *Disputacion* refused to accept. (This was for $8000 only).

Hartnell's final inventory of the Mission (now church) was made on August 24th, 1844 and read: "buildings, $3435; furniture and utensils. $59; 2 gardens with 22 fruit trees and 210 vines, $2629: lands about 16 leagues, $8000; livestock chiefly at Nicasio, 266 cattle, 593 horses, 310 sheep, total $3051. List of church property and utensils, no value; total $17,230. Signed by Pico (Governor) Masso (his secretary), and Murphy (*administradore*). The auction was held in October and realized $17,000. Vale the Mission San Rafael Archangel!

Singularly enough, and yet typical of so many western cities, San Rafael has never valued the only remaining evidence that there was once a living, vibrant Mission Community here, rather than the merely vague tradition of its existence many years ago. Some wonderfully old and weather beaten pear trees of the Mission orchard still remain. They have been woefully (better stated wholly) neglected in the past years, the greater number and the largest specimens having been cut down to make way for buildings. There are still five left in a row, almost unnoticed on a side street, where if some cities had them they would be cared for far more tenderly and reverently than the choicest greenhouse plant. They exist merely as a memory of the past, have no particular attraction, and few of the rising generation know little and care less about their strange and eventful history.

Doubtless they were brought here by Padre Amoros about 1819, for he was a Catalan native and therefore a lover of fruits and vines, and having been at the San Jose Mission for years before coming here, some of its stock was probably obtained for his new field of endeavor. We can picture him sitting beneath their grateful shade, and thinking of them as the link between Missions of the olden days and of those to be formed on up along the northern coast to complete the perfect western chain.

---

[87] Pío de Jesús Pico (1801–1894) was the last governor of Alta California (now the State of California) under Mexican rule.

This stately row of old pear trees of the Mission Days are now only witnesses of their own great age. They are twisted, gnarled, and bearded with age, and at this season bereft of any hint of life. They look more like the ancient oaks and give every evidence of having passed through most severe treatment in wintry gales in the days long passed. If they were able to speak what a wealth of old tales they might unfold! They could tell of the joys and the sorrows of the old Padre, of the tolling of Mission bells for prayers and for the passing souls of epidemic days, or of sharp ringing for alarms. They could tell of the peaceful calm of successful days or the pain and sorrow in the closing years of San Rafael Archangel's period. Or they could now express an idea of our present neglect of a pitiful claim to better treatment at the hands of a people who owe all they have to the hands which guided this land down to us and to our children. Shall we let them pass as others did the helpless Indian of aboriginal days, or shall we take steps before they are destroyed, to retain this only living link of the old Mission Days in Marin to the present happy prosperous period filled with the fruits of the then Mission efforts? What better purpose could we plan than to so care for them that in all future years we can have pilgrimages of children to view them and listen to stories of the olden days when these bare trunks were fruitful parts of a vast Mission domain which nurtured the pioneers of Marin County for years after the passing of the Mission San Rafael Archangel![88]

So ended the Mission Period Days in Marin County to be, the lasting benefits of which are a never ending theme. It was about a twenty-eight year period which some may claim left nothing of material evidence but an historic building in crumbling ruins; or of mental impression on the one hand of an exalted example of unselfish effort for humanity without hope for personal reward, and on the other to-be-forgotten reminder of the later day record of oppression and injustice of simple minded, childlike natives doomed to be eventually swept away by an advancing new era.

---

[88] The trees survived another forty years, until only one tree remained, in a lot on Fourth Street. The property was bought by Jacob Albert, who planned a parking lot for his new apartment buildings. He planned to save the tree, but died before he could notify his contractor. The tree was destroyed in December 1963, at 144 years old. Then it was found that in 1929, nurseryman Richard Lohrmann had taken cuttings from the tree. These cuttings were grafted onto other pear trees and survived. One was planted on the Mission grounds; another is at the Marin Art and Garden Center in Ross.

Out of the thousands of Indians who directly and indirectly came under the instruction and influence of the Mission San Rafael Archangel in these twenty-eight years the record shows of but one—Camilo Ynitia— who rose to the standard set out for them all. He was eventually given a United States Patent (titled) to his Olompali Rancho. He alone seems to have succeeded while the others had no chance to do so, typifying with his family in the future years the new standard of life which his beloved Padre Amoros so earnestly taught him in the early days of the Mission San Rafael Archangel. Olompali, 1776 to Olompali, 1846 is a strange and suggestive coincidence.

Yet was that all that the Mission San Rafael Archangel left Marin County? Decidedly not. It should be forever considered as developing the county, not San Rafael or the southern end of Marin. For by the Mission development and complete isolation from entry, San Rafael was held back and Sausalito afforded a first start in the county from trans-bay activities. By its Haciendo ranchos, the most fertile territory in all Marin, was farmed and forced almost world-wide attention to its wonderful crops and to the far-seeing, keenly alert settler who knew that land pursuits must in the end support all other developments. By its surveys and reports of all Marin points the resources of entire Marin were listed and ready for the prompt development of materials collectors for early San Francisco. By its position on the northern frontier the Marin Mission Days were wholly free from the political turmoil of earlier Mission territories, and was enabled to develop slowly, surely and permanently. Best of all the Mission perfected the clearest of all land titles in California, matters which have always been in trouble without end elsewhere; for its lands were all Mission or specially exempted government territories under Mission direction, hence clearly titled since the Cortez order of 1513.

Its purpose of foundation here, and its exceptional development under Marin's matchless climatic and soil conditions, and the claims of its fertile lands, —were known the world over through comparative Mission Reports. In those days every foreign visitor of note to the coast came to San Francisco as the port of entry, and there were scores of official expeditions including Marin sections in their travels for home reports. Had it not been for matters noted in another article, the old Mission town would have sprang up almost overnight when restrictions were released; for the charms of Marin were more widely known than those of any other California unoccupied territory. But who shall say that it was not better to have had it develop more slowly, more solidly and in the end more intellectually than some overnight growths of that period?

In a spiritual sense lies the really undying evidence of the Mission Days in Marin. We have had the (for the most of us) intimate feeling in all these years of a participation in carrying out the carefully laid, far seeing plans of old Padre Sarria and Padre Amoros; and of making Marin county a section of homes, and of peoples in search of the health giving, peaceful Marin Days. They were the hope and the final reality, of those early neophytes who were with good intentions robbed of their life in other sunshiny California Valleys and marooned on inhospitable peninsular shores. There they stood shivering in nature's garment and at the mercy of her varying moods, dying for want of the more generous silvery skies just across the Bay in Marin. But once in Marin territory they became our first advertisers.

It is Marin's north country which should the more heavily value and claim the benefits of the Marin Mission Days, for it was there that old Padre Amoros spent most of his traveling periods, guarding against encroachments from the north, and organizing a closer connection to his great work with a view of direct dependence upon northern products for subsistence in the southern section. And have we continued his work in like manner, and continued to consider our northern neighbors to be our best assets?

"From Arroyo de los Animas, down the Canada de los Baulinas to the shore, and on the opposite or north side the Canada of the Arroyo de San Antonio to Los Tomales, and from Punta de Quintin to the mouth of the San Antonio Creek along the Bay shore," was the old Padre's domain, later added to by the forts freed government peninsulas of Tiburon. Sausalito, Bolinas and Point Reyes sections. Shall the traditions which bound this territory together in a spiritual effort for common good from 1776 to 1845 and by the succeeding years for a community cause be now divided by the whims of 1922?

Rather shall the work of the Mission San Rafael Archangel for Marin County and the efforts of the beloved old Padre Amoros be perpetuated in the peace of our homes and our much needed farms, in our schools and our colleges, in our churches and our lodges,—in all that goes to make up the life which owes the "Padres of the Missions" a grateful memory for developing and saving this fair land for us.

Let us pass on to our children and to our children's children the words of Padre Sarria in dedication of not San Rafael but this county to be, for he planned no north or no south but a heritage for all "which shall be called San Rafael Archangel in honor of that prince who in his name expresses the 'healing of God,' in bodies as well as in souls."

27 April 1922

MARIN'S LAND GRANT DAYS

It is not difficult to understand just why Marin County started with such a homogenous and progressive people throughout its entire area, if the general facts concerning its Land Grant Days are known. There are certain features of this period which every present landholder should know and for which he should still further revere the memory of Marin's pioneers for saving him the many years of unending and expensive titles litigation many other sections have had.

The period of land grants began about 1832 and extended well on towards the 1850 years. Its story is really that of the beginning of the interior settlement of the county and rightfully deserves a place in a general review of its history as well as providing a framework into which later mention of the Post Mission Days naturally falls.

Came a time when the California Missions rule was plainly near its end. And about this time began the land grants to soldiers who had served at the presidios for the allotted ten years before obtaining the land pledged to them by the Government as a bonus for faithful service. Therefore, when the Mission days were over and the presidios closed, these soldiers had the first choice and could practically choose whatever lands they liked best, —and well they knew from frequent journeying in the territory which were most suited for their particular purposes. But they had competitors also, for the various *administradores*, major domos, *comisiandos* and other officials had their turn, usually selecting the best of the haciendo ranchos. And now and again a high Government official had a brother or a particular friend to be taken care of or to hold title subject to future changes in officialdom. Especially was this latter case true in the closing days of Mexico's control, when the Governor in every way attempted to keep the land from falling into the hands of American settlers. But any unprejudiced student will admit that the Spanish and Mexican laws were most explicitly clear and definite and it was not easy for any official to ignore their plain intent. Yet now and again it was done, and especially in the chaos of changing control.

And so in this land distribution, the poor Indian for whom the years of endeavor had been carried on by the Missions, and for whom was held in trust all the fruits of the years of his labor, —was practically forgotten in the lands matter until it was almost all in private hands. He seldom had ability enough to claim his own, and in some cases a white man "friend" claimed title for him and then obtained it personally through connivance of officials.

But here in Marin County we had few of these Land Grant troubles. A number of false claims were presented, which were usually attacks on existing titles that courts of reference promptly disallowed. Probably the blocking of well laid schemes for private sale of Missions as occurred with the San Rafael Archangel when the Governor's brother and a friend obtained it privately but the Government refused to confirm the transaction and ordered all others to be at public auction thereafter, prepared the way for more straightforward dealing. And so Marin county, in comparison with many other territories, is noted in all records as "it has clear land titles." a priceless boon because elsewhere there has been and will be unending litigation about this matter. Practically in only one case, noted later, was there any real trouble and this was summarily and effectually settled by combination of determined pioneers who had implicit confidence in the justice and fairness of the court of last resort.

As before stated, the entire present county territory - except the reservation of coast lands, was Mission controlled. In consequence the resulting Land Grants left only the extreme northern section, at first under land grants but on a resurvey became public domain and was quickly taken up. It was to this Mecca of the particular soil chooser that men gathered who for years were the strength and leaders of Marin County.

While very little remains of record in early Marin days concerning the Indian question of distribution of land and property following the secularization order, one neophyte as before mentioned was confirmed in the ownership of the Olompali Rancho. Later the Nicasio Rancho which included about one fifth of the entire territory, was given in full ownership to such Indians of the Mission as cared to reside thereon and make use of it. But they failed to do so, and little by little it was cut off in sections until their old major domo, Timothy Murphy, made a claim for the Tinicasia Rancho[89] for them; but the Court denied the claim. Then indeed came distress to the Indian, for he had no land, no home, no aid, —and eventually became free labor to any settler who would subsist him. What property was distributed to him was promptly gambled away or traded for trifles, and if his small dwelling lot at the pueblo was deserted then its title went to the state.[90]

4 May 1922

While we have every sympathy for the Indian, his fate seemed foreordained and would probably occur in much the same way in modern times. The Spanish laws for division of the lands matter were explicit and fair, and made as the foundation plan for the Missions when they were first authorized. It was to be expected that in some cases the officials appointed to carry out their provisions were tricky, incompetent, or careless. The title of all lands in a new territory remained with Spain. It recognized the Indians as owners of all lands needed for their support. The Missions had no title to any land as is popularly supposed, but could use it only to subsist and prepare the Indian for his own possession later. It was an understanding of record that in all cases as soon as this work was accomplished, secularization was to follow and all temporal control of Indians and property was to pass to an "*ayuntiemento*" (town council); the Missioners were to enter new Mission fields or return to their Colleges; and the religious work was to be continued under curates much as at present in any church. But the Missioners naturally attempted to delay any such action, because they realized that settlers of any kind would in the end disrupt a Mission community.

This granting of land in Marin county and even location of settlers in any manner was delayed as it was all over California, by ten years of strife in Mexico; but in 1833 the Mexican Government notified all that the old Spanish decree would be carried out at once. Then applications for land grants quickly followed and settlers gained a start. Yet on getting these lands if they did not till the soil or graze lands the title lapsed to the state

---

[89] A tiny grant of one square league.
[90] In 2000 the Coast Miwoks were finally granted the 15-acre Graton Rancheria near Sebastopol, containing one house. In 2008, the tribe bought an additional 254 acres.

again. In 1834 Governor Figuero issued a *Reglamento* protecting the Indians in their land rights and noting the amount of land and the share of property each was to receive, but few of them knew how to retain it.

So in the end the Mexican Colonization Laws, in reality those of Spain as at first issued, governed in Marin County. Such grants as were given here were issued by the Territorial Government, hence there was little delay except through careless officials and changing control. The Treaty of Guadalupe Hidalgo[91] guaranteed that all settlers' rights would be protected, yet in 1851 land schemers persuaded Congress to institute a Court of Claims to pass on all land titles and so for a time put some claimants to endless and unnecessary trouble and expense. The matter of the Court of Claims was proper, but the manner of its execution proved to be faulty to some entirely innocent persons.

Applications for Land Grants in Marin county could at first apply for land only up to a *"sitio"* (eleven leagues), and a league, or more properly a square league, was 4,408.402 acres[92]. Proper assurance had to be given that a claimant could and would use the land for agriculture or grazing before it was granted. The request was made to the Governor, stating quality, location and description (sometimes with a rude map), and the age, nativity and vocation of the applicant. This was referred back to the district Alcalde for an "informe" (comment or verification) and on the Governor's approval was filed in the state archives. The entire papers were called an "expediente," and while settlers often occupied the territory even before making the application, the title was perfected only when the Governor had referred the matter to the Territorial *Disputacion* (legislation) where a committee on Land Claims seldom refused it. But the Governor sometimes failed to do this, or his secretary failed to make any record of his so doing; hence the settler had to apply for the *Disputacion* Certificate, and this completed the title.

The district Alcalde was then instructed to "place suitable marks" to designate the boundaries of the claim. This was usually done by measuring it off with riatas, beginning at some supposedly imperishable object, point or hilltop. It is astonishing how accurate most of these crude measurements

---

[91] The 1848 treaty that ended the Mexican-American War, granting to the U.S. the territory of California and much of Arizona, New Mexico, Nevada, Utah, Wyoming, and Colorado.

[92] One square Spanish league is actually 4,317 acres.

proved to be on later surveys. The point is therefore clear that the Missioners had nothing to do with the Land Grants except to occasionally have a claim referred to them as to interference with Mission lands, and incidentally to indicate to particular friends the best locations left.

But even with the perfected title the landholder was not always safe from unscrupulous practices, especially the small holder who purchased from a large claim, the records of which he knew nothing about. Our own Government was unjust to some grantees in that the act of 1851 compelled all to defend their fully proven titles, which oftentimes the grantee had held undisputed for years and his family long after his passing. This being at the owner's expense, a sad predicament resulted, if rich and influential opponents disputed his title. The title being questioned he could not sell to legitimate purchasers, but in order to pay court charge in advance, obtain tax moneys, secure lawyer's fees and continue development costs, there was no other way than to sacrifice the rancho piece by piece to sharpers and rascally land speculators. If by any chance he won a decision before the Court of Claims, the opponent would appeal from one court to another, in some cases keeping matters in litigation for as much as twenty years. If by that time the title was finally shown to be good the original owner had long since spent his last dollar and was an outcast and forever a poor respecter of citizenship rights under Government guarantee. Many a present day fortune was laid in this manner, and it was the driving out of small settlers in this way that for a long time retarded proper development in many parts of California. But in Marin county there were but few of such cases. In one some outside citizens acted foolishly and submitted to extortion, and in another the settlers won out by showing a united front in opposition.

11 May 1922

Perhaps a mention of two of these cases in Marin County merits mention in this account. The first so directly and vitally concerned Uncle Sam's own properties that Congress promptly appropriated $200,000 to expose fraud. As noted before, the Spanish and Mexican Governments had reserved the Bay islands, the Farallones, Tiburon and Sausalito peninsulas and the Bolinas-Pt. Reyes territories (Sausalito was shortly afterward granted to

Captain Richardson). One José Yves Limantour[93], a French trader along the coast, presented a grant title of 600,000 acres of this territory and about 17,000 acres of San Francisco's choicest lands, stating that Governor Micheltorena had given it to him in payment for aid furnished troops in southern California. Notwithstanding the fact that no special grant of over eleven *sitios* (about 48,000 acres) could be granted to anyone except by consent of the Mexican Senate, a puzzling decision was handed down by the Court of Claims. He was confirmed in title to the San Francisco lands, but denied the others. In spite of Uncle Sam's prompt action, and the opinion of the best lawyers that the claim was a fraud, citizens became frightened and paid Limantour $300,000 in buying titles to the property they already owned. Then Professor Geo. B. Davidson[94], an expert, painstakingly and clearly showed that the claim was a fraud and the testimony in the case was plain perjury. Limantour was arrested and put under a $30,000 bond, whereupon he placed this amount with his bondsmen and disappeared. Eldridge clearly states this matter, noting that the proceedings are of record in the Court Papers. And yet Marin County has always retained the name of Limantour Bay, probably from the trading days of this individual!

The second matter was more directly a county affair, though one of the apparent attempt of wealthy foreigners to influence the court itself, and blocked by an irresistibly sturdy Americanism. Its story can be noted in full from the notice sent broadcast by the settlers of Tomales, as framed at a settlers meeting thereon Feb. 16th, 1851. Many old scrapbooks probably have original copies of the following (names are omitted as of no import now):

Whereas the latter action of Judge ... in confirming the claim of .... to the Bolsa de Tomales, after he finding the same to be infected with Fraud

---

[93] Joseph Yves Limantour (1812-1885) was a Breton trader and captain who traded from Chile to California. In 1841 his schooner *Ayacucho* was wrecked on the beach in Marin that now bears his name. He sold his cargo to General Vallejo in return for a new schooner. In 1853, Limantour filed claims for 200,000 acres of California, including much of San Francisco, which by then was a sizeable city. His son José was Finance Minister of Mexico.

[94] George Davidson (1825-1911) was an American geodesist, surveyor, astronomer, geographer, and engineer. He built Davidson Observatory in San Francisco, the first observatory on the Pacific Coast. He was president of the California Academy of Sciences and a Regent of the University of California.

and Forgery, is in our opinion contrary to all law, all justice, and common sense: and

Whereas the action of the District Attorney of the .... District of California, (one .... Esq.), in his refusal to take an appeal in the case, is in our opinion unprecedented, (considering the character of the claims, — the character of the claimants being rich and powerful, and being a combination of English and French capitalists), and exercise of powers that if delegated to a public officer, argues something radically wrong in some quarter: and

Whereas, in our opinion no such power has been delegated to this officer so as to make his action binding upon the Government, therefore be it

Resolved by the citizens of Tomales in mass meeting assembled, that we will use all honorable means to have the case carried before the Supreme Court for its final adjudication, believing firmly as we do, in the integrity, wisdom and justice of that tribunal, knowing that no social influence, whether of wealth or poverty, can warp its judgment.

Resolved, that while we accord to all men equal and exact justice, whether grantees of Spain, Mexico and others, yet in our opinion the action of a portion of the claimants, viz.. (naming six), in instituting actions of ejectment against parties whom they supposed to be in the neighborhood of said Bolsa de Tomales, and before a final adjudication and survey of the same, and their evident desire to dispose of their interests at once, holding out at the same time threats and inducements to effect such purpose, is in our opinion an attempt to perpetuate a legal fraud, a fraud in magnitude that the lesser crimes that fill our penitentiaries with the outcasts of society, sink before it in utter insignificance; and we hereby recommend to all parties interested to make no compromises with the said parties, or their agents in the premises, as we firmly believe that they will finally fail to carry out this fraud successfully, and

Resolved, that we now do organize to carry out the object of the Resolutions and that they be published in the *Petaluma Journal* with a request to all other papers that are friendly to the cause of even handed and exact justice, to copy the same. (Signed by Chairman, Mel Osborn, and Secretary, Wm. Vanderbilt.)

Evidently these bold words and the bristling front behind them had some effect for the District Court in the next session, "continues the twenty-eight ejectment cases of settlers on the Rancho Bolsa de Tomales until the next quarterly session." Evidently, also, very fast work was accomplished by someone, for the famous Pony Express brought news on March 13th that "upon the motion and order of the United States Attorney at Washington, the United States Supreme Court had granted the appeal of settlers on the Bolsa de Tomales Rancho."

The *Marin Journal* of April 6th, 1861, notes "that there was much rejoicing at Tomales upon the receipt of this news. A gun was fired for every state in the Union including South Carolina which has just seceded. A large bonfire illuminated the whole country around and a platform was speedily erected. Then Settler John Keyes (the "Father of Tomales")[95] was loudly called for and addressed the audience, being soon followed by Dr. Dutton, Messrs. Vanderbilt, Brady, White, Jacobs and others. The crowd retired at a late hour." Perhaps things were not always thus in Tomales, for the article closes with the statement that "nothing had occurred to mar the jollification."

18 May 1922

Since preparation of the foregoing, a final mention of this matter is noted in an advertisement of 1863 which reads as follows:

"Grand Barbecue at Tomales! The citizens of Tomales will on Thursday, April 2, 1863, give a grand barbecue in honor of the triumph of truth and justice over fraud and falsehood backed by all the influences of wealth and position as evidenced by the recent decision of the Supreme Court of the United States rejecting the land claims in Marin county known as the Bolsa de Tomales, being for about 25,000 acres of the finest Agricultural Lands in the State, and worth in the neighborhood of half a million dollars. The undersigned, committee of arrangements, respectfully announce that preparations will be made for at least two thousand people. A band of music will be in attendance and a good time generally is anticipated. The barbecue will come off at one o'clock p. m. The friends of the Honest Settler in Marin and adjoining counties are cordially invited to

---

[95] John Keyes (1824-1873), born in Ireland, planted the first potatoes in Marin and built the first house at Tomales.

attend. Signed by committee: G. W. Burbank, Mel Osborn. Wm. Vanderbilt, Warren Dutton, John Keyes."

Somewhere between the filing of the ejectment suits in 1861 and of this celebration of victory in 1863, there must be an interesting story of shoulder to shoulder co-operation and of sternly patient tolerance toward the horde of squatters who flocked to Northern Marin in hopes of an unfavorable decision or were sent there under pay by the foreign claimants. Perhaps someone can offer this story for the later Tomales items. The successors to these sturdy Tomales pioneers should for generations to come be proud of this stand of their forefathers in first attempting to effect by peaceful means what they had every right to attain by violence in its every essence, since all over the state these foreign interlopers had attempted (and at times succeeded) by questionable means and subtle influences with some governing powers, —to suborn justice and to defraud the settlers of their lands after years of hardship and earnest endeavor in good faith with the Government. Casting its shining light through such difficulties as occurred on the Bolsa de Tomales Rancho was the calm assurance of our pioneers that somewhere in this Government of ours there could still be found justice and principles of fair dealing for the average man in spite of the frauds and forgeries of the Government's sometime tricky underlings. And again the issue is thrust forward of how easy it is for a party of citizens, sure of their rights and steadfast in their confidence in one another, to effect any proper purpose in view. How interesting indeed it would be to read the minutes of the meetings which must have preceded this open notice for all to beware "until all peaceful means" had been taken. What confidence the men at those meetings must have had in their leaders! So it is in our day, if we could only band together and effect our aims one by one with such singleness of purpose and with such confidence in leaders we ourselves select, and are too often afterward accountable for.

The entire State of California profited by this action at Tomales for the sharp Government rebuke to the Courts and especially the forces of attention on foreign claimants brought an end to such claims. But there was another pest to the settler of small means in the person of the so-called "squatter," an individual who settled on land after full knowledge that it was already taken, but who either sought to be bought off, stayed in hope of the title being disproved, or, and this was the troublesome type,—had been employed by powerful interests to stay and to either intimidate or annoy the settler so that he would sell at a sacrifice. The "squatter" noted here was therefore the unscrupulous party who "jumped" a title, rather than hunt for a place of his own. To decide such matters was the real purpose of the Act of 1851 but in its execution the small settler was badly handicapped before he could obtain a United States Patent or title, which all the time was fully and clearly guaranteed by the Mexican Treaty which the United States had signed. Some of these squatters were prospective settlers with the best of intentions, because it had been heralded everywhere in the East that all California lands were the public domain, whereas they were nearly all taken up in Mexican Grants by earlier settlers and Indians before the United States gained control. Therefore on arrival with all their goods and chattels and at an expense which exhausted the savings of years, they found hardly a foot of ground that was not controlled by immeasurably large holdings, the smaller grants, or by unscrupulous land speculators. One can sympathize with them, but like the final comers to a new mining camp, they were too late.

Thus San Francisco especially had become a nest of squatters, — hundreds and hundreds of families constantly arriving and with no place to go, for there were other hordes returning from unsuccessful attempts to find locations. Hence the only plan was to "squat" on any vacant space, from which came the general name. But of course turmoil resulted, and riots, fights, and disturbances of all kinds followed. When it was announced in 1850 that San Rafael had been surveyed and laid out in lots, which were to be auctioned off at thirty dollars apiece to the first applicant arriving, a multitude of speculators and locators rushed across to Marin territory. But the town developed very slowly from several natural causes, and fortunes in trading lands did not materialize. Hence the tax collector soon had most of the lots back again.

In consequence came the San Rafael "Squatter Riot," which in itself was a small matter but which set the example all over the state for a growing resentment against the lawless acts of the squatter element which was not only increasing but in places organizing to resist lawful authority with arms.

25 May 1922

The remaining Mission land in San Rafael had been set aside by Mexico for religious uses and purposes. The Mission was practically in disuse and the still extensive orchard and vineyard lands had been neglected for years. So the squatters organized, seized these lands and staked them off. Finally on August 7th a Church party of about twenty-five men "attacked them with sticks and staves and drove them down to the Bay and off Marin's shores." This action, slight as it was, started the flame of resentment in other places. Oakland followed with a serious fight; then Sacramento followed with several days battle in a veritable "Squatter's War" with a number of casualties. Then outraged public opinion took stern measures and city after city effectually brought matters to an issue, —a general cleanup as started in Marin county. Much the same attempts were made on the Bolsa de Tomales Rancho during the pending suit, but in the general jollification following the end there the bona ride settlers rather pitied the disappointed squatters and aided them to locate elsewhere or retained them for general work.

Thus the unending difficulties of land matters all over California practically passed Marin County by, and its settlers by their forethought and early perfection of titles have saved our farm owners endless subsequent litigation. Every school room in the county should have a Marin County Map of the Land Grant Ranchos, and every school child should be told of the struggles of the Marin pioneers to attain them. Those Tomales Resolutions should also have a place if for nothing else than to indicate that pioneers were dignified, law abiding and homes protecting citizens, as well as to remove a too prevalent idea of their being the wholly untrue type usually represented. We little know how sometimes these early stimulations fix the character and aims of the fast developing child and serve to firmly shape his or her ideals of true citizenship.

There is a current belief that the original locators of these early Marin Land Grants were not representative people. Nothing could be further from the truth. These articles on Early Marin Days are in no sense to be geographical in the case of individuals, yet in them sufficient statement ought to be made to remove this wholly unwarranted idea.

This mistaken impression is a fair example of the senseless comment one so often hears on the "foreign element." If the average one of these critics would scan their own family tree they would soon be convinced that the *Mayflower* was not such a large vessel after all. Further, and more important, they would find that its passengers were from the solid citizen type of bread earning English people and not the so-called aristocracy. It is true that a few outsiders were included among the early Marin grantees, who by government positions or favors were awarded grants and then promptly sold them for immediate gain. But Marin did not suffer by the exchange, since the real homebuilding, ranch developing citizen usually succeeded to these lands. Then among so many, there was certain to be a few to whom such sudden wealth of opportunity appeared in the same light as our present lottery drawings,—something for nothing and when so easily gained was easily lost.

Marin County unquestionably gained its best citizens in these early times from among retired soldiers and some immigrants in both Spanish and Mexican periods and later in the Gold Rush times, who saw surer opportunities in agriculture and stock raising than in the wild scramble for preference or for gold recoveries in the short lived placer mines. Up to 1774 there were only thirty-one Spanish soldiers in all California, nineteen at Monterey and twelve at San Diego. These were men of families, of good settler promise, whom the Government signed up for ten years of frontier military service, after which they were to receive a bonus of land grants if they would make proper use thereof. So when the service expired the land was virtually theirs for the asking, even though the Missioners attempted to in every way block their final reward. Many attempts were made to get settler's parties to come to the new lands, but the sea trip was so disastrous to explorer after explorer and the accommodations so extremely poor for the trip for any one, that no applicants could be found.

Then occurred the famous land trip of Juan Bautista de Anza, making a journey to San Francisco from Sonora and return, and bringing with him the first party of settlers for the new land. This journey across the desert wastes of northern Mexico, over the Gila and Colorado Rivers, through a bitterly hostile Indian county, and thence up through the uncharted, unknown territory of California,—should be a tale available for every school child in the West. Think of a land trip of nearly fifteen hundred miles, half of the distance with a large party of men, women and children, and brought through in safety against every natural obstacle. The thirty settlers were carefully chosen; were to be soldiers first; and each family allowed eight hundred dollars for the equipment and trip expense. The party consisted of

Don Anza, Fray Pedro Font[96], eighty men, and two hundred and forty women and children. The party is mentioned here because from it arose the well-known first families of California, several of whose descendants afterward came to Marin County when the San Francisco Presidio was abandoned.

So when one sees some comment of the early Californians being drawn from the most indolent type of aged soldiers and turned out office holders and their resulting descendants, read over this Anza journey in Bancroft, Eldridge, Chapman and a score of other references, then see if you do not just as quickly resent this statement as you would a claim that our across-the-plains pioneers were the worthless, wastrel, loafer element of the Eastern States, —even yet made by land grabbers who gained California lands by one means or another from early pioneers who developed homes in the West.

The record of these Ranchos is by itself a most interesting story, but much too extensive for present mention. There were eighteen original grants in Marin county in the following order of granting: Baulinas, Corte Madera del Presidio, Sauzalito, Punta de los Reyes (later divided to P. del R. Sobrante also), Tamales y Baulinas, Canada de Herrera, Corte Madera de Novato, Novato, Punte de Quintin, San Jose, Olompali, Blucher (partly in Sonoma county), San Geronimo, Point San Pedro - Santa Margarita - Los Gallinas, Nicasio, Soulajule, San Antonio Laguna, Bolsa de Tomales (afterward cancelled).

Of the grantees who became long time pioneers in Marin, there were Rafael Garcia, Pablo Briones[97], William Richardson, John Reed, A.

---

[96] Pedro Font (1737-1781), Franciscan missionary and diarist for the Anza expedition, was born in Girona, Spain. He selected the site for the San Francisco mission and named the Sierra Nevada.

[97] Dr. Joseph Pablo Briones (1823-1897), son of Gregorio Briones, an early settler at Bolinas.

Randall[98], Domingo Sais, John Martin[99], R. Buckelew[100], Ignacio Pacheco, Timothy Murphy, William Reynolds, James Black[101], J. Cornwall and B. Bojorques[102]. Four of these men were Presidio soldiers and five were either guards or officials at the San Rafael Mission. Nine Ranchos were granted to either soldiers or Mission officials, one and part of another to Christianized Indians, one to a settler, and six to Government officials. This data is for principals in the applications for lands, some of them having a number of sub principals named who developed the grants. Therefore the Marin county grants were fairly representative of those who had worked to develop the territory either intimately or indirectly, and in accord with the original aims of the Spanish and Mexican Governments for the new territory. Few sections can present a better showing in this respect than Marin County, if this point alone can be thus brought out as to the type of the original grantees, the effort of these notes will have been well repaid. Of the sub-principals of the warrants involved, two were American ex-

---

[98] Andrew Randall (1819-1856), born in Rhode Island, came to Monterey in 1849 as Customs Inspector. A geologist, he founded the California Academy of Science. He bought Rancho de Punta de los Reyes and 110,000 acres of land elsewhere in California.

[99] John Martin (1787-bef. 1860), born in England, came to California in 1822 on the *Orion* with William Richardson. He owned a league of land between Sonoma and Petaluma, but Indian attacks caused him to move south. He bought the Rancho Corte Madera de Novato, two square leagues, roughly Marinwood and Hicks Valley today.

[100] Benjamin Rush Buckelew (1822–1859) and his wife, Martha, came to California in 1846 with the Hoppe and Harlan wagon train. In San Francisco, he founded a watch making and jewelry shop, and manufactured gold scales for use by miners. He owned and operated the San Francisco newspaper *The Californian* (1847-48). In 1850, Buckelew bought three Marin County ranchos in 11 days. Besides Cooper's Rancho Punta de Quentin, Buckelew also purchased Cooper's Rancho Nicasio and John Reed's Rancho Corte Madera del Presidio. He became embroiled in lawsuits that cost him much of his land, and he fought them until his death.

[101] James Black (1807-1870), born in Scotland, was a seaman who became ill with typhus and was put ashore in Monterey in 1832 to die. He recovered, was helped by B. R. Cooper, and became a trapper for the Hudson's Bay Company. General Vallejo granted him land near Fort Ross as a buffer against the Russians. He married Maria, daughter of Domingo Sais of San Anselmo.

[102] Bartolomé Bojórquez (1780–1863) was the son of Pedro Antonio Bojorques, who came to California with the De Anza Expedition. Bojorquez, a soldier serving at the Presidio of San Francisco, was granted the six square league Rancho Laguna de San Antonio in 1845.

soldiers from the Mexican war, and one was the Halleck who afterwards was so widely known as General Halleck[103] in the Civil War.

1 June 1922

FREMONT IN MARIN

Comes now the so-called Fremont[104] episodes in Marin County, which clearly evidence how careless we are concerning the nature of the history which our children often learn as authentic, when at the same time the original and correct sources of such data are easily obtainable. It is indeed puzzling to at times understand just who is or what influences are responsible for current acceptance of some historical writings. We in Marin County should at least feel responsible for accepting and passing on current accounts of happenings in our own midst to outside peoples; and in any event showing that there is a decided difference of record on certain matters. Our own people ought to know what has occurred here and be able to present the best sources of local history to our children.

Two painful memories remain of early day happenings, yet each was the act of an individual and not of a community. The Indian massacre near San Rafael has been noted and the second appears in the resumé of the Fremont matters. This latter was an incident over which a storm of bitterly unfavorable comment arose and which has left questionable influences on many matters pertaining to the so-called Bear Flag war. Its discussion passed to foreign countries, became an issue in the halls of our own Congress, and eventually a vital cause for the defeat of John C. Fremont in the presidential election of 1856. Therein he received only one fifth of the total vote of all California.

The Marin County History of 1880 vividly portrays some thrilling days in Marin County of the Bear Flag-Fremont period, matters which are eagerly listened to by our children as facts of early times. The writer does not seek to in any way detract from this youthful interest, but rather to

---

[103] Henry Wager Halleck (1815-1872), chief of staff to U. S. Grant, helped draft the California Constitution. He owned Rancho Nicasio and 110,000 acres of land elsewhere in California.

[104] John Charles Frémont (1813-1890), illegitimate son of a Virginia planter, explorer, surveyor, military officer, first Republican candidate for President.

present the proper vision as detailed by several of the best research historians and a multitude of specified additional references which are listed in any reliable review of the period. And with such changes, there is still a wealth of inspiration and interest for the younger folk in the tale, as there is in almost any story of the early day matters. If any doubt remained about the Marin episodes of Fremont, a thirteen day speech by Senator Benton[105] in the United States Senate in the early '50's in defense of serious charges of similar misrepresentation in Fremont's behalf elsewhere, gave the historians and his political enemies in the presidential campaign ample chance to disprove Benton's version with innumerable items of local and eye witness evidence everywhere. The Nation then gave an unmistakable verdict at the polls in 1856.

While Fremont was at San Rafael the distressing and seemingly inexcusable slaying of the inoffensive and well-known across-the-bay citizens occurred. In view of the fact that the former Marin County History details this matter as not only justifiable but rather creditable, and with such accompanying data as seemed impossible, the writer compared this data with the research evidence of Bancroft, Eldridge, Historical Papers, Political Campaign Records of 1856, etc. It then appeared that our Marin History writer took his account from that of one Lancey[106], who in turn obtained the data from the writings of a mariner named Phelps[107], whose mention in a later note herein rather indicates why he states matters which have no mention in any of the existing writing of that period.

It therefore is advisable to present the historians' view rather than that of Captain Phelps, whose writings are not accepted in other matters. While probably presented in good faith at the time, the data was undoubtedly gained merely from hearsay evidence of Fremont's followers who in turn had it through several other sources, since but few of them were eye witnesses. So a restatement of the case is made as based on the evidence noted by the historians mentioned and from the bitter debates in Congress

---

[105] Thomas Hart Benton (1782-1858), Senator from Missouri (1821-1851), Representative from Missouri (1853-1855). He was Fremont's father-in-law, but despised the man for his Republican affiliation and his actions in California.

[106] Thomas Crosby Lancey (1824-1885) was a coxswain on the US Sloop of War *Dale*. He later ran the first stagecoach from Sacramento to the gold mines.

[107] Captain William Dane Phelps (1802-1875), of the American bark *Moscow*.

on Fremont's career. Whether Fremont personally, or Kit Carson[108], or Carson's Delaware Scouts, or a desire to retaliate for atrocities on Americans near Santa Rosa supposedly at the hands of Castro[109] forces, were responsible for the outrage has never been settled. Therefore the reader must judge whether there was any excuse for the crime.

It appears that a boat containing four men was seen coming from San Pablo toward Point San Pedro. It proceeded up the San Rafael Estero, where three men disembarked, placed their saddles on the beach and started for the Mission with evident intention of borrowing horses for the northern trip as was then the custom. Fremont and his leaders were standing in the corridor of the Mission San Rafael Archangel when this approach was reported, and the commander directed Kit Carson to intercept the visitors. Taking two men, he returned after going a short distance and asked as to the arrest of the party of strangers. To this Fremont replied that he wanted no prisoners. Whereupon Carson and the two men rode on for a time, dismounted, and calmly shot the three visitors at rifle range distance. The bodies were stripped and allowed to remain there several days. It then developed that one was an old man and a respected citizen of Santa Clara, Don Berryessa[110], whose son[111] was in arrest at Sonoma at its Alcalde and in the hands of Fremont's men at that point. His wife had sent Berryessa north to look into the matter. The others were twin brothers of the De Haro[112] family, both mere boys and whose father had been Alcalde at San Francisco. They had been sent from San Pablo by Castro with a message to his Lieutenant

---

[108] Christopher Houston "Kit" Carson (1809-1868), mountain man, guide, Indian fighter, and brevet Brigadier General in the Civil War.

[109] José Antonio Castro (1808–1860) was acting governor of Alta California in 1835-1836 and Commandante General of the Mexican army in Alta California at the time of the 1846 Bear Flag Revolt and the Mexican-American War of 1846-1848.

[110] José de los Reyes Berryessa (1785-1846) was born at Mission Santa Clara and served as a sergeant at the Presidio de San Francisco. In 1842 he was granted Rancho San Vicente, at the south end of the Almaden valley, which included a valuable mercury mine. He had thirteen children. He was 61 when he was killed.

[111] José del los Santos Berryessa (1817-1864), born at Yerba Buena, was alcalde of Sonoma. In 1843 he received the grant of the Rancho Mallacomes in Napa. In 1846 he and two brothers were captured in the Bear Flag revolt. He served on various land commissions.

[112] Francisco and Ramon de Haro (1827-1846) were twin brothers of Francisco de Haro (1792-1849), first alcalde of Yerba Buena. They were 19 at the time of their murders.

de la Torre[113] in Marin County, neither Castro nor the De Haro's knowing anything about Fremont's being here. Yet in spite of all these facts, and of the boatman returning with report of where he had left the messengers, the accepted Phelps' account lands the party at San Quentin, where they were arrested, searched and found to be spies of Castro. Moreover that they carried a message to kill every foreign man, woman and child of the north of the bay territory, upon which they were promptly shot. But a searching and painstaking inquiry followed by responsible people and by friends of both well-known pioneer families. This showed that in the presence of all, these unarmed, non-combatant citizens were shot without a hearing and avenged only by the later civil results to Fremont.

8 June 1922

On return of Fremont's party to Sonoma, Berryessa's son begged the commander in presence of witnesses to give him his father's serape which a soldier was wearing. But Fremont declined to interfere, whereupon it was purchased for twenty-five dollars and doubtless returned to the sorrowing old wife at Santa Clara. Many accounts of this San Rafael matter followed in the press of the period and numbers of letters written East and to the continent were afterward located which detailed the circumstances of the crime. One must consider that it was one of the lamentable acts always accompanying unorganized war times, yet the historian accounts should replace the Phelps' version. The Mexican Military Governor demanded explanations from the *U. S. S. Portsmouth* Commander at San Francisco, who replied that "Neither the United States Government or its subalterns had any part in the insurrection, (Sonoma and Olompali incidents) and that the Mexican authorities ought, therefore, to punish its authors in conformity with the law."

But the Mexican war broke out a few days later and action could not follow, which prevented an inevitable international incident arising therefrom. No authority seems to have yet published the official Mexican account of this affair. But for our purposes a list of thirty-one standard references discuss it and historians do not hesitate to state that the early

---

[113] Lieutenant José Joaquin de la Torre, born in Santander, Spain, was a soldier at the Presidio de San Francisco. He later became a captain and served as Alcalde of Monterey and secretary to Governor de Sola.

Marin History version is not only decidedly in error but intentionally misleading. A Los Angeles paper[114] published an affidavit of an eye witness, and but one copy thereof is now preserved, which evidences an attempt to secure and destroy them.

Fremont declined to afterward discuss the facts other than noting it as a trifling matter incident to a state of war, and once said that it was an act of Delaware Scouts only known to him afterward. Yet out of the incident arose far reaching consequences, not the least of which were the subsequently more vigorous control of the followers of other filibusters[115] of later years.

Whoever chronicled the deeds of John C. Fremont should take rank with some of the famous press agents. In spite of the innumerable official and authentic reports of his so-called skirmishes, battles, engagements, campaign, etc. of the Bear Flag War days, and the consequent open reference thereto, this individual seems to have surrounded Fremont's even minor acts with a halo of heroic leadership and result. It is inconceivable to believe that an engineer of his ability, education and frequent concise reports to Governmental superiors, could have sent on such lurid accounts of his exploits as are noted in accounts of him. It seems more reasonable to think that he had the misfortune to be in the hands of well-meaning friends who, when once committed to statements, Fremont did not wish to embarrass by contradictions. However this may be, we in Marin county having the Marin History account noted, should also have the historian's version of the matter; yet at the same times remembering that these were frontier times and occasions when there was little chance of other than hearsay evidence to the learned unless principals themselves gave personal versions. Bancroft made repeated personal requests to Fremont for facts of the matter but without result.

So the scenario accounts of the Marin History of 1880 deals with the strenuous days of Fremont in our territory; of the dashing attacks on General Castro's men (whom not one of his force ever saw); of the capture of the Mission San Rafael (which ruined building contained only some discouraged and hopeless native families); of the execution of spies at San Quentin (who were peaceful citizens of the best repute shot down near San Rafael); of his race to Sausalito in pursuit of Castro's men (who left there

---

[114] *Los Angeles Star*, 27 September 1856.
[115] One definition of a filibuster is a person engaging in unauthorized warfare against another country.

before the pursuers had started from Sonoma); of the thrilling incidents of a hurried trip across the bay to spike the Presidio guns and dismantle its fort (which fort had been abandoned and guns dismantled long before); of his finesse in dealing with the de la Torre Mexican soldiery (when he was easily and thoroughly outwitted by them in spite of his famous Kit Carson Scouts); —only a few of the accounts which once served their purpose and must now be viewed with the charity of later years. Yet our children believe them and accept them as authentic local history.

Fremont was our one time Governor for a short period[116], and in justice to him it should be said that up to the Bear Flag days his results as a United States Officer on topographical survey work received unstinted praise from the highest authorities everywhere. Let us also grant that he was probably acting here under at least quasi instructions from Washington, details of which are still well guarded in Government archives. Yet to continue to eulogize him in our schools as a California military leader in face of Government, Western, individual, and historian records to the contrary, is a plain sample of the kind of history which is furnished our children today. By all means have them admire this picturesque figure of frontier days in his success as an explorer and mapper of much needed trails for coming emigrants. But in Marin County at least let them know the truth of his "brilliant campaign which drove the enemy entirely out of the north of the bay territory, destroyed his transports and spiked the guns of the Presidio."

15 June 1922

Account of the Bear Flag war began with General Castro's visit to San Rafael in 1846 to requisition horses for the plainly growing need of an expedition to escort Fremont out of the State, — the Mexican authorities having so directed after his defiance near Monterey. Obtaining these, Castro's Lieutenant took them to Sonoma to receive others, after which he started to return by way of Knights Landing. But they were captured by Fremont's sympathizers who sent the officer back to Castro with an invitation to come and get the animals. Castro, as Mexican Military

---

[116] Fremont was self-appointed Military Governor of California from January to March 1847, when he was removed and court-martialed for mutiny. He served as US Senator from California from 1850 to 1851, and Territorial Governor of Arizona from 1878 to 1881.

Governor, then sent Lieutenant de la Torre from San Pablo to southern Marin with instructions to hold the territory and observe Fremont's actions until a main body could be marched around the bay and attack Sonoma which was reported as about to fall into Fremont's hands. De la Torre established a base at Olompali and connected with Padilla's[117] small force near Santa Rosa. Two Americans[118] were captured by this latter party and murdered after unspeakable tortures at the hands of some desperadoes of this force, which then came south with other prisoners.

Lieutenant Ford[119] hurried down from Sonoma, surprised and routed a few men at our Laguna San Antonio and advanced to attack the main body at Olompali. A sharp engagement resulted, the much larger Mexican force retreating toward San Rafael after severe losses. Ford released the prisoners[120] and returned to Sonoma.

This was the first battle of the Bear Flag War. Thereupon Fremont garrisoned Sonoma and marched to San Rafael, his party being made up of his across-the-mountains expedition, with Kit Carson and his Delaware Scouts; John Marshall (of later gold discovery fame); and a fast accumulating number of adventurers, filibusters and camp followers; also a number of Americans joining from the best of motives. Altogether there were 165 men in the force which entered Marin County. Fremont's chronicler tells of the "surprise attack" on the De La Torre's camp near San Rafael, and of the "capture" of the Mission San Rafael; but those statements are only samples of many illusory items of the brilliant campaign of ridding all Northern California of enemy forces; of destroying his transports and effectually scattering his followers.

---

[117] Juan Padilla, sometimes called Captain, was apparently not a soldier. He is sometimes called a Californio vigilante. He apparently gathered a group of like-minded men to resist the Americans. After General Vallejo was taken prisoner, Padilla sneaked into the Americans' camp, met Vallejo, and offered to free him, but Vallejo refused. There was a soldier named Juan Padilla at the Presidio de San Diego, but it is not clear if this is the same man.

[118] Thomas Cowie and George Fowler. They are sometimes described as "two of the youngest" Bear Flaggers.

[119] Henry L. Ford (1822-1860) was a deserter from the US Army who had impersonated his brother to escape. He was appointed Lieutenant by William Ide, leader of the Bear Flaggers.

[120] William L. Todd (1818-1876), designer of the Bear Flag, was a nephew of Mary Todd, wife of Abraham Lincoln. He was released from the house by a California woman. The other prisoner, an unnamed Englishman, was killed in the fight.

Fremont's party spent three days at San Rafael searching for the enemy. But in all of his trips in Marin County not one of his force ever (of record) met a combatant enemy. Meanwhile Kit Carson's Delaware Scouts were busily engaged in trying to locate the de la Torre's forces but without success. One would like to read de la Torre's report on his duty here, for he plainly and cleverly outwitted these seasoned campaigners. He had Indians "captured" both at San Rafael and at Sonoma, bearing a message to Castro to the effect that an attack was planned on Sonoma in the morning. Though his officers objected, Fremont failed to note the ruse, and by an all-night march managed to arrive at Sonoma just before daylight. There he narrowly escaped having his party blown to pieces by his own garrison who were ready for a supposed attack, and who on hearing the approach stood behind loaded canon with matches aflame in readiness for the firing command. So the Fremont party hurried back to San Rafael, de la Torre meanwhile quietly departing from Sausalito at daybreak by embarking for San Pablo. Thence he went to Santa Clara. In spite of Castro's command being still at Santa Clara, Phelps notes that from the ridge back of San Rafael Carson's scouts "saw Castro's army marching around the head of the Bay toward San Rafael."

Fremont next "pursued" de la Torre to Sausalito where Phelps of the "*Moscow*" trading vessel informed him of the escaped soldiery. Then Phelps took Fremont and ten men to the Presidio (the Marin History says "half of his force"). This party "captured and spiked its guns and dismantled the fortifications," thence returning to Sonoma for a general jubilation on July 5th, 1846. While these matters should not detract in any way from the stirring incidents occurring at Sonoma in the Bear Flag matters, this heroic gun spiking episode suffers somewhat when unimpeachable facts prove that the guns had been dismounted for a long time and the post abandoned. Bancroft slyly adds "So far as it is known not one of the ten guns offered the slightest resistance."

The wide variance between the Phelps' account of this matter and the historian's facts caused further search for comparison by the writer. Eldridge presents practically the foregoing facts also but closes with the original wording of Government records, no doubt with intent to show his impartial discussion of Fremont's expedition. It seems that long afterward Phelps sent a sworn statement of a claim to Congress for ten thousand dollars for transporting and aiding the Fremont party on this Presidio trip, as taken under great danger to himself and his property. Fremont certified to the correctness of this aid, not mentioning its worth in money. But the California Claims Committee in Congress thought otherwise and reported through its chairman, Major Gillespie of the Marine Corps, in an endorsement that "the party was transported seven miles, to spike guns of a fort so badly dismantled that it could not be occupied unless entirely rebuilt: that no enemy was present, and the sole object of Fremont was to prevent future use of the guns; that there was no personal danger incurred and that the service would be well paid at fifty dollars." The bill was accordingly settled for this amount! This result alone would seem to indicate that Fremont never made any explanations of any matter, being already hard and fast in the hands of friends determined to magnify his exploits for his ultimate and disastrous presidential candidacy.

We should of course like to consider that Marin County had some thrilling part in the Bear Flag War which began as a filibuster following a long series of disturbing matters but happened just on the eve of Uncle Sam sending our Navy here to seize the California territory. The Bear Flag party knew nothing of that proposed action. In consequence we should give full credit to Sonoma, whose Lieutenant Ford's prompt efficient work at Olompali caused immediate withdrawal of Mexican soldiery from Marin County and doubtless saved our residents from serious consequences. (This was before Fremont's assumption of leadership). Our small boys can still revel in the thrills of Kit Carson and his Delaware Scouts being here, and of the Fremont party with its picturesque assemblage of hunters, trappers, adventurers and eagerly patriotic American settlers from Sonoma and Sacramento; yet local incident should in some measure conform to fact or be plainly noted as tradition.

22 June 1922

EARLY MARIN INDUSTRIES

Long ago the first Spanish explorer passing through Marin territory was impressed with its natural charm, and others later considered that there are few places indeed which were superior to it in the matter of natural beauty. In later years its comparison vies with any section anywhere for wide variation of topography, climate, resources and possibilities. With a multitude of esteros and inlets and the San Pablo, Richardson's, San Francisco, Drake's and Limantour Bays, it yet has the gem of them all in the inland water area of Tomales Bay. This extends for sixteen miles into the very centre of the county, a land-locked, sheltered sheet of quiet water which appears to be an inland lake of wonderful beauty in its setting. If any doubting Thomases on this matter will take a trip out toward Tomales Point from the Inverness Road, or climb the slopes of Black's mountain near Point Reyes Station, and look out over this beautiful land locked bay,— there is small question of any doubt in the matter.

As yet Marin county has taken little account of this advantage of an almost continuance of shore line as its boundaries. Long stretches of deep water frontage are still bought and sold as grazing lands, and little or no attention has been paid to the wealth of water approach which this section has over less fortunate neighbors.

Probably the first business in Marin county territory other than the routine Mission trade lines was that of the fur hunting Russians. They had a base at Fort Ross and farming lands at Bodega a few miles south of the fort. From there, posts were established on the Farallones and on the Santa Barbara Channel Islands, They proceeded to strip Tomales Bay, Drakes Bay, the coast line, San Francisco Bay and its many inlets of thousands and tens of thousands of fur bearing animals each year. A flourishing business was developed on the Farallones, where a Russian or two and from six to ten Aleuts from Alaska remained for several years.

From 1812 to 1818 they obtained twelve to fifteen hundred seal skins a year and thereafter only about two or three hundred annually. The kill also included some two hundred sea lions and from fifty to a later five thousand gulls. The skins and sinews were used for making boats. The meat was salted and dried for use as food at Fort Ross and faraway Sitka. The bladders made water tight sacks for oil intended for food and for lamps. Gull meat was also dried and the feather down collected for exporting. Great quantities of sea fowl eggs were gathered and also prepared for later use elsewhere.

The Russian fur company found rich pickings in the tremendous numbers of sea otter which were found all along the western coast and the inlets and bays therefrom. The Aleuts came down the coast from Fort Ross and also from the Farallones in the frail skin bidarka[121] boats and stole into

---

[121] Baidarkas, or kayaks.

San Francisco Bay in spite of the orders of the Spanish authorities and of the Mission Padres. By hugging the Marin shore they kept out of range of the Spanish guns at the Presidio and then plundered the bay territory and well up the Sacramento and San Joaquin Rivers, since the Spanish officials or the Indians had no boats at all. Still later these Aleuts came up to the head of Tomales Bay and carried the light canoes overland at night to San Pablo Bay to continue these raids after the Spanish boats arrived. Sir Francis Drake's chronicler aptly described this Farallone Island wild game in the log of his voyage here in 1579, which shows why the Russians had a post there: "Not far from this harbour (Drake's Bay) did lye certain Islands,—we called the Islands of St. James, —having on them plentiful and great store of seales and birds; with one of which we fell (landed) July 24: whereon we found such provision as might competently serue (serve) our time for a while. We departed against the day next following, July 25." So it was Marin County's coast which subsisted Drake for his long journey home.

29 June 1922

It seems that the valuable sea otter was found in exceedingly great numbers all along the Western Coast, but at a price of sixty and later one hundred dollars a skin in China the poor animal had few chances to escape prompt extinction in even those early times. A few of them are still occasionally found in the extreme north and once in a while one of them is shot off the Marin Coast line. Many Marinites can remember shooting sea otter in off shore waters in modern years. General Vallejo probably had the last lot of sea otter on San Francisco Bay, having carefully protected and built up a colony at the head of Sonoma Creek. But the fame of them reached some poachers in southern California, who raided the place one night and decamped with their ill-gotten gains. A Spanish visitor to Marin County tells of lassoing numbers of sea otter at San Quentin Point in early days. Vallejo says that from five to ten thousand sea otter skins were each year sent to China markets, and at sixty dollars a skin, the business was more profitable than anything else in the early days. There were also great numbers of beaver here in the bay territory, and they likewise fell victims to the fur hunters. At the present time there are several colonies along the

San Joaquin and Sacramento River countries, but thoroughly protected by Government game regulations.

While the limited exchange of Mission products with the Presidio for other supplies was the first business dealings of that nature in Marin territory, and to a slight extent some means of water transportation had to be evolved therefor, agriculture in its larger sense was not developed in the early Mission years because with the exception of local demands, the trading vessels visiting the coast would accept no cargoes except hides and tallow for many years. When sea otter became scarce and considerably more wary as well, Don Timothy Murphy found a means of continuing their capture by the importation of some beagle hounds at forty dollars apiece, which animals became adepts in capturing the last remaining otter and beaver in the bay and along the shore. The Indians of course had nothing of trading value to exchange for crops products. Therefore beaver trapping and cattle raising were the leading industries for a long period.

Cattle were slaughtered merely to obtain their hides and the tallow in each carcass, and when a vessel arrived for such a cargo great droves of cattle were slaughtered for this purpose. The hides were sold green as there was no cheap salt then, and a vessel carrying them was usually given a wide berth to windward in consequence.

It was about 1846 that Americans first began to get the rich lands of Marin territory and to cultivate it. It was sold by the grantees for about twelve dollars an acre. Oh, for those chances again! In a later period lumbering opportunities brought many companies into Marin territory for that purpose, notes thereon being found under some later localities reviews.

A few items of early Marin farming methods ought to be of interest to modern specialists equipped with every possible labor saving aid, yet who are in turn only now beginning to realize how much better results are still to be evolved by more patient and painstaking endeavor. In mission times wheat was cut by hand by means of short tree limb sections made with sharp edges and forming a cycle [scythe] like implement. On gathering up the grain stalks and heads, it was threshed by being placed on the ground in a circular corral-like lane, through which horses were made to race around and around the circle. The Indians would toss the resulting chaff into the air with wooden shovels on a windy day, whereby the straw blew away and the golden, shiny kernels fell to ground again. It was then usually washed before being ground or smashed between heavy stones for breadstuffs. The crop was plentiful, horses for the asking, the labor cheap, —altogether an Elysian field for the ranchers as there was an ever growing demand for the grain.

Plows were exceedingly primitive affairs, merely a crooked limb of a tree with a piece of flat iron for a point and a small tree for a pole. To this there were sufficient oxen attached to perform the needed ground "stirring." If no iron was available, a number of extra crooked sticks were carried along for emergencies and used as others gave out. The vehicles were great unwieldly carts with green hides stretched on the bottom, sides and at times the top also. The wheels were pieces of hard wood fastened together with cross cleats or a double thickness of planks at right angles. They were not always round, and when revolving on varying diameters on either side at the same instant, afforded plenty of diversion to the rider or to the driver in his attempts to keep his load properly fastened. Occasionally enough iron was obtained to fit the wheels with tires. Naturally enough the axles had to be of wood and as tallow was cheap the result was satisfactory if constantly attended to. Yet occasionally a worker forgot his grease supply and the country for miles around was very soon informed of the fact. Those who have attended the old time "chivari," with its resined plank for music, will understand how a heavily laden, wooden-axled, dry wheeled old time cart of this kind had a tendency to attract undue attention unto itself. A story is told of the first of these carts to be made at the Presidio to transfer goods to the Mission Dolores some miles distant. When the wheels began to protest in good earnest the reverberations so resounded in the San Francisco hills as to scatter the neophytes far in advance of its advance. The Indians had never heard a noise like it or as loud as it was except thunder. So the driver proceeded to the end that only an angry old Padre met him on arrival at the Mission. No Indian appeared until after nightfall, and meanwhile the driver had to shift the load to the accompaniment of the Padre's choicest remarks on his ancestors, his intelligence and other equally instructive comments.

The high priced milkers of our day should know of the efforts of their earlier compatriots. There were children to be fed then also, and an occasional cow to be milked in consequence. It was a neighborhood affair and usually heralded long before. Three persons commonly joined in the effort and the rancherio, his family and the neighbors watched the episode. One vaquero held the impatient cow by the head at the end of a trusty riata; another secured her hind legs by similar means; sometimes an extra assistant fought off a hungry calf during the process; the third party obtained what milk he could with one hand, while holding a crock or other receptacle in the other. More often this third party used his two hands to milk, to hold the crock and to discourage the hungry calf. Sometimes the second helper busied himself with the young bossy between plunges of the angry bovine mother.

The neighbors, as spectators, were not supposed to say anything, being present by invitation to merely take notes on how things should be done. But the rancherio, his wife and his children made the most of their privilege in consequence, keeping up a running fire of suggestion and comment as to the poor results of the workers in calming the cow sufficiently so that she would offer the milk supply. Great was the joy when a chance came to ridicule the milkers if they failed of results. Somehow the children thrived on this milk supply, in spite of the present multitudinous dairy inspectors, pasteurizing necessities and certificated supplies of which those times knew nothing.

Crimes were very seldom unpunished in those days, and if committed it was almost a certainty that strict enforcement of penalty would follow. Aside from their fondness for stealing cattle and horses from the big ranchos where no record of numbers was ever kept, there was little need of a juez de paz (justice of the peace). Ranching was very simple. The rancho was a huge domain upon which lived numbers of Indians ready for any labor required in return for their own subsistence and for the privilege of horseback riding on the rancho. Only the Haciendo proprietor, or his principle foreman, etc., etc., were allowed to ride elsewhere. One southern writer of those times describes at great length his amazement on first seeing the Indian woman ride astride (who incidentally never rode at all): but failing in any ability to properly express himself except by the statement that a particularly handsome young Indian maiden "exhibited a small foot and neat ankle on either side of the horse." The rich lands had been fertilized for unknown ages by annually recurring growths of rank grasses, hence if only its surface was stirred or a stick point made a slight furrow for the sown grain, it provided an ideal start for the quickly growing crop. This in turn so far overtopped the weeds and native grasses and its upper section later harvested by hand. —that the native growths never interfered as they do now.

6 July 1922

Inquiry has often been made as to why the Marin County History of 1880 dwelt at such length on details of homicides of the county. This is better understood when it is known that between the deserting whaler element, at Sausalito, the thieving fraternity of some "respectables" and many vagabonds trying to obtain Indian properties, and especially the relics from San Quentin, —the interior and northern Marin ranches of outlying districts were at the mercy of predatory characters. Hence those old pioneers banded together in much the same way that they did in the Land Seizure days, and pledged the "one for all, all for one" idea. This guaranteed protection to the humblest settler and an unrelenting justice upon criminals of any sort. Southern Marin was very sparsely settled and then only in groups of respectables; therefore the roving loose-charactered individuals resented the northern attitude. But the northerners attended all criminal trials of moment, not from mistrust of justice, but to impress upon the criminal element that northern Marin never let up on their transgressions. In consequence it was made a condition of rendering assistance to the history issued, that only straightforward facts of these murders be presented and not the lurid crime incenting accounts of newspapers concerning the outlaws of early days. By such action it was hoped to establish a remembrance to the lawless fraternity anywhere and at any time, that citizens once banded together for a common aim were a force to be carefully considered before lawless acts were consummated.

LUMBERING IN MARIN

The Russians produced the first sawed lumber north of San Francisco. This was by means of the old time whip-saw and pit. Stumps of trees then cut are still standing in the West Mendocino coast region and about them have grown from one to six shoots to a size quite sufficient for present day lumbering of certain type. So much for the western climate which reproduces redwood time [trees?] in fifty years or more.

What a wonderful heritage we would now have in Marin County if some of the mammoth old redwoods of pioneer days still grew in our midst! Our railway travelers can note what first appear to be groups of these redwood trees from Kentfield to Corte Madera and one often hears a stranger ask why they were so planted. Yet closer examination would show that they are but sprouts of the original tree which stood there towering up into the sky and with a base of from twenty-five to fifty feet in circumference. It is still living in that its shoots appear as the present day growth, but wholly robbed of the dignity and beauty of the single giant of the old days. Down in the Muir Woods we have some of the original trees of Marin County, yet none are in any way as large as those which stood in the Mill, Ross, Nicasio, Bolinas, Liberty and Lagunitas valleys of the county. One used to stand near the old Liberty Ranch and is now probably gone before the Alpine Dam assault. Another old timer stood out Camp Taylor way. But both of these were either too much branched for timber or had been topped by storms some centuries ago, seem to be but mourners of a lost race. One has to journey up to the Bohemian Grove in Sonoma County to see an even older generation of trees which resemble the former giants of Marin; or to the Armstrong Grove at Guerneville and the Hendy Woods of Philo to be able to compare with our own destroyed specimens. Nothing like them remains south of San Francisco in the Santa Cruz region. What a priceless link between the old and the new days there would be now, for no city in the world has any nearby trees like those at Muir Woods which are almost within the City by the Golden Gate.

It appears that Marin County was the centre for practically all the lumbering and wood getting for early days. All of the Mount Tamalpais slopes on the north, east, south and west sides of the mountain, and Nicasio, Lagunitas, Olema, Novato, Bolinas and the west side of Tomales Bay sections were ruthlessly denuded of the irreplaceable heritage of centuries. Thus has it ever been,—this generation bewailing the action of the last, yet making no provision for the next. It is each era for itself and the future takes its own chances. Some old oak, madrona and laurel trees that would have been world famous were sacrificed over wide areas of Marin County merely to provide "ship knees" for the main trunk crotches, and the remainder of the old giants either burned up or if near transportation facilities taken over the bay as fire wood.

The timber resources of Marin territory were very limited in a general sense and quickly cut down. The pine and fir trees in the Woodacre Valley, then too small for use, are about the only general forest area now remaining as of the old days. The Muir Woods Grove was preserved on account of inability to remove the timber and a group or two above Mill Valley hint at the wealth of old time giants on the mountain. There is a madrona tree of tremendous trunk girth on the shores of Lake Lagunitas, which aptly indicates a comparison of former companions[122].

Marin County narrowly escaped becoming a colony of Mormon settlers through its lumbering interests. There were many parties made up in the East to make the journey to the western land of promise by cooperative pooling of interests and resources. Among these the Steamer *Brooklyn* brought several hundred Mormons to San Francisco as an advance party of the great body driven out of Nauvoo Illinois, in 1845-6 and who started on an overland journey in search of the Promised Land of Joseph Smith's prophecy.[123] Upon arrival at San Francisco that city was for a time a Mormon town in reality, since these emigrants virtually outnumbered the residents there. They were orderly, moral, honest and industrious; and generally camped on vacant ground while the strong young men scattered to earn money to pay for passage out and for a new fund to proceed onward again. Numbers of these workers came to Marin County to engage in lumbering industries then thriving here. This party would have probably settled here and in fact some of them made tentative plans to do so. But Brigham Young's halt in Utah instead of continuing West as at first planned,—made our visitors trek again. Time has shown that these people became some of the best settlers elsewhere.

The discovery of gold in California and the resulting turmoil and excitement on the western coast brought thousands of new emigrants. The first came from the nearer points of Mexico, Central America, China, and later Australia. Then England and other European countries sent their quotas; while all the time across-the-plains-parties, around-the-Horn-voyagers, and across-the-Isthmus-adventurers were constantly arriving. Even in Marin county heads of families, vaqueros, farm hands, and anyone able to leave rushed to the famous placer diggings and the fabled mountains of gold. This great California mining boom was of exceedingly short

---

[122] One of the largest and oldest madrones in California, the tree near Pilot Knob died in a storm in 2009.

[123] Samuel Brannan (1819-1889) brought 245 other Mormons around Cape Horn, to Honolulu, then San Francisco in 1847. He brought a printing press and started a newspaper, the *California Star*. Two years later the paper merged with the first paper in California, the *Californian* (1846) to form the *Alta California*. It ceased publication in 1849 because everyone left for the gold fields.

duration for the average man. The at-first wonderful gain for little endeavor soon gave way to a meagre pittance for heavy labor. Rich placers changed from an average of an ounce and more per day per man to a half, a quarter, and an eighth of an ounce only. Finally they paid less than the cost of the tools employed, much less a living return. Quartz claims and workings were an impossibility without great capital to work them, and were bought for a song by those who afterward became the bonanza kings. The quickly changing fortunes of many mining camps ruined the average merchant there, whose business could not become stable. Men began commercial trading on small capital, managed it loosely, had frequent fires, and gradually began to see that the mining game was not for the fellow who expected greater returns than the slowly accumulating yet nevertheless sure returns of home pursuits. Hence hundreds of men who had passed through fertile Marin on the journey north, remembered its solid promise of returns from the agricultural products which all mining camps must have and hastened back again. Hence agriculture and stock raising gained its real start, and lumbering and manufacturing had to await better transportation facilities. So also did the Marinites remember the rich home soil and its opportunities and saw that this horde of searchers for the Golden Fleece must eat and have someone provide the eats for them. They too returned and Marin's agricultural days began in earnest. Great droves of cattle were gathered here and driven into a ready market at the mines, and all available wheat was bought in the field for prompt transportation at purchasers cost. Rancherios named their own prices and the farmers were the section plutocrats.

In the manufacturing line early Marin territory pioneered in several industries, but as other sections developed and transportation of raw materials became cheaper there, Marin's early manufacturing days died away. One of the first was the flourishing paper mills below Camp Taylor[124], which for years supplied all demands for book, news, wrapping and print paper of the bay region. Some distance above this a powder mill flourished until suddenly vanishing from any records in an explosion of the

---

[124] Started by Samuel Penfield Taylor (1827-1886), who bought a schooner with some friends in Boston and sailed around the Horn to the gold rush. Later he built the first paper mill in California on Papermill Creek. It later became a popular resort called Camp Taylor.

plant[125]. Tomales started the first county cheese factory[126] and found an eager market for the product, and its potatoes were the first staples from the north. Over in the Olema Valley insistent attempts were made to develop a lime burning industry but it is probable that limited capital prevented proper results[127]. Lumbering at Novato, Nicasio, Tomales Point, Olema, San Geronimo, Bolinas, Corte Madera, and Mill Valley, was a flourishing industry for a brief period. Shipbuilding at Bolinas formed the largest ship yards in the west for a time; and Black Point, Sausalito, Tomales Bay, and the "inland port" of Gallinas (noted in San Rafael review later) made rapid additions to the fast growing San Francisco fleet of trading vessels. The names of Corte Madera del Presidio and Corte Madera de Novato indicate the wood supply centers of those times. The Nicasio timber was hauled via the present Lucas Valley road to Novato and Ross Landings for water transportation to San Francisco. The Lucas Valley road was built for this purpose, or rather it became the trail over which logs were hauled to water points. Oxen being plentiful, the shortest distance between two points was the chosen route then, regardless of the little matter of grades which troubled the next generation of wagon transportation.

End of Lumbering in Marin

13 July 1922

MARIN'S ORGANIZATION PERIOD

We have noted that Marin County had a number of world voyagers on its shores from 1542 to 1775, and from then to 1817 was thoroughly explored by numerous Spanish expeditions for future purposes. From 1817 to 1834 it was actively the Mission Lands, and then until 1845 only partly so. For a time its northern boundary reached the Russian River but was afterward brought back to the present line of the Estero Americano. Until 1845 there was practically little general development other than the occupation oi the rancho land grants, which varied from 450 to 80,000 acres,

---

[125] The Pacific Powder Mill blew up 29 November, 1867, killing three men and wounding one.

[126] The Marin French Cheese Factory, started in 1865, is still operating.

[127] Several old lime kilns still survive along Highway 1 near Dogtown.

yet even before 1845 some sections had laid a proper foundation for future success. But Marinites should know something of the successive steps in this development, and especially should the school student know how its political organization was effected.

Too few of our elders and in consequence still fewer of our children know how political government started in this country, or by what names our nation became listed as town, county, city, State and national domain. Towns were first known in New England. They were formed by reason of the necessity of cooperative protection from hostile Indians, and as refuge bases for outlying farms and forest clearings in time of need. Those old time "towns" meant about what our "townships" do now insofar as extent of territory under that name. In consequence there was a central village, and the "town meetings" arose as a means of transacting all public business. Later a "state" was made by a union of the "towns," which units then practically operated as our "counties" do. Down in the Virginia country there were a number of very large landed estates, each one usually including an entire watershed, and no "towns" at all except at the river's mouth. Therefore in this region a certain number of these estates formed a "county" and these in turn joined to form a "state."

But Marin county began as a domain occupied by more or less roving tribes of Indians having no settled interest in the land other than as a means of natural subsistence and did little or no cultivating of the soil. Then in the Mission Days it was one large holding, which extended its borders just as fast as Indian neophytes could be sufficiently developed to carry on the Mission lands development. It was known as a part of the Sonoma District, a territory of vague boundaries but including all lands from the coast to the Sacramento River line and as far north as the Spaniards hoped to control it.

In 1844 the Marin District was separated from the northern territory in its civil jurisdiction and its boundary simply mentioned as the Russian River. It remained thus until the organization of California counties. The seat of justice was of course at the Mission and A. M. Osio[128], a Mexican official and afterward a Marin grantee was its first juez de paz (justice of the peace), though soon succeeded by Timothy Murphy, also a later grantee. In consequence Marin County first began its organization as seventeen land grants of territory, and villages sprang up here and there as trading or supply

---

[128] Antonio Maria Osio (1800-1878) married the sister of Governor Arguello and was granted Angel Island. He later acquired Rancho Punta de los Reyes.

centers in connection therewith. Next followed the townships and in later years parts of these townships have been set apart as incorporated cities such as San Rafael, Sausalito, Mill Valley, etc., so that in some cases there are two or more incorporated cities and a remnant of the original township, all conducting separate government system and in consequence just that much more needless expense to the taxpayer, who is of course in the large minority as to numbers.

In addition to this there are numerous Commissions and Districts set aside by Legislative enactment which are wholly independent of county control or of county oversight concerning expenses and tax levies. Someday the public will unite and clear all such cumbersome and extremely expensive methods of government. Marin lands therefore at one time included Bodega, where Indians told of the "Valley of the White Men" back of Bodega Bay, so called because in the long ago a ship was wrecked at Bodega Heads and its sailors chose this valley as their dwelling place. Perhaps these men were the fabled ancestors of the Indians thereabout, who by intermarriage with the natives produced a race of people with characteristics found nowhere else and from whom our Chief Marin and his people may have been descended. They were very courageous, preferred death to the rule of the Missioners and never allowed themselves to fall under Mission control. No record has been found showing how far east this Marin District extended but it probably went to the head waters of Petaluma Creek and thence south to the Bay.

Marin territory had its first settlement at San Rafael if the Mission can be so considered, but was distinctly not a pueblo (village) open to outside people and under their own control after 1845. Towns sprang up here and there in the country by a few residents grouping about a base for supplies or for sale of products. Thus Sausalito was really the pioneer town in this sense, it being called the Puerte do Balleneros (Port of the Whalers) because it was the place where the great fleet of whaling vessels gathered for outfitting and between cruising seasons.

Bolinas began as an early land grant and suddenly developed from lumber and shipbuilding industries.

Nicasio was at first set aside as the village for all Marin Indians desiring to accept the Mission property distribution.

Novato was a cross roads point from the already developed Black Point section, and a base for the interior lumber and wood workers, as well as a rest point on the frequent Sonoma and Petaluma journeys.

Tomales originated as a purely agricultural center from settlers coming from Bodega.

Since we had no hostile natives, and but few of them here at the period of county settlement, country farms began to spread out from these centers mainly for grazing purposes. But there was still no county or any approach thereto.

By reason of the Mission regulations, none but Mission people were allowed near San Rafael. Sausalito being a whaling vessel base was neither an attractive nor a particularly safe place for settlers or residents other than those directly in business there, and most of these people declined to remain there at night. Therefore Sausalito continued to develop as an equipment base. San Rafael was circumscribed by the Mission and in consequence outsiders could not enter and much less settle there. The remainder of the county had only seventeen land grants and consequently about that number of families. The Blucher Grant[129] in Sonoma County extended somewhat into Marin territory, and all central Marin up to a point below Marshalls was Indian lands. Hence the only public domain was from about Marshalls north to the Blucher Grant beyond Tomales. To this flocked the true agriculturist, pioneered by John Keyes in 1850. Therefore the Tomales country was the first in Marin to be settled in reasonably small ranches and with many families. They were mainly peoples who knew the value of good land and in search of permanent home sites. In consequence this circle of settlers for one or two generations steadily and cooperatively developed Northern Marin. It will be noticed on a map that roads in the north take a checker board pattern, the early settlers each taking a section and donating roads portions for easy cross country trips. But as the years passed many of these "squares" roads have been abandoned as to repair work and are passable only in summer months. Nevertheless they remain as an evidence of the thorough plans of the early settlers and some day will be a valued asset to that country. Meanwhile each large Marin Rancho was little by little cut up into smaller sections as new settlers arrived exception the Pt. Reyes domain

---

[129] Rancho Blucher was named for the Prussian field marshal Gebhard Leberecht von Blücher. It was granted in 1844 to Jean Jacques Vioget, a Swiss sailor and surveyor.

which was held together until more recent years. It is said to easily excel any similar extent of isolated grazing territory anywhere in the West.

20 July 1922

When the American Government gained control of California General Riley, U. S. A, was appointed Military Governor[130] and proceeded to call a Constitutional Convention in 1849 at Monterey (then the executive centre). Shortly thereafter the County, Assembly and Senatorial Districts were formed and in 1850 Marin county boundaries were designated as at present. Later some slight changes were made along Petaluma Creek and the mid bay lines. There has been no surveys as yet and this boundaries description is interesting as a concise, brief statement of those times; and might be an excellent example for comparison with present day methods.

Thus Marin County came into official existence, bounded on one side by the ocean, on another by the Bay, and on the remaining two sides by Petaluma and American Creeks, with a narrow land strip between watersheds of the two latter streams. Note that the words "The seat of justice shall be at San Rafael" was appended to the boundaries direction as probably a continuance of Mission Days practices, and also because other sections were not then easily accessible. In 1845 Captain Richardson had applied under the Mexican regulations for the appointment of a juez de paz (justice of the peace) at the Mission. In closing the Mission period anywhere such an appointment was usually made to settle disputes as to property, etc., though doubtless Captain Richardson had many troubles at Sausalito from turbulent whalers there and desired to transfer the increasing difficulties to an official center.

Later, when the pueblo was formed at San Rafael, this juez de paz gave way to an Alcalde (Mayor) and an Anunciemento (town council). In 1850 a Court of Sessions was formed consisting of a County Judge and two justices of the peace as Associate Judges. This Court of Sessions had practically all the duties of a Board of Supervisors and held six bi-monthly and four quarterly sessions each year at various points in the county. It is interesting to note the report of this Clerk as appearing in the Marin County History of

---

[130] Brevet Major-General Bennet C. Riley (1787-1853) was the last military governor of California 1849-1850.

1880, apparently had his own way of spelling Spanish names though some of them have materially changed since then. Perhaps also, the printer "pied" his type[131]. Districts noted were South Salieto (South Sausalito), San Rafael, Navato (also Navat), Boulinas, Logonitia, Guenas, Portos wella (Puerto Suella, Pounte reys (Point Reyes, Turmalas (Tomales) and Necatio (Nicasio). The South Salieto mentioned was from Old Sausalito around the coast to Bolinas Bay. A redivision next made townships of South Salieto, San Rafael and Boulinas, to which Corte Madera, San Antonio and Tomales were soon added.

This Court of Sessions ruled the county until 1855 when it was abolished in the somewhat ridiculous attempts of a badly disorganized legislature to try out new and fanciful schemes of government. A Board of Supervisors was substituted having greater powers than the previous body, yet including duties almost down to the details of one's private affairs. No doubt the legal gentlemen strenuously objected for the County Judge was retained and the section adds a note to possibly reassure "His Honor" of good intentions, stating that this Board "need not audit the County Judge's salary."

This Act established the three Supervisor districts of Novato-San Rafael-Corte Madera townships; Sausalito-Point Reyes-Bolinas townships: and the Tomales-San Antonio townships. On November 7th, 1855, two school districts were formed, viz.: Tomales-San Antonio townships; and the remainder of the county. This latter is emphasized because it is the only record found which indicates where the greatest number of families.—and therefore smaller ranches. —were to be found, at that time. In the following March each township was declared to be a Road District and overseers were appointed therefor.

Next came a scheme which if not blocked by the people would have entailed eight times the cost of public government. A second legislature attempted to try another experiment, and in its analysis seems to have been directed by some hidden purpose toward checking co - operative effort to counties as a whole. In 1861 this body provided that each township would become practically a self-governing body but still linked into a county government by a County Judge, District Attorney and County Sheriff. In a different period and where each communication exists between townships,

---

[131] To "pie your type" was a typesetter's expression meaning to drop a loaded tray of type.

this plan has elements worthy of earnest consideration, —but in those days would have been a disastrous check to general county development. The settlers were hard pressed as it was to provide necessary tax moneys, and almost as a unit voted against such a plan.

Comes now a report which extends somewhat in advance of the period of previous notes, but which is one of the few located records that indicates the comparative growth of Marin county communities. If we could only now have these records filled in with accompanying local incident, there would indeed be an interesting story. In the following list of 1880, San Quentin was then known as Marin City until the Prison was established: and Preston was a busy point referred to later in Tomales notes.

On November 6, 1851 the first Marin post office opened at San Rafael, and no date has been found for its removal to Tomales later or of its re-establishment. Doubtless this was some years previous to 1851. Next came the others in order, viz: Pt. Reyes, 1853 and cancelled 1855, doubtless after the period of shipbuilding thereabout; Tomales, 1854; Novato 1856 and cancelled 1860; San Quentin 1859, cancelled in six months and restored in 1862; Olema, 1859; Preston, 1863 and cancelled 1866; Bolinas, 1863; Black Point. 1865; Sausalito, 1870; Marshall, 1872; Angel Island, 1875; Hamlet, 1876; Corte Madera, 1878 and cancelled 1880; Fairfax, 1879 and cancelled in three months. We still hope to find reasons for post offices at some of these points and for the frequent changes mentioned.

As before noted, long before the legislature directed that "the seat of justice shall be at San Rafael," an Alcalde (Mayor) was appointed for the Mission in preparation for forming the pueblo (village) of San Rafael. The Mission Hall was the Juzgado (court room) where all settler's disputes were brought for adjustment,—and there were plenty of them. This was, so to speak, the first County Court House from 1851 to 1853. It then removed to Don Timothy Murphy's adobe building, from which he had departed to his land grant east of San Rafael. No doubt the Mission was practically uninhabitable then, for in 1849 it was reported as in ruins and the Alcalde probably used it merely as an assembly room because Murphy resided in his adobe structure which was the only house outside of the immediate Mission grounds.

So in 1872 it was determined that the county had grown sufficiently and that its future was so assured as to warrant the erection of a proper court house. Thereupon Sheriff Austin sold the old adobe for fifty dollars to Isaac

Shaver. Court House bonds were sold for 98¾ cents on the dollar, or $59,250 in all, —specified as for a building only. All parts of San Rafael and adjoining sections competed for the location. Finally owners of the present block offered it for $12,000 less the difference from the sale of the old property.

As indicating the speed with which public business was transacted in those days in comparison to many present day matters, the following record is a commentary for all to read: Proposals for land purchase, March 27th; purchase. April 9th; acceptance of plans and specifications, April 10th; erection bids asked for April 13th; accepted May 18th; bid cancelled June 4th for non-start of operations; second highest bid accepted June 6th; cornerstone laid August 22nd. Could this be duplicated today?

27 July 1922

In 1863, a petition originated at Bolinas and was freely circulated throughout the county, to remove the County Seat to a more central point, and recommended Olema as a proper place. But Nicasio was almost the central point of the county, hence its residents erected a huge flag pole on the Nicasio heights and flew their "County Seat Flag" which could be seen from every high point in the County. The law of 1859 had established the seat of justice at San Rafael, leaving the matter of a subsequent County Seat designation to the voters. Then the matter was taken up again, and the claims of Tomales, Nicasio, Novato and Olema all weighed in comparison with San Rafael;— meanwhile the great Nicasio flag was streaming its challenge to all points. If such a move had been made at a later date when easier methods of travel and communication had been effected, it is extremely probable that the County Seat would have been located somewhere at a compromise point of Nicasio-Point Reyes Station-Olema territory, which action would have unquestionably more rapidly and more thoroughly developed the county and more solidly knit it together against past, present and future designs for its dismemberment. But the conditions were so different at the time of the attempt to locate a new County Seat that a few of the items are of present interest.

Tomales was even more remote from the county as a whole than San Rafael was, and reached only by way of Petaluma or by boat from San Francisco through Tomales Bay. It had the most people and by far the most thriving business and promised development. Nicasio was the central point but again was as yet inaccessible as to roads, etc., from other points for general purposes and had very few people. Novato was accessible by road and water from the Bay region and from the southern part of the county, but an equally long trip from the west and north sections of the territory. The county Scrip was then at a 25% discount and the change would entail an expense or some $75,000 for a new centre. The Grand Jury met and deliberated on the question, and several settler's meetings were held for calm consideration thereon in spite of the vociferous demands of the boosters for each section.

In those days nearly every settler was constantly in litigation over land and property matters with squatters or with neighbors over boundaries, since there were no fences and it was difficult to control the wandering stock. Only a few of the San Francisco horde of so called lawyers were trusted in such matters, and the expense of getting them into Marin county for legal purposes was a heavy burden to all. It was therefore decided that for the best interests of all, the trip to San Rafael would be the least expensive in this growing items, and that settlers would prefer their own inconvenience to that of still heavier taxation and greatly increased legal expenditures.

But about this time some trickster overreached himself. Sufficient signatures were obtained to have the legislature authorize an election choice in the matter, whereupon instead of leaving the question open for choice, the ballots read "For or Against" OLEMA ONLY. This incensed all concerned. Since Northern Marin had the large number of voters, it was by the concert of unselfish and united action of the northern settlers that San Rafael came into its own for all time. Those old pioneers were keenly alert to the future promise and development of Marin County and by their foresight and cooperative effort on this and a score or more of later county matters, enabled Marin to move steadily and surely forward to present status. Yet southern Marin now calmly ignores the northern section and the concerted and steadily progressing attempt of Petalumaites to have northern Marin secede from the rest of us. No impartial citizen can blame Petaluma for wanting the choicest of Marin county territory since it does not seem to be wanted at home, and could, with a little more county recognition readily expand to many times its present development and future worth to the entire county. Doubtless few of the later residents of southern Marin know of these old matters and fewer still consider how the far seeing old timers threw the northern support to southern Marin and enabled it to have the position now afforded. All that this territory in the north has asked for many years is an entire county support of a plan to have a shorter and direct road put through to the County Seat, instead of the roundabout trip through Petaluma which by that means retains all but a small portion of the rich trade of Northern Marin.

Notwithstanding the decisive stand of the County as to the County Seat location, the Nicasio Flag was still flung to the breeze. A story of the whole matter has been more or less current for years which differs somewhat from the official record and is of interest in these notes.

In those days of the carpet bagger who flocked to Marin as the place of some of the choicest agricultural lands in the State, in attempt to find an entering wedge between the rancherio and his grant, or to smoothly separate the Indian from his rightful properties.—Nicasio had its full share and San Rafael was not entirely behind in this roster of that gentry. While the story is told as a joke on Nicasio, an analysis offers some evidence of a deep laid plan of both that Valley and others to once and for all be rid of this type of trouble maker. Hence to the writer it appears that there may have been some deep laid scheme of the wise old Nicasioites to with the help of some San Rafael colleagues turn the laugh where it belonged. This idea is reached because in no record thus far located has there been the slightest hint of any one set of the real early settlers in any way attempting to take unfair advantage of those of another section. There was an unwritten combination between the solid citizens all over the County to make things unpleasant for the unscrupulous outsider, and many tales are told of humorous matters by which such plans were effected. Any student of these old measures and who has been close enough to the old pioneers to get an inkling of the inner workings of those days, cannot help but smile when some present day plans, political, commercial and otherwise are most carefully evolved, built up and flourish. Then when the crash comes suddenly the manipulators recall the famous statement of Abraham Lincoln about fooling "some of the people all of the time, all of the people some of the time, but not ALL of the people ALL of the time."

So the story goes that matters were taken to the County Sessions Court for its recommendation as to whether its recommendation to the Legislature would apply to San Rafael or Nicasio. Whereupon the greatest number of signatures was asked from each lobby.

Then the nimble witted gentry scurried over the county and searched out every bona fide citizen they could locate and as many more they could call in from elsewhere. San Rafael successively matched each new accretion to the list until the fateful day arrived for a show down. Then the so-called Nicasioites, heavily burdened with a voluminous manuscript took up the journey south. Their courage mounted by leaps and bounds as they paused here and there on the trip to exchange ideas on the coming victory. On arrival at the County Seat they first made the rounds of supposed sympathizers, steadily accumulating more and more enthusiasm for their own plans and an increasing sympathy for the downhearted San Rafaelites. At the appointed time for some unexplained reason no opposition was presented to the Court to its San Rafael endorsement, an extremely long petition made up of the signatures of almost every bona fide citizen of the County to the request, and only the names of a small coterie of outsiders accompanying the rival paper, while explanation was made that its sponsors were incapacitated and could not appear but left the matter to the excellent judgment of the assembled judges. The smoothly handled delegates later viewed their petition from which the merit names had been neatly clipped and affixed to the major parchment. So everyone was satisfied and Nicasio never again saw its sponsors in this matter.

Chosen for a humanitarian aim; occupied without bloodshed; pacified without opposition; developing one of the most successful of western Missions; its land granted in somewhat more strictly legal form than in any California county; its people effecting a political organization without friction or rancor; and thence solidly developing as an agricultural sections; Marin county can well claim that from its earliest beginnings its progress has been systematic, orderly, progressive and successful. Look over the features of the Marin pioneers as portrayed in the Marin History of 1880 and note the predominantly square jawed, firm lipped men of that time who were intent on progress and personal rights no matter what obstacle had to be overcome. Note also the kindly, humorous lines about their eyes and know that they could also be genial, co-operative, home loving people. It was their insistent strength of purpose and shoulder to shoulder cooperation that started Marin County on a steady journey into the future. It is to them that we owe every reverence for guiding early Marin County from difficulties which have ever since then handicapped some other communities, and would otherwise have been with us also.

(End of Marin's Organization Period)

3 August 1922

MARIN'S MINING DAYS

The northern California territory did not by any means have all of the early day mining excitement. There the turbulent period was from 1849 to about 1855, and long before that date the Bay cities were filled with both sadly disappointed prospectors and enthusiastic late comers eager to show how little the old timers knew about mines. These latter individuals were in just the proper frame of mind to be stampeded, and again and again they would rush off to some new "strike." So it was in Marin County a few years later. One day Sheriff Van Doub[132] was handed ore samples claimed to be from Marin County which assayed $235 to the ton. On publication of these facts it was assuredly thought that here at the threshold of the metropolis was a veritable true Mother Lode of which the northern mines were mere outcroppings. Within a period of three weeks Marin County had been combed from shore to shore, rancho to rancho and valley to mountain top. To better understand what followed it should be understood that Sir Francis Drake had reported that wherever his men went here in Marin, there were evidences of gold even in the soil itself. Further, at almost any rocky point or ledge in Marin territory traces of gold can be found, and in addition the abundant "fool's gold" or pyrites exists in such form as to sometimes puzzle even experienced miners without proper test.

Also, in many of the streams high up in the western ridges, an easily disintegrated granite leaves prettily shining particles of golden mica in the shifting sands of the smaller streams. So an "assay" by looks and weight was the amateur's natural mistake. Quantities of these materials were gathered here and there and pronounced the proper and much envied ore. But before the bubble burst it was found that a distinct mineral ledge

---

[132] Valentine David Doub (1829-1877) was a gold miner, sheriff, and county clerk.

extended from Point Benito[133] straight across the entire county and almost in a line with the eastern peak of Tamalpais. Then a second great ledge of fine looking quartz was discovered elsewhere to the east of the main line. In consequence there were no less than thirty-two mining companies organized and claims filed to ninety-one thousand feet of mining claim frontage,—nearly eighteen miles long, besides innumerable prospects staked off and some work done before paying the filing fee.

An old mining record gives these locations, and alluring descriptions and assays of the ore, which we omit in sympathy with present ranch owners and cottage garden folk who do not want curious fellows digging holes promiscuously over their grounds. It would not be so bad if they filled these excavations up again, but they never do.

The legion of claim owners, in some cases a dozen or more to a claim, now hints to us of an overweening desire to have a bonanza within easy commuting distance from San Francisco, where one might take a few hours off now and then to gather up an income. One company announced a fifty ton shipment for which returns were claimed of twelve to fifteen dollars per ton in gold and silver. No further mention is found of the first mentioned $235 ore, but a certified report of a mining engineer is noted later which put this badly behind in the telling.

Some of the names of these mining companies may be of interest, though often the local name as it would now appear, designated some far-away claim. If one adds "Gold and Silver Mining Company" to each of the following, the record is as follows: Keystone; Brigandello; Corte Madera; St. Vincent; Central; Briar Clif; Angonetti Ranch; Reed Ranch; White Horse; Landslide; Fashion; Novato; Deer Island; Schwiesau; Peacock; Indian Valley; West Spur; Black Canyon; Blue Ledge; Smith's Maria; Alpha; Daniel Webster; Hog Eye; Crosby; Stove Oak; Von; Lone Tree; Pacific Laguna; Mountain Spring; Coast Range; and San Rafael. Even the huge rocks on the top of Tamalpais were claimed and assayed and other locations placed all around it. One claim on Angel Island gave great promise as also another at Fort Baker until Uncle Sam put a stop to further workings.

Away back in the Spanish records of 1777 an expedition named one of the small Upper Bay Islands "Del Oro" and some wag started this story as well, to the end that considerable muscular energy was expended against

---

[133] Point Bonito.

the stiff Bay currents. One company spent what must have been other people's money on such a "certainty" that a 200 foot shaft was sunk and some 500 feet of crosscuts continued at its bottom. Yet the huge dump pile now assays only a few cents per ton by the best of modern methods. Another on the same ledge sent a tunnel far into a huge rock wall and during the operation erected a complete operating plant outside in readiness for the harvest to follow. Numbers of copper ledges were found on the slopes of Tamalpais but in those days copper was of no value.

Let us present a statement of only one of these Marin Mining Reports, issued by a mining engineer of supposed repute, records of qualified assayers, and suspicion of a good press agent, altogether making a report which in a faraway country would seem to be a rival of the King Solomon Mines. Yet we are liberal enough to think that there must have been supposed evidence of something good there or such an expenditure would not have been made. Had it been a "wildcat" or a "salted" mine there would doubtless have been some highly lithographed stock shares still on file somewhere. Perhaps some old attic trunk contains them.

Suppose you had money and from far away had word of this glittering prospect. Would you have taken a chance and helped to finance somebody? And yet there are still more uncertain chances sold every day. The following is a summarized report from the original historical account of the Official Report to the Directors from their engineer:

"The mines are almost alongside a railroad. The ledge is easily seen to be fully four miles in length, and shows a deep and true fissure. Croppings are very heavy, and in some cases several feet high and eighty feet wide. I took 900 pounds of ore from several places and had many assayers test it. One assayer by fire test gives twenty-five dollars gold and eleven dollars silver; another assayer by fire test gives eighty-five dollars gold and twelve dollars silver (exact cents value omitted). On the other side of the ridge the vein is traced as an out crop for 3600 feet. The (omitted) Company has a 200 ft shaft and a 200 foot cross cut below. One assay gives ninety dollars gold four silver; another (of the same ore) gives seventy-seven dollars gold and nine dollars silver. The vein of the 200 foot level is remarkably strong and the entire formation indicates that it will improve both in width and quality as depth is obtained. There has been no water,

In closing I can say that the outlook for the future of these mines, located as they are, convenient to everything necessary to work a mine cheaply, with the finest climate in the world, and with an outcrop of ore of wonderful richness, and in such large quantities, and, extending already 200 feet in depth is very favorable, and as a prospective investment when it looks so nearly certain of success, I know nothing equal to it." An appended note adds "There has been some difference among assayers as to the first assay noted. To satisfy myself and before distributing this report, I have assayed it in two ways. By chemicals showing gold $210.15 and silver $6.65."

We must not unduly criticize this report, since there was many a slip between the natural rock, an honest engineer, and to the time of its assay. It would be interesting to know just what the backers of this "mine" were leading up to. It is still undeveloped and the great dumps offer some excellent rock for purchase at rock prices. The dump samples show a very good grade of feldspar and limestone and practically without mineral content other than pyrites. Just how such an assay value could be arrived at is a mystery in this period.

10 August 1922

To show that to this day certain people have had their eyes on this property, when the recent White's Hill tunnel was bored, every carload of rock thrown on the dumps was carefully scrutinized; and a number of around the bay assayers gained a goodly revenue from embryo geologists,—though no mining claims were filed.

So the matter rests. But ever since those days some ambitious real estate or farm-for-sale advertiser has some fellow "find" one of these old ledges again which gives the space writers a chance to display their mining knowledge. In later years an assay of some of the huge masses of rock found near Tomales has caused new prospecting ventures there, but failed to disturb the people of that locality. It should by now be generally understood that the old land titles carry with them all possible rights to the lands described.

Gradually however, it began to dawn on Marin's new mining fraternity that agriculturists and stock men were not at all averse to accepting money from purchasers of options on good, rock hillside "lots" for any purpose in view. Then the "all that glitters is not gold" idea came into the limelight again. Nevertheless these frequent mining excitements of Marin County brought out the fact that within our borders there are promising deposits of copper, chrome, manganese, lead and slight evidences of coal and oil. This does not mean that there are rich enough deposits to apparently pay for further exploitation, and on a thorough study of the geological reports on the county it is highly improbable that there will be any mining industry here in the minerals sense. Yet two manganese deposits exist in thickly settled districts, where the residents prefer the beauties of nature rather than to duplicate the experience of Southern California in its present predicament of some shore residents' substitution of great oil derricks for former beautiful door yard trees. One shipment of Marin manganese ore is recorded as sent to one of the largest of eastern steel mills and bringing an offer of thirty dollars a ton for all that could be delivered there. This is not surprising since it is yet impossible to make steel without an admixture of the "spieglesen[134]" ore which is imported from Northern Sweden and which closely corresponds to our own deposit here. Some day when the western section of these United States has the inevitably coming steels mills. Marin County may be called upon for this supply if it is then considered abundant enough.

But Marin's present wealth in mining work is along the line of building materials of a permanent nature. In the aforementioned prospecting days here there were numbers of localities found where these stones and clays rivalled any about the Bay region. For many years San Francisco's supply of granite was quarried near the Point Reyes lighthouse and lightered down to the city yards. Old timers remember the street curbings and large flat street crossing stones of this material.

Finally when other deposits were located Congress was persuaded that it was not right for Uncle Sam to rival other companies and the work was stopped. This granite is much softer and less durable than the present hard grey material from mountain quarries. But after an enterprising quarryman located a better grade and sent out seven thousand cubic feet at a handsome profit before he was probably offered better opportunities elsewhere. In later years also, the entire supply of paving blocks for San Francisco streets were quarried in Marin, and the six Marin county brickyards furnished the material for the greater part of the San Francisco commercial district buildings. In these days the discouraging fact is presented to present day residents who want to put up permanent structures here, that in those times

---

[134] Spiegeleisen (literally "mirror-iron") is an alloy containing approximately 15% manganese and small quantities of carbon and silicon.

hand make brick, kiln dried, and much better than present material, —sold for six to eight dollars per thousand f. o. b. the car, and there were dozens of later yards about the Bay in direct competition. Now only one is in action in Marin County and a purchaser is asked fifteen to eighteen dollars a thousand for machine-made, oven-baked, mechanically-handled brick. One wonders whether we in these days are really profiting by the modern methods in all cases.

A great wealth of building was shown in these early days to be in Marin County, but has been almost wholly neglected in succeeding years.

The retaining wall about the well-known Stanford mansion in San Francisco and the lower portion of the Mark Hopkins home nearby were built from Marin stone after the best geologists had searched far and wide for the most durable known stone for the purpose. It was very expensive in those days to cut such material but later methods would easily allow of it at the present day. Down at San Rafael and at San Anselmo several churches have also been built from the southern Marin stone quarries material and vie with any on the coast for beauty. A northern section church built of similar material was demolished by the earthquake; but the construction was at fault,—not the stone.

There is a tradition that the Ft. Ross Russians operated lime kilns in the Olema Valley though this probably means that some men of Russian nativity had them. Considerable work seems to have been done there and the old tunnel mouths are still in view, though no record remains of the character, quantity and duration of the lime operations.[135]

Down on the Pt. Pedro peninsula the only remaining crushed rock quarry is in operation, having supplied San Francisco with a major portion of concreting material for all of the larger structures since the earthquake days. Several of these plants were in operation in Marin County and rock was purchased from $1.25 to $1.75 a yard. Now, with all modern machinery and quarry equipment and motor transportation it has in recent years advanced as high as $3.75 a yard at times. So much for specialization, yet there are many difficulties in present day business concerns which the casual reader knows nothing about.

Nevertheless, what a wealth of materials Marin county has for the erection of the type of permanent buildings which will of a certainty finally

---

[135] Three lime kilns were built beside Highway 1 near Dogtown in 1850 by James A. Shorb and William F. Mercer. They only operated a few years, but still stand.

find a place here and in the bay territory! The most durable building stone known; an inexhaustible supply of the best grade of brick clay found anywhere; whole ranges of rock for concreting purposes which is preferred over all other kinds; many square miles of foundation and wall granite; unexplored wealths of limestone of varying worth; and indications in several places of fairly good building sandstone. Cement works ought to be here for the materials are all at hand; and these deposits of many kinds all have water or rail or highway transportation facilities. Has any Bay county greater undeveloped resources for building activities?

17 August 1922

Marin County has also had its oil excitement, although it is difficult indeed to find anyone here who will admit that the savings of years were put into the still remaining oil well pipes in western Marin. Two or three times oil companies have been organized and carried on development work there, and mainly sold stock in Europe and elsewhere. There was a good basis for the work however, and no doubt the poor drilling machinery in those days, and the small capital involved, did not afford a proper test. The last time oil was struck there the coincidence of the same grade of oil being pumped up that had been laboriously hauled out for fuel seemed to affect matters, though one of the drillers there still claims that prospects were exceedingly promising and some day would prove his judgment. Several of these huge pipes were driven down much below the Ocean level from the top of the broad table lands north of Bolinas. The matter of there being oil there is certain to come up again, since along the low water line there are oil seepages in abundance, and on the cliff side appears evidence of asphaltic matter. Some miles out from the shore near the point of Duxbury Reef, it has long been known that a natural gas jet can be lighted at low tide, which burns with a reddish smoky flame. Old timers tell us that long before the lighthouses were built on the coast, there was a tradition of the Bolinas sea folk having fastened a pipe over this gas flow and to have had this as a night beacon for a long period. It is possible, but hardly probable that in those days the pressure of high water about the lower pipe end would have allowed this.

Unfortunately for a long-suffering public, which is just now coming into its own through a coal dealer's war in Southern Marin, five purported discoveries of Marin county coal have proved to be disappointments. All were very dark shales, and some so impregnated with oil materials as to be slightly burnable. Nevertheless one of these finds was heralded as the hope of San Francisco Bay people for "after thorough tests by experts the prospect was heavily bonded to San Francisco capitalists." Natural gas was also once reported from the Nicasio Valley but cannot now be located.

Someday Marin County may also use part of Nature's bounty in conformity with the original purpose of entering its territory: the relief of suffering humanity. We have had some excitable mention of several sulphur springs, at least one creditable hot spring, and a number of medicinally valuable mineral water springs, two of which have been capitalized for years and are furnishing bottled supplies of their product. Some fine agate, garnet, and especially some fine serpentines for polished stones effect have been known since early days. Except for the Exposition[136] Exhibit of polished Marin stones by Dr. Augustine, very little attention has ever been given to them. Over on Pebble Beach above Bolinas the moonstone varieties are much sought for at especially low tides. One thoroughly defined fossilized sandstone cliff was found in Northern Marin and only superficially investigated because many more accessible deposits then existed elsewhere. As these become more and more torn apart, our Marin fossils' deposit is certain to be looked into.

So when people remark that Marin County's future is merely that of a fringe of suburban residences on the southern border, a Petaluma county on the East and Northeast, and a dairying industry over the remaining section, they are hardly in a frame of mind to be interested in matters of this present review. It is what Marin has always had, does not at present consider of worth enough to develop, and which in the future years is certain to come into such competition with monopolies in building supplies and other industries —that interests the far seeing citizen of today who wants to do his share in planning for the future generation instead of controlling matters for present periods. Marin county has an enviable position and a wealth of natural advantage in the dairying, grazing and agricultural industries, but poultry is looming in the near foreground; the potato crop in the northern section is regaining lost ground as a leading county total of wealth

---

[136] The Panama-Pacific International Exposition, held in San Francisco in 1915 to celebrate the opening of the Panama Canal.

production; and the Novato section has every reason to plan a most successful vine and fruit center of activities.

What will assuredly make this Marin County retain an especially strong position among all others in California, and what if properly capitalized by smoothly co-operating communities in the county, is its peculiar situation relative to the rest of the state, and its universally recognized natural wealth and advantages. This is held to be its future because once the proper roads are provided, ninety-five per cent of the tourist auto travel to and from the East and Middle West which now centers at Los Angeles and the Portland-Seattle territory in such numbers as to make their care most difficult in those places.—will prefer to motor through Marin county on the coming coast line route to connect extreme north and south sections of our State. These people will not locate here, but through their accounts of our broad, fertile and sparsely settled land, the unexcelled beauties of landscape, of good water, and delightful climate, others will come to us to stay.

(End of Marin's Mining days)

24 August 1922

SAN RAFAEL TOWNSHIP

The Settlement of San Rafael was a natural evolution from the early Mission establishment in 1817. In the previous notes it has been stated that the Mission San Rafael Archangel was in every respect an entire Marin territory institution and not a local one because its lands and activities practically covered the present county area. While a majority of western Mission centers ultimately became pueblos (villages) by official decree, a number of them did not remain so. In San Rafael's case this would also have been the probable result because there were not any naturally developing activities in its vicinity. Therefore its people should now know that one of the first steps towards its real foundation, aside from the earlier Mission beginnings, was the application of Captain William Richardson of Sausalito, for the appointment of a juez de paz at San Rafael. In consequence it became the territorial center and the consequent permanence for a later city. Thus San Rafael came to be called the "seat of justice" where settlers were wont to bring their troubles for review and adjustment, and where the malefactors of all descriptions in the troubled 1844-1850 period were sternly halted in their evil ways. Had there been a building of consequence anywhere near the center of the county, or in the Novato region where a greater number of people then resided, the general distaste for San Rafael in its closing Mission Days and the following Indian resident period, also the nature of the then Sausalito activities, —would have inevitably established this "seat of justice" elsewhere. Once so located, the legislative enactment of 1850 might have then perpetuated it as was done for San Rafael. But the Mission buildings were the only structures available in the county for the purpose. In consequence San Rafael became the seat of justice and our Mission city may well pay honor to Captain Richardson of Sausalito as one of its early founders. Without this seat of justice, around which gathered a real community beginning and led to the present County Seat, San Rafael would have develop[ed] very slowly and most certainly in quite another way.

It is also to be remembered that by his action in this respect, Captain Richardson not only made San Rafael a later city but the immediately resulting conflict of authority with the juez de paz at Sonoma promptly led to the official segregation of Marin territory from the Sonoma District of those days for its own judicial control. Therefore the oft recurring question of Petaluma being a New County centre was settled in the beginning by Captain Richardson's action in 1845.

At that time the Sonoma District included all Spanish lands north of the Bay and west of the Sacramento river and extending "to the furthermost limit of Spanish Discovery"—a very indefinite boundary. For governmental direction it was usually considered up to about the present Mendocino line. Therefore Marin territory had remained in the Sonoma District, the latter legislative division of counties would have undoubtedly established our northern boundary as due east from the mouth of the Estero Americana, a natural topographical line along the American Creek through the valley of the same name until joining the headwaters of Petaluma Creek. In consequence Petaluma would be in Marin County and that city in conjunction with the Tomales and San Antonio territory would by virtue of the joint population transfer all official Marin activities to the north. Marin county people must therefore also recognize the result of Captain Richardson's action in locating the juez de paz at San Rafael.

John J. Reed was the first English-speaking resident of Marin County, locating at Sausalito in 1826 and later in San Rafael where he held the position of majordomo at the Mission under Padre Quijos. Then he was juez de paz for the northern district, Indian Agent for the Nicasios, and later a lumberman and land grantee near Sausalito. To him belongs the title of "Father of Pioneers" of Marin County.

Timothy Murphy or 'Don Timoteo' as popularly known, was the Mission Majordomo from 1837-1840 and had the first house in San Rafael outside the immediate Mission grounds. This was a large adobe structure built as a centre for his ranching activities and the then proposed grants of all contiguous San Rafael lands. It is said to have stood about where the Tamalpais Bank is now located[137]. As noted below, this Rancho headquarters was occupied by lessees of Murphy's properties for a time. Then, inasmuch as Don Timoteo continued to reside at the Mission, the adobe house was leased to Don M. Osio at about the period when San Rafael became the headquarters of wealthy rancho owners in Marin County. Osio had been a Government Official at Monterey and was granted the great Point Reyes Rancho properties in Marin. This same building was occupied by Fremont during part of his stay in San Rafael, and was used as the county Court House in early Marin days.

Murphy was appointed the first juez de paz but resigned and Osio succeeded him. Then Murphy was elected to the position in 1845 with Ignacio Pacheco as *"supplemente."* Sometime later Pacheco and Damaso Rodrigues became Alcaldes and were succeeded by William Reynolds and James Black in 1846.

31 August 1922

The first mention in old Marin records of San Rafael "citizens" was in 1844 when Don Timoteo apparently appreciated the dignity of his position, for the juez de paz at Sonoma vigorously complained to the Military Governor "that Murphy, a citizen of San Rafael, declined to take his authority or to report to a summons." And again later the Alcalde at Sonoma complained that this same Murphy "directed certain citizens of San Rafael to disregard his authority," as indeed he had a right to do.

---

[137] Now 1300 Fourth Street, on the northwest corner of C Street.

The second house in San Rafael was that of J. O. B. and Jacob Short who in 1846 made some additions to a Mission adobe outbuilding located on the upper line of the present Court House square[138]. Their mother, Mrs. Merriner, resided there with them until they became interested in Nicasio and later Fairfax properties. From there they returned to San Rafael and in 1868 laid out the extensive Short's Addition[139] which is still regarded as one of the choicest residence sites in the Mission city.

For a long period San Rafael was not populated beyond the transient wood cutters, lumbermen, trappers, explorers and other wandering strangers using the city-to-be as a centre for their activities. But with the gold rush years San Rafael came into its own and attracted settlers who quickly saw its advantages and promptly made plans for its permanency.

The first house in the township outside of San Rafael, was the Miller[140] home at Gallinas. This was erected in 1845 as a shake shanty, changed in 1846 to a split-redwood shack, re-erected as a large adobe dwelling in 1847, and in later years the substantial Miller Hall was built nearby. No more striking evidence of the perseverance of the early pioneers can be shown than in this steady prosperity of James Miller on the Gallinas property. Choosing a site for his homestead which in many respects resembled one of the old country estates, his activities quickly broadened to include a major share in all public and community matters of adjoining territory.

One can visualize Mr. Miller daily viewing the many small vessels passing up and down the Bay within easy view of his home, and therein gaining inspiration for the following venture. —another typical incident of the stubborn determination of those old pioneers to overcome any obstacle in their paths. Gallinas is a section just north of San Rafael, so named on President Prefect Payeros' visit here in 1818 to decide whether San Rafael should be the northern Mission stronghold or outposts pushed still further north to block reported moves of the Russians at Fort Ross. Gallinas was and still is the site of the old Miller home, one of the earliest and finest

---

[138] Now 1050 A Street, on the southeast corner of Fifth Street.

[139] Short's Addition was that part of San Rafael around Gerstle Park.

[140] James Miller (1814-1890) was born in County Wexford, Ireland. He led the first wagon train from Missouri to California in 1844. After arriving in San Rafael, he became friends with Timoteo Murphy (another Wexford man) and bought the Rancho Las Gallinas from him. He sponsored the first school in San Rafael, as well as St. Vincent's School. He donated the land for another school. Some Southerners helped build the school and dared him to name it Dixie School, the name it still bears.

residences of those days in all Marin County. It provided one of the most interesting and striking incidents of early times in the West, in the launching of a ship built several miles inland from the bay shore and at this old Miller adobe home.

It seems that in the intervals of busy days of ranching, stock raising and rancho developing matters, Mr. Miller determined to not only have his own means of transportation but to embark in the ship building line himself. He had one of the old time "whipsaw" outfits and plenty of timber, and determined to try something new in ship launching methods. Notwithstanding the jibes of the countryside, the building of a large three-masted schooner proceeded at his home, apparently on the plan of Noah's Ark insofar as its indicated proximity to any navigable water.

Numerous indeed, were the conjectures of curious travelers constantly passing to and from Petaluma, Sonoma, and San Francisco sections, as to what manner of man must live at this point and steadily proceeded with such an odd undertaking.

The fame of this inland ship plant spread up and down the coast and the north of the Bay region, and each party reaching San Francisco brought new tales of the vessel that in our day might be related to those of the famous Swiss Navy. But this old gentleman, a genial Irishman of long past type, bided his time and piece by piece added the full equipment of spars and ropes and sail, altogether a ghostly hint of some great storm-driven craft cast far inland in a heavy storm. It was a common joke to have night travelers halted to enjoy the Miller hospitality and to note their amazement in the morning on seeing such a dooryard ornament far from the Bay waters.

Then came invitations for a grand gathering at the Miller home to view a site [sight] unseen within the memory of man,—of a vessel built far back on a farm yet to journey over the meadows to its home in the sea. Every vaquero within traveling distance was summoned to report with his trusty riata and a truly picturesque assemblage must have made up the guests on that day. So on a winter's morning, when constant storms had softened the adobe bed of a trickling brook, these lusty horsemen lassoed every available projection of the schooner from stem to stern, fastening their ropes to mast, to spar, to deck side and to figurehead, each man in his place and awaiting the word to move. Then when the stiff west wind began to blow, up went a square rigged mainsail, the doughty skipper took the wheel, and amid the huzzas of a countryside this land ship started on its journey to the sea.

Great indeed was the gathering afterward at the old Miller homestead, and well filled tables under the ancient trees of the Rancho easily recompensed the drovers who had become ship yard workers for a day. And we can well believe that in the sharp interchange of wit and story at these tables, this Miller gentleman slyly alluded to the wealth of lore some dry-land sailors did not know concerning the way to properly launch a ship.

What a chance there is for an artist familiar with the old time setting to properly portray this incident! A square-rigged three-masted schooner waltzing along on dry land toward the bay, led on every side by a legion of joyous early day vaqueros in all their finery and colorful dress: and their sturdy mounts dragging this vessel over the slippery ground. Truly a story which even in our day would not be believed if we saw it as a painted view or on the movie screen.

7 September 1922

The preservation of old time land marks is universally recognized as a distinctly definite indication of community pride and community endeavor. It is a puzzle to all California and to the Nation as well, why certain California Mission towns seem to be utterly oblivious to the heritage they have for future generations in property preserving traces of the old Mission settlements on the western coast. Perhaps it is because these have always been mentioned as having been a strictly sectarian affair, but the impartial reader knows better and even though they were, the subsequent developments gathered about them as central points, indubitably brought California and all of its wealth into our own hands in the end, if not also blocking the grasping world nations' attempts to occupy it themselves.

So it is with our own city. To the Mission establishment Marin County owes its deliverance from having been the battleground of opposing world forces; from having been freed from being a point of many later disputes; and of still more significance to us, of having been the means of publishing all over the world the fact that in Marin county could be found a veritable Ponce de Leon territory for quiet, health-giving, happy days for the ill and afflicted and for those in search of the perfect combination of sunshine, soil and pure water. Yet here in our midst the still-living reminders of Mission Days stand silently begging for someone to preserve this link from the past.

The San Rafael Mission was a most unpretentious affair as previously noted, being built for temporary purposes and therefore quickly crumbling away after it had served its purpose.

But our entire county territorial development was a result of it and before its passing the San Rafael Archangel Mission became one of the most important and flourishing posts of the old Spanish Padres. Probably its short duration tended to deaden public interest in its preservation, but that is no reason why present day folk should neglect its treasures now. It astonishes one to learn that in the year 1921, when excavations were made for the new church on the old Mission site, the only use found for the Mission tiles unearthed there was for filling in marsh lots! It is doubtful whether the workmen or the foreman there knew what they were, or cared to.

So it is with our Mission pear trees. What a price some American cities would pay for them, yet one by one they have been cut down and the remaining five will soon disappear unless some action is taken to preserve them. No one seems to care whether they live or die. and the comment in the Marin County History of 1880 might well have been a note of yesterday for all the affect it has produced in the intervening forty-two years relative to preservation of these ancient old trees now well beyond the century mark in age.

Two more interesting old buildings of early day periods still exist near San Rafael. One of these adjoins the E. B. McNear residence and furnishes as definite an example as can be given of the fast disappearing items of interesting local incident, accounts of which can easily be preserved for future generations by proper effort of public schools centers. At first glance this old building seems to be merely a ranch hands dwelling and is heated accordingly. But what a treasured volume its old associations and memories would be now! At the time of its erection there were no marsh lands there, and boats landed about where the school house now stands. In fact it is only a few years since duck hunters lay in wait just outside the McNear garden fence to shoot their birds in the open water beyond.

In the early days of the trading activities in San Francisco Bay Captain Simpton, an Englishman, made several trips to the Coast. It is said that he purchased the present McNear ranch on one of these, returning the next year with the present house made up in sections after manufacture in France. Upon discharging the cargo at San Francisco his ship proceeded to the San Rafael shore and landed the house material as stated above. Doubtless he left an expert workman or two here, because the building had been made to be put together wholly by means of wooden pins instead of nails. Then the next trip brought the Simpton family to the house that had been so carefully and thoroughly prepared for them. The Daniel T. Taylor who is noted as having been intimately connected with all early Marin matters, married Captain Simpton's daughter. Although there are five grandchildren of the Simpton and Taylor families still residing in Marin County, this interesting incident of early home building, and the existence of such a valuable old-time relic in our midst was apparently forgotten in the community, and only persistent inquiry located this information. But what a wonderful story there is between comparisons of this early structure and the present modern building adjoining it. And yet how much further back such still existing buildings as the adobe Burdell walls, seems to carry memories of early days.

Though erected long afterward, a second old-time building construction is found in the four-inch hardwood inlaid floors of the old O'Connor home now occupied by the military academy[141]. This too came from Europe, in blocks fifteen inches square, each one built up of innumerable pieces and then mortised together here with corner "stars" of white and red maple.—a striking example of painstaking joinery seldom seen nowadays.

14 September 1922

The year 1849 was indeed a fortunate one for San Rafael and Marin County in that it brought settlers who had come to the coast in response to the chance of commercial enterprise rather than the uncertainties of mining excitements. From the remnants of two of these companies, Southern Marin county obtained a start under men of means, of education and of wide experiences,—all planning to remain here and grow up with the territory. As the result their names are household words with us, the result of their work is to be seen on every hand, and their faith in the development of southern Marin has long since been fully realized. In distinction to these men one can select twice as many names of individuals who came here for purely exploitation purposes, who remained here long enough to accumulate property and incidentally to greatly complicate community matters, then left at the first opportunity and were long ago forgotten.

---

[141] Now Marin Academy private high school.

The Baltimore Company came from the South with intention of engaging in the lumbering industry and had a vessel laden with a full equipment therefor. On arrival in San Francisco it proceeded to erect a fifteen-saw lumber mill at the Corte Madera del Presidio Rancho. But before beginning operations the company disbanded. Only two of its members came to San Rafael, Messrs. Ai Barney[142] was later the first Marin County judge and founder of the *Marin Journal*. D. T. Taylor[143] opened San Rafael's first store and afterward held county offices, in fact was an intimate part of all government activities for the county for many years.

The Virginia company was organized in the South also and came to California to embark in general business matters, bringing with it a cargo of supplies and having within its membership capable, educated, energetic men who had come west with the definite intention of staying in the new country and assisting in its development. But this company also failed to withstand the excitement of mining tales and promptly disbanded in San Francisco. This was fortunate indeed for Marin County because one party of five and another of eight from this organization formed partnerships and came to San Rafael. The five men leased Mission lands from Don Murphy and engaged in farming the territory in vicinity of the Robert Watt home (Hotel Rafael grounds now)[144] and the Saunders Addition (out Petaluma Avenue)[145]. The eight members formed an organization and proceeded to engage in trading in stock, beef and other indirect lines of agricultural industry.

Fortunate indeed was Marin County in having the solid men of these two trading companies settle here in the days when qualified leaders and men of education were needed to assume the difficult task of instituting and proceeding with the beginnings of County Government and far reaching community. For example, from these men the beloved Doctor Taliaferro[146], Dr. J. A. Sharp, J. A. Davis[147], S. S. Baechtel[148], Ai Barney, J. L

---

[142] Ai Jerome Barney (1804-1866), Forty-Niner, judge, founder of *Marin Journal*.
[143] Daniel T. Miller (1830-1916), Forty-Niner, county clerk, recorder, and auditor.
[144] A 100-room five-story luxury hotel at the corner of Rafael Drive and Belle Avenue.
[145] Now Lincoln Avenue.
[146] Doctor Alfred Walker Talliaferro (pronounced Tolliver) (1827-1885), Forty-Niner, Marin's first physician. He partnered with Doctor Henry DuBois to found Mount Tamalpais Cemetery.
[147] John A. Davis (1808-1859), merchant and the first county auditor.
[148] Samuel Simon Baechtel (1826-1915), Forty-Niner, the first sheriff.

Poindexter[149] and Daniel T. Taylor were all chosen for Marin County's first Assemblyman, Senator, County Judge, Sheriff, Treasurer and Clerk respectively.

Fragmentary notes and items concerning these men have been collected with the view of finding just why San Rafael attracted them at the time their company disbanded. It seems to have been a period when southern Marin was a topic widely discussed as to its future possibilities and the immediate chances in agriculture and stock raising for those desiring to follow such occupations. Moreover it was then clearly shown that the mining tales were gross exaggerations and that the common man had very little chance in the mining fields except the hardest kind of work without adequate reward. Marin's rancheros had for the most part stampeded to the mines at first but quickly saw that someone must raise food for the multitude and remembered their own broad lands at home. In consequence Marin's rancheros were among the first to return from the mines to resume stock-raising and agriculture and this immediately focused attention to the fertile lands north of the Bay.

So the reviews of the period indicated that Marin county and its possibilities was decidedly in the public eye and offered the best opportunities anywhere in the Bay section for capable agriculturists and traders. Several of the Virginia Company selected San Rafael with the definite idea of its possibilities as a residence and consequent business activities.

Prior to this period the Bay was crossed only by a whaleboat from San Rafael, a trip which at times was extremely dangerous and at all times very destructive to the property carried on board. But when Davis and Taylor opened San Rafael's first store, they added a small sloop to carry supplies to and from San Francisco, which made regular trips for the purpose. Their store opened in November, 1850, and was located on C Street at the water's edge, which again shows how far the Bay once extended into San Rafael[150]. While there are many ideas as to who must be considered the real founders of San Rafael, the establishment of this first local store and the freight route to San Francisco, with the consequent immediate organizing of local business, is entitled to be listed, as one of the initial matters of a start for the real permanency of San Rafael.

---

[149] James L. Poindexter (1828-1855), Forty-Niner, county clerk and recorder.
[150] Probably near Murphy's Wharf at 1st Street and C Street.

It was in 1850 that San Rafael was officially surveyed and blocks were laid out 300 feet square. In that year there were twelve houses consisting of residences, barns, stables, etc. Timothy J. Mahon[151] came in this year and afterward built San Rafael's first hotel. He it was who in later years imported and propagated several thousand grape vines and distributed them in southern Marin territory, and was one of Marin County's contingent in the Civil War.

The impetus given to San Rafael and its contiguous territory by the energy and ability of the men from the Baltimore and the Virginia Companies, and the vigorous trading activities of such rancheros as William Black with the mines territory, not only thoroughly established San Rafael's future but in connection with the activities in and about the Mission City, many new comers to San Francisco and some of its business men like U. M. Gordon[152], William T. Coleman and others focused attention on the southern Marin section for country residence. Thus the initial period of San Rafael passed by and its real development rapidly followed.

21 September 1922

In 1851 the Mission City had ten residences, the crumbled Mission buildings, one store, one boarding house, and one saloon or "whiskey still" as then commonly termed[153]. Don Murphy's house was the only substantial structure. There were no fences except for a few corrals; no home grounds or gardens; and no general town improvements. No data has been located concerning the next ten year period in this connection, but in 1866 all these things had changed. There were then eighty residences and many of them were of a decidedly pretentious nature and with well-arranged grounds. This indicated the demand for suburban residences in San Rafael.

In addition, the rapidly increasing number of commercial houses showed a definitely increasing population, for there were three stores, two hotels, two boarding houses, a restaurant, two livery stables, a public school, an Academy (the Gilbert School)[154], a newspaper, telegraph office, three

---

[151] Timothy J. Mahon (1824-1905) ran a store in San Rafael.
[152] Upton McCrae Gordon (1831-1888) married Elizabeth Meriner, half-sister of the Short brothers.
[153] De Hierry's Bar, at the corner of 4th and A Streets.
[154] Northeast corner of 4th and E Streets.

bootmakers, two blacksmiths, a harness maker, butcher shop, clocksmith, barber, three lawyers, and one physician. Prior to this San Rafael had been merely a meeting place for clearance of county business, but from about 1865 had begun to attract statewide attention as a popular and exceptional site for country residence. If there had been others to take the place of its earlier admirers, who for the most part either lost their properties in the oft recurring San Francisco financial crashes or were for other causes denied the completion of their plans here, —San Rafael would have been just such a center of wealthy home makers as the Peninsula has since become. In general, at that period the Murphy, Black and Short Ranchos supplied the greatest number of cattle, and the stock and beef trade was the central point of all local business matters. Steers brought twenty-five dollars a head which provided a profitable margin; and the smaller stockmen joined with the above gentlemen in making up great droves of cattle enroute to the mines markets.

Now and again we hear of a proposal to have some observance of October 24th as "San Rafael Day." Various versions have been given as to the special significance of this date and a diligent search finally seems to arrive at the facts of the matter as this date being the "St. Rafael's Day" of the church calendar observances. In the Mission period it was celebrated with all proper respect and religious solemnity. But when the influence of the Mission passed, this date developed into a season of general celebration much like a public community Thanksgiving might now become, being merely a day set aside as an outlet for a community rejoicing and pleasure.[155] Finally its gatherings sank into such disrepute and public censure as to arouse the united wrath of the community to a point where the evil was promptly eliminated. In consequence if San Rafael desires to set apart a "day" of its own, its people are free to select such a date as seems most appropriate in the matter, or to resume more orderly observance of the Saint Rafael's Day on October 24th.

From the earliest years of the Mission San Rafael Archangel, the 24th of October was the annual date set aside in recognition of the Patron Saint of the Mission in order to recognize the religious observance of the Feast of St. Rafael, a long standing church festival date. A similar custom was followed at each of the Western Missions.

---

[155] First celebrated by John Reed and Timothy Murphy on October 24, 1842 as a barbecue at the Murphy house, to which all the local settlers and Indians were invited.

At San Rafael the native Californians were assembled by the venerable Padre Amoros from the furthermost points of the extensive Mission lands, arriving on the twenty-third and returning on the twenty-fifth of October. On the twenty-third, church services and ceremonies, festivities and games, and the usual holiday observances were followed by all. Then after the next morning's special religious rites, a great feast was provided in display of the products and resources of the Mission lands and in gratitude to the memory of St. Rafael.

It was an extremely spiritual occasion, probably intended to bring the Mission folk together once a year and at a time which least interfered with the ordinary duties. It provided much closer contact between Christian Indians, the Neophytes and the Gentiles not yet under the Mission influences, and especially in relation to the idea of the direction by this Patron Saint for their ultimate share of the Mission lands and properties.

But what a change took place in the nature of these assemblages at the Mission city when the Mission Days were over! An enterprising hotel proprietor seems to have years afterward revived the celebration by widely publishing the following advertisement in about the Bay papers:

"San Rafael Festivities! Bull Fight; Bear Fight; Horse Races, etc.! According to ancient custom, the festivities of San Rafael, the Patron Saint of San Rafael, will be observed on the 24th of October here in the following manner: Bull and Bear Fight; Sending the Traitor Judas adrift, Mazeppa-like[156], on a wild horse; horse racing; cock lighting: and a round of other amusements. To conclude at night with a display of fireworks and a grand ball. The hotel will be gorgeously decorated and every convenience afforded for all. An excellent band of music will discourse enchanting strains for the benefit of the Public."

The "Sending the Traitor Judas forth on a wild horse" was an old Mission custom, wherein a figure was bound on the back of a wild horse and the animal driven out into the wilderness, evidently a spectacular item to impress the Indians with the seriousness of betraying the confidence of

---

[156] Mazeppa is a narrative poem written by the English romantic poet Lord Byron in 1819. It is based on a popular legend about the early life of Ivan Mazepa (1639-1709), a Ukrainian Cossack. According to the poem, the young Mazeppa has a love affair with a Countess Theresa while serving as a page at the Court of King John II Casimir Vasa. Countess Theresa was married to a much older Count. On discovering the affair, the Count punishes Mazeppa by tying him naked to a wild horse and setting the horse loose.

the old Missioners. It was only one of a number of similar features usually carried off at the Mission-Indians gatherings elsewhere and which are omitted in these notes because of no definite knowledge of their being offered at San Rafael.

This particular boniface seems to have been a typical pioneer hotel man. A prevalent hotel sign of those days of "For Epicures and Hungry Men" might infer that the gentler sex did not need any man-made meals or did not frequent such places. So it would seem that the inclusion of the "Grand Ball" idea was a wily plan or inducement to attract them on this occasion. No doubt he was the center of community activities and while undoubtedly handsomely profiting by the initiative, had in mind the re-awakening of old time spirit here.

But as the years passed on this festival day changed from the earlier religious nature to one of bullfights, horse races, gambling of every description, whisky drinking and all manner of excesses typical of an uncontrolled early community. At these times San Rafael began to be the meeting place of the nimblest of all gamblers and green goods men[157] on the coast; of every manner of device and plan to separate the trusting and unwary visitor from his properties; and an assemblage of that fraternity which can only get together because citizens ignore the inevitable consequences. But when successive years brought an ever increasing horde of these gentry a time arrived when, figuratively speaking, the angry shadow of old Padre Amoros attended the roisterous meeting and fell upon these unworthies in the shape of an outraged public opinion and drove them forth to other lands. So "San Rafael Day" went unobserved for many years thereafter.

28 September 1922

Several accounts of these old annual festivals are of record and the following will summarize their main features. As early as the twenty-second of October the town began to fill up with a collection of nimble witted gentlemen from all up and down the coast, for they traveled from Mission town to Mission town where these days were held, much as the circus

---

[157] A well-known con game purporting to sell counterfeit bills.

followers did in recent years before outraged communities held the circus management to account for their actions.

On the twenty-third of October either a Rodeo or a Bullfight or both were scheduled in which anyone could enter. That evening there was a grand ball which lasted all night, and a punctilious ceremony at these affairs was the official bestowal of such prizes and awards as merited unusual mention from the day's festivities The next day, the twenty-fourth, old settlers gathered from far and near for a barbecue or great feast and for the flow of oratory which had been pent up at isolated points for many months. This feast was a typical reunion of settlers and woe to the individual who attempted any disturbance thereat. In fact it was an unwritten law that no violence would be countenanced at this general celebration hence those who had been fleeced in the earlier periods had little redress. This last day was one of full rejoicing and happy memories. So ended the annual three day gathering, of a character in some respects which in our day might be severely criticized. Yet some of the present day assemblages that are not so clearly in the public eye would not stand analysis by ourselves, and most assuredly not by those old time folks.

These local bull fights are said to have been very tame affairs, since so far removed from experts at the game. A few vaqueros would tease protesting animals and promptly vault the surrounding fence at the slightest approach of angry bovines. It is said that at a later day Rodeo and Bullfight the enclosure included the present Pfeffer Store block on E street[158] and that the visitors viewed the spectacle from the slopes of the sharply rising hills at the end of E street. This was probably so because the Mission Garden extended to Irving Street on the East and to the water on the south, while the San Rafael Creek extended beyond D street at that time. This statement may be doubted but if the note of the Davis and Taylor store and wharf on C street is correct the matter is plainly true.

Aside from the Mission efforts along that line, an interesting horticultural item of early San Rafael days appears in the mention of John Sims submitting a sample of cherries on May 18, 1861, with statement that the tree had been planted only the previous December. Since then practically every San Rafael back garden plot includes one or more flourishing fruit trees.

---

[158] Southwest corner of 1st and E Streets.

San Rafael lost its post office in 1862. At that time mail was sent via Benicia, Napa, and Sonoma and by mounted carrier to San Rafael. Afterward it came from Vallejo to San Quentin by Petaluma steamers, whence it was taken to San Rafael by stage. But an agreement had been made by the community that if the route was installed, a proper road connection would be afforded to San Quentin. After repeated complaints by the contractors and following more direct demands by Uncle Sam, the route continued to be an almost impassable matter and the Government suddenly canceled the privilege. Thereafter the mail was taken to Tomales via Petaluma, and sent from the post office there to San Rafael by pony carrier. One can imagine the strenuous attempts that were made to restore the continuous mud-hole route to San Quentin to passable condition. But for a long time Uncle Sam did not forget the exasperation of previous matters and Tomales continued to be the distributing post office for the county territory, until the pressure of a growing southern community developed proper roads.

In 1863 the State Telegraph Company located an office in the County Court House and Daniel T. Taylor manipulated the key as a side issue from duties as a County Deputy. In July of the same year a stage route was instituted to Petaluma and another from San Rafael to Tomales via Novato, Petaluma and Two Rock.

5 October 1922

Since so much has been written in later years of the advantages of climatic conditions of San Rafael and its environs, note of its charms in 1861, mentioned in the Journal of that year are now of interest. "The Institute" (The Gilbert School), is situated in one of the most beautiful and loveliest places in the country, in the quiet and pleasant town of San Rafael. Nature has strewn with a profusion of the generous gifts, the most picturesque scenery around our pleasant little village, and blest with one of the most delicious climates on the habitable globe. We may not be permitted to boast of our snow covered sierras covered with the snows of eternal ages, nor of the glittering gems which encircle her brow, —but we can turn with feelings of admiration to our Tamalpais rising far to the Southwest in stately and majestic grandeur, whose lofty crest is watered by the dews of heaven;

and raising his hoary visage as if in mockery to the storms of ages and in defiance of the decays of time."

In the matter of publicity, probably no wider circulation of the claims for any new community occurred in early times, than was obtained for San Rafael by Doctor DuBois[159]. He was a specialist on climatic conditions for certain types of invalidism and had spent periods in all of the then reported health centers. But when reaching San Rafael he at once located here and proceeded to collect most painstaking and accurate data concerning daily temperature changes, rainfall, sunshiny days, winds, humidity, etc., etc., and submitted a voluminous report of his findings to the New York Medical Society in vigorous endorsement of the Marin advantages over others in direct comparison. The Society published it in full in the New York Medical Society Journal. In this article Dr. DuBois made direct comparison with Mentone (France), Santa Barbara, Los Angeles, San Diego, Denver, Colorado State, Minneapolis, Minnesota State and New Mexico.

A third article in the 1880 Marin County History, closes with a note seldom considered nowadays in health localities comparisons, but which is nevertheless one of the things which our best physicians consider to be a vital assistance to convalescent cases or the general results to cases of mental overwork. The item explains itself: " But while the equability and salubrity of such a climate must exercise a healthy influence upon persons of impaired health, who seek this locality with a view to the restoration of enfeebled physical energies, the beauty of the valley and its surroundings may also claim a charm and a share in the healing processes; for it is well known that scenes which charm the eye, and which constantly gratify the innate sense of the beautiful, do much to give tone to the feelings, and reach and influence the physical organism through the pleasurable action of the imagination."

Father Gleason's "History of the Catholic Church in America" gives the following account of the St. Vincent Seminary foundation a few miles north of San Rafael. "Moved by a laudable desire of providing for the moral and intellectual culture of the Catholic youth in the vicinity of San Rafael, Mr. Timothy Murphy donated three hundred acres of land to the Church for the purpose of establishing and maintaining a school."

---

[159] Henry Augustus Dubois, Jr. (he pronounced it Duboys) (1840-1897), Union surgeon, Marin physician with Dr. Talliaferro, and founder of the Mount Tamalpais Cemetery.

Thereupon the Archbishop appointed the Sisters of Charity to form and direct the institution. These Sisters had their foundation in Paris and headquarters in Maryland. They erected a $5000 building and two Sisters with one assistant for the direction took possession in 1825 with four children enrolled. The school included facilities for neighboring children also and was called St Vincent's Seminary. Don Murphy's original deed of gift (a copy) is framed in a local clubroom and is a prized possession indeed. There are few institutions in California which carried on such earnestly constructive work as St Vincent's in the early California period.

In the literature of the mining days on the Coast the expression is often noted of Marin County being dismissed with the single comment of "notorious throughout the West for its Lime Point and San Quentin," for reasons easily imagined.

In 1861 a call was made for a mass meeting in San Rafael to take steps to mitigate and to once for all settle the pressing question of depredations of men discharged from San Quentin. Under direction of Ai Barney and Dr. D'Hiery the struggle with State authorities began, which extended over a period of many years before outraged public opinion forced the issue. On the other hand it is to be remembered that prisoners from the mining districts virtually suicide if they returned thereto, and in San Francisco when the public cleanup of Mexican and Australian deported convicts took place, the Bay City held out no olive branch to any ex-prisoner. In consequence the nearest territory was the only refuge on discharge from San Quentin, while awaiting a chance to ship on some vessels departing from Sausalito Bay or on the other side. Nevertheless San Rafael suffered for years in the eyes of prospective residents and in fact this proximity to the institution which was then so widely known for scandals in its management and for frequent escapes of its prisoners.— militated against a steady development of San Rafael's earlier promise. Under present efficient prison management, Marin County is now seldom aware that it has a State Prison within its borders.

Oliver Irwin owned all of the present valley extending north from Union Station, which was called "Magnolia Valley" in recognition of the long lines of magnolia trees planted there in earlier periods.

Then William T. Coleman, whose name may be said to have been known in every English-speaking section of the globe, purchased this beautiful valley and proceeded to spend a fortune in attempts to re-forest its denuded ridges. He was a general Commission man in the metropolis, and like many of his friends could not finally stand the repeated disastrous San Francisco fires, financial panics and mining failures,—and did not complete his earlier plans. But he installed a very large nursery in what is still called Coleman Park[160], for his tree planting project. He practically covered the entire valley with pepper, magnolia, lemon, orange, almond, acacia, ash, chestnut, cypress, maple, pine, walnut, and various assorted fruit and ornamental trees. At the time he announced that at the conclusion of its nursery use, this beautiful piece of ground would become a public park. It is still held intact and practically in primitive state other than in the exceeding height of the trees then planted. It contains one of the largest undisturbed Indian Shell Mounds north of the Bay, and is occasionally opened for public festivals and children's days.

12 October 1922

It is to the far-visioned purposes of William T. Coleman that San Rafael is indebted for its beautifully laid out avenues and wooded roads, for he had the true idea of future beauty in a city where conditions were ideal for buildings on the heights and winding roadways on the lower levels. What would some cities now give for an opportunity to rebuild in such a way! In consequence San Rafael has its beautiful winding drives, on easy grades and of great widths, and it was these factors which attracted the earlier wealthy homemakers to Marin shores where country estates could be built up in such naturally beautiful, healthful surroundings.

William T. Coleman also spent considerable money in the Laurel Grove Valley which became the community picnic grounds and gathering place in after years; and also effected the grade on the ridge and on into Ross Valley over the later title of "Brewery Hill," —a long neglected yet still appealing beautiful drive. Mr. Coleman's plan (years before the coming of railroad) was that in driving from Sausalito or Ross Landing all Ross Valley was opened to view on climbing the ridge, and the view therefrom included the entire San Rafael territory. Then a grade here and there, and winding roads throughout enabled one to make the entire circle about San Rafael. Houses now materially interfere with the beautiful views on the circling ride down San Rafael Avenue, Grand Avenue, Petaluma Avenue, Fifth Avenue and

---

[160] Now the Dominican neighborhood.

Forbes Avenue, which was once the famous "Coleman Drive." Many interrupting changes have since been made in this route. All visitors of any prominence arriving in San Francisco and wishing to see some of the country districts were taken over this circle and San Rafael was known all up and down the coast as "The Sanatorium" by reason of its growing popularity for country homes.

Thus the Mission City finally began its steady growth and has indeed been fortunate in escaping any "booms" or speculative realty movement in later periods. Its residents came to it for a definite requirement of sunshine, climate and pure water, and finding it as stated everywhere, remained as permanent citizens. The Baltimore Company's men took the Don Murphy Rancho house for farming activities headquarters; lumber men cut down the forests on San Rafael's surrounding ridges; small vessels opened the way to water routes to San Francisco; the Davis and Taylor store and their freight route paved the way for steady supplies;—and as settlers began to pour in, the town was surveyed and officially laid out in 1850.

In paying tribute to those early residents of San Rafael who should be included in the list of its builders, the name of E. B. Mahon[161] ought to be mentioned. While he was for many later years the County Judge, it was his much earlier efforts which virtually forced the Narrow Gauge railroad to include San Rafael on its route. The facts of Stockton's predicament in being isolated after advancing a subsidy for its railroad, was sufficient reason for Citizen Mahon to unite with the Tomales Group (who had the money and offered rights of way to assist), and insure a definite result before the County Bonds were authorized. He began his Marin residence at Bolinas.

The first frame building was erected in 1849 by James Miller for school purposes, and the Court Room maintained in the old Mission building until 1853 when the Don Murphy home was substituted. In 1864 there were 108 children of school age, including only four of Indian parentage. The Baptist church was organized in 1868, though no building was erected. In 1869 the Catholic Church was built and in 1870 the present Episcopal structure. No details of the early membership are at hand. The Presbyterians organized in the same year and later built what is now the Congregational church

---

[161] Edward B. Mahon (1834-1907), born in Ottawa, came to San Rafael in 1857, where his brother had purchased the old Murphy house. He kept a store, then became a lawyer, county treasurer, and Marin's first District Attorney.

building on E street. Mrs. H. B. Shaver is a surviving charter member and resides in San Rafael, while the names of former heads of the Murray, Dickson, Barney and McDonald families of San Rafael appear in the list.

19 October 1922

In 1865 the sad news of Lincoln's assassination reached Marin County; and at San Rafael appropriate observances followed. In the same year occurred the disastrous earthquake of early days but San Rafael suffered no damage[162]. The pleasure seeking public was more and more attracted to San Rafael and in 1866 when the marsh road was completed, there was a rush to purchase town lots.

The Masonic Lodge came in 1867 and about this time the Tamalpais Water Company was formed to bring water to San Rafael from Lagunitas Creek and thence on to Oakland. While not effected, it paved the way for a local Water Company, upon which installation and the building of the railroads, San Rafael may be listed as having fully passed the probationary period and to have entered the modern era—of progress.

Time has not permitted of a more extended search for San Rafael's early settlement days' record in this series, but enough has been presented as a basis for others to now add to. There are a number of sources of old family records which would afford an invaluable insight of the local incident of these old times, if they could be opened to proper view and selection. As time passes there is less and less chance of the preservation of these old matters, which if not of documentary proof, ought to be disseminated as a source of tradition for future generations. Of all cities north of the Bay, San Rafael should have the greatest wealth of local incident history of the early California period. Who has available data? While this general account brings its early record down to the early 60's, there was a wealth of happenings here in the early days which were of statewide significance and ought to be of record for the future years.

San Rafael Township has been divided into districts of several incorporated cities and in consequence there has been no general unity of effort throughout its territory. Yet a time must come when each of the

---

[162] An estimated 6.3 magnitude quake in the Santa Cruz Mountains on October 10, 1865, caused heavy damage in San Francisco.

several localities will recognize that through co-operation and co-operative effort this district can become almost one continuous city. Its natural situation as a choice suburban residence section, and its unexcelled advantages of sunshine, climate, and pure water seem to definitely point to its probable future. As a section for homes and schools, of beautiful drives and matchless natural scenery, and as a nearby resting and recreation place for the busy San Francisco Bay region it is certain to have its various sections combined into a more smoothly co-operative district. Various agencies are slowly effecting this and little by little some forward looking people are beginning to consider permanent steps to attain it. The Marin Municipal Water District serves the entire territory; the Gas & Electric service likewise: the school facilities of differing nature now afford opportunity of interchanging students; the railroad has finally recognized the fact that the needs of one section are identical with all of the others and is therefore working to provide adequate transportation facilities for the entire district; various municipal matters are beginning to be of a cooperative nature; —in fact all signs point to the evolution of leaders who will be able to clearly show how all of the different districts may come together to natural advantage yet still retain the major items of individuality and local endeavor. Alameda, Oakland, Berkeley. Santa Rosa, San Mateo, San Jose, Seattle, Spokane, Fresno, Los Angeles, and many other western cities have each had similar conditions and have come to recognize the advantages of combining outlying districts into one central control, which in several instances has not eventually been that the originally largest district. One eminent gentleman who visited San Rafael recently after trips to every California county and also city of any size, stated that San Rafael and its adjoining districts had but two comparisons in all the West, and of the three, this southern Marin county section was the most attractive by reasons of its beautiful hills and opportunity for claiming the ideal requirements for perfect homes and schools surroundings. Another gentleman has traveled all over the world, to practically every place renowned for climate and homes advantages, yet returns to San Rafael with the intent to remain here now in preference to any other locality visited.

[Note: The series did not appear in the *Marin Journal* for the next three weeks. No explanation was given.]

16 November 1922

SAUSALITO

The first men of the white race to visit Sausalito were those in the Spanish expedition to Olompali in 1776, who probably landed at Lime Point and gave the name Sauzalito to the present settlement as the Spanish word for "a place of small willows" on account of the brushy willow thickets covering all the low land of that territory. The name has since changed through Salieto, Saucelito, and is now Sausalito.

While the Ayala party previously referred to anchored off Sausalito Point and then moved to Richardson's Bay, the diary of the trip mentions fhe first landing on the opposite shore, though it is probable that it may also have been made near Sausalito for fuel or wood. Then various exploring vessels anchored in the sheltered Sausalito Bay from time to time and northern whaling vessels wintered and outfitted there, which gave it the name of Bahia Balleneros (Whalers Bay). They were compelled to do this because the Spanish Government forbid any foreign vessel or crew to land anywhere at Pacific ports except at Monterey. When its advantages for wintering and outfitting became known all over the world this "Whalers Bay" was made the rendezvous of great numbers of whaling vessels, French pearlers, Honolulu traders, exploring expeditions, Russian traders, and the English, French and American navy vessels. At first all trading with them was illegal and from this side they procured fresh water and beef from the shore peoples.

But Captain William Richardson, an Englishman, arrived in San Francisco and shortly thereafter married the Commandant's daughter[163]. He was then appointed to take charge of the rapidly increasing troubles with foreign vessels entering San Francisco Bay. He was quick to see the opportunity of establishing a business of outfitting these ships which were not in a "port" and proceeded to build up a very profitable business

---

[163] William Richardson (1795-1856) arrived in San Francisco in 1822 as second mate of the British whaling ship *Orion*. He went to an all-night dance and met Maria Antonia Martinez, daughter of Ygnacio Martinez, Commandante of the Presidio. He jumped ship, converted to Catholicism, became a Mexican Citizen, and married Maria. He was granted Rancho Sausalito and established a watering and supply station for visiting whalers. He built the first two-story house in Yerba Buena and laid out the street plan of the city.

therewith. As he was later appointed Captain of the Port in San Francisco (until 1844), it was an easy matter to prevent any opposition. Ships' captains made strenuous endeavors to arrive at this Whalers' Bay for the annual Christmas week festivities, details of which would make interesting reading nowadays. It can easily be imagined that a prized opportunity was thus presented [to] meet crews and officers of other vessels, many of them spending years away from the home port.

One must know something of the early whaling days to understand why this annual gathering did not promptly start a Sausalito town since at times scores of vessels gathered there and seldom any month passed without several visiting ships on exploring tours. But since the business at Whalers' Bay was wholly controlled by Richardson, and no object for building houses existed, it remained merely an outfitting and watering port. In fact it was a venturesome individual indeed who went there in daylight, and after nightfall prudent gentlemen boarded ship early or departed in sunlit hours. That partly explains why Captain Richardson, after moving his family to the Rancho home near Sausalito, applied to have a juez de paz appointed in San Rafael: because the Spanish authorities at San Francisco cared little about matters at Sausalito and each ship's captain ruled the affairs of only his own crew. Yet deserting sailors, wandering vagabonds and occasional troublemakers had to also be taken care of. It was a common saying up and down the coast that if one wanted trouble, "Go to Sausalito and fill up a beach grave."

Richardson conducted a thriving business at this point. He led pure spring water into huge tanks on the beach and sold it to the vessels there and when the volume of this business became an important item, the San Francisco authorities made a number of attempts to find water across the bay but gave up the matter after sinking a number of wells near the shore. One can easily read between the lines of the news of this period, that a thriving business with Honolulu traders was also developed at Sausalito. Someone should still have the carefully kept diary of Captain Richardson unless it was lost in one of the frequent San Francisco fires of later date. If it is still extant, its contents would afford an intimate view of those times.

The early history of Sausalito centers around five main events and with the activities of only three men. There was the early outfitting activities of Captain Richardson, the lumbering of John Reed, the Government Stores plant, Captain Storey's Ferry, and the Sausalito Land and Ferry Company.

23 November 1922

Sausalito's first resident was Captain John Reed in 1826. Inasmuch as he was the "Father of Pioneers" in Marin county and it was his activities which practically started all southern Marin's history, a more extended mention of him should be made in cases of other early Marin settlers. He was the first English speaking resident of Marin County, and is said to have been the first Irishman located permanently on the Pacific Coast. The Spanish Government refused his application for the Sausalito Rancho grant as being territory reserved for future military purposes. Thereupon he took up a Rancho at Cotati in Sonoma County, but the Indians destroyed his property and drove him out of that territory. Next he was majordomo at San Rafael Mission until 1832, when he again applied for the Sausalito Rancho. Meantime Captain Richardson had made application for it in 1828 and received it later, much to Reed's disappointment for it was a valuable property and of great extent. Another version states that Reed occupied the Rancho and expected the title, but when the papers arrived they were in the name of a third party, whom Richardson paid for the title. Thus it happened that in the meantime Reed resided near Sausalito and built the first house there, if a shack shanty could be so called.

During this time he established the first ferry on San Francisco Bay, in fact the first in all California. This was merely a small sailboat making a few trips a week to San Francisco yet nevertheless the forerunner of our modern system of Bay Ferries.

In 1833 he applied for the Corte Madera del Presidio Rancho ("place where wood was cut for the Presidio"), which was granted to him in 1843. But he seemed to be assured of the title this time and proceeded to develop his property before the grant was awarded. He built an adobe home with the help of Indian labor from Sutter's Fort, which seems to indicate that at that date the remaining Marin Indians were not of the working type. This was the old Deffenbach[164] home in later years.

---

[164] Thomas Boileau Deffenbach (1822-1884), born in Pennsylvania, came to San Francisco on an English brig in 1850 and spent three years in the gold mines. He then opened a printing business. He married John Reed's daughter Donna Inez in 1864 and bought Reed's house.

As stated above, long before this Captain William Richardson had extensive business interests at Sausalito, though residing in San Francisco as an official of the port thereof. On the granting of his Rancho in Marin County in 1836, he moved across the bay and was therefore the second settler at Sausalito. He lived on the Rancho property and though in San Francisco office until 1844, devoted his energies in the meantime to further developing the outfitting and watering business with foreign vessels.

While San Francisco had small quantities of drinkable water at first, its rapidly increasing population brought on a serious question of adequate water supply. Bancroft mentions this in his gruesome tale of the "'Sailor In The Well."[165] In consequence Richardson expanded his Sausalito business to the point of furnishing water to San Francisco. We can infer from this the fact that early records describe his wooden troughs leading trickling streams from Sausalito hillside ravines into large beach tanks, that the Sausalito slopes had to have been heavily wooded in those days to have supported such an all the year round supply. Its ridges certainly must have been an inspiring sight if that was the case.

One early Spanish explorer records a party naming Angel Island on viewing it from the Presidio Heights. They named it Nuestra Sonora de los Angeles (Our Lady of the Angels), mainly because great towering trees extended up through the low hung clouds on its peak. If Angel Island still had such treasures it would be known the world over and perhaps if present reforesting efforts proceed there, it will once more be covered with beautiful trees.

28 December 1922

John Reed built the first saw mill and gristmill in Marin County. This was on the Corte Madera del Presidio Rancho. The mill stones were purchased at the sale of the Russian Colony equipment at Fort Ross, and ought to be still existent in that they were made of the hardest basalt blocks. This mill ran by water power just back of the Reed home, which again gives a hint of what a forestation must have been there to conserve a sufficient supply for the purpose, where now only barest of dry ridges are shown. His

---

[165] Bancroft relates that when customers at A. J. Ellis' boarding house and "groggery" complained about the bad taste of his beer, he discovered a drowned Russian sailor in his well.

mill was of the "sash saw" type and the first of its kind on the coast. Then he built the first steam sawmill plant at old Sausalito in 1849 and ran it until 1852. His logs were cut on the ridges and the low lands at the head of Richardson's Bay. What a wonderful panorama our commuters would now have on their daily trips if these immense tracts of redwood forest were still about Richardson's Bay! It takes some imagination to visualize the primeval forest of that period where now all that one sees are the bare hillside and dry ravines.

In 1849 Captain Storey[166] brought the first immigrant family to Old Sausalito. Then others arrived and in 1850 the first Government store and outfitting warehouse was established there. Captain Storey developed the real beginning of the present extensive trans-bay ferry service.

Sausalito then advanced rapidly until in 1852 the great fire at Sacramento in turn demolished Old Sausalito and checked its further growth for many years. There were a number of boarding houses, warehouses and other large buildings in Old Sausalito and the U. S. Government had added a second great warehouse there, from which navy vessels of all nations drew supplies. But Sacramento was the central distributing point for all the mining territory and after its disastrous fire its merchants offered such tremendous prices for immediately delivered lumber, that Old Sausalito was "wrecked" almost overnight and its building material shipped to Sacramento for immediate use. The Government thereupon moved its supply depot to Marc Island.

While it was indeed a sad day for Old Sausalito, yet it proved to be a blessing in disguise, for the business of the port had declined as soon as San Francisco anchorage was opened to foreigners, and the space there was much too limited for any extended development.

Captain Storey continued to run a large vessel to San Francisco to transfer piling and large timbers across the bay, from which nearly all the early San Francisco wharves and large buildings were constructed. Charles Lauff[167] of later Bolinas fame, and his partner William Hodd, floated a raft

---

[166] Captain Leonard Story came to San Francisco in February and arrived in Sausalito Christmas Day of that year.

[167] Charles Augustus Lauff (1822-1917), born in Strasbourg, Alsace (now France). He married a daughter of Gregorio Briones, founder of Bolinas, and became the first Anglo settler in Bolinas. He published his memoirs in a series of newspaper articles in 1916.

of 80,000 feet of timber to San Francisco. This was the record for all time of a raft timber cut on the shores of San Francisco Bay.

In 1850 Captain Richardson formed the Sausalito Water Works to add to his former efforts in supplying San Francisco's needs. He built a 30 by 30 by 8 foot tank on the beach and soon added another one 60 by 60 by 8 feet, from which steam schooners transferred the water to San Francisco. This was its only supply until the birth of the Spring Valley Water Company in that city.

In consequence Sausalito was born by reason of its safe anchorage; next developed its resources of pure water and abundant beef supplies for the whalers; next supplied San Francisco with timber; and finally established a flourishing ferry system thereto. Though its whaling trade visitors dallied for a time only, they established a rapidly populating graveyard along its shore line and on the hillsides to the south. Pest stricken Russian ships added large quotas to this gathering and the turbulent sailor crowds likewise. Up to a few years ago some of these old graves were fenced off on the slopes above Old Sausalito.

Though the old town was torn down and remained "wrecked" after 1852, it was reborn in 1868 when the far-visioned men of the Sausalito Land and Ferry Company organized and located there. They proceeded north from the old site and laid out one thousand acres into lots and established a then modern ferry line to San Francisco. The steamer "*Princess*" ran until 1875 and then the "*Petaluma of San Francisco*" continued until about 1880. It would be interesting indeed to look over the records of this still existing company and note the local incident of Sausalito's later history, during which its permanent prosperity was developed and extended to its present promise.

Point Bonita was first a "Fog Cannon" station, whose guns roared warnings at intervals in all foggy periods. In 1855 the first lighthouse was established there and a fog "siren" added to replace the cannon, all other fog whistles on the Coast being of the steam type. A new light was secured in 1877 and is still there.

How many of us know where the attractive "Tennessee Cove" obtained its name? It is a small bight just north of Sausalito and now a favorite picnic place. In 1853 the large Panama-to-San Francisco steamer "*Tennessee*" went ashore there in a dense fog, and happily all on the heavily laden vessel were saved[168]. Anyone who has been there will agree that only the hand of Providence could have saved those people, because a deviation of a few feet either way would have brought the vessel squarely against extremely high rocky cliffs where not a foot of landing is available. As it was the officers thought they were entering the Golden Gate and came in on a high tide, landing well up on the narrow sand beach in the small valley there. Almost as soon as the passengers and crew were removed, an angry sea arose and quickly demolished the huge vessel. Of all maritime disasters this wreck of the *Tennessee* and of another vessel at Bolinas under almost identical circumstances, must rank as among the mysteries of early day Guiding Hands, since the chances of such miraculous escapes were against all precedents of the kind.

4 January 1923

In 1856 the *San Francisco* was wrecked at the heads to the south of Sausalito and again all hands were saved by passing boats. In 1849 [1878], a smaller vessel, the *Fourth of July*, was driven into this same Tennessee Cove and under pressure of immense waves was rolled over and over far up on the land beyond the beach.

In 1857 the *General Story*, a sloop enroute to Bolinas struck on the "Potato Patch" west of Bolinas. Three men, two women and a small child were on board. The boat was overturned and the women and child imprisoned in the cabin, whereupon a Kanaka dove underneath and fished them out with a boat hook. The party was picked up by a passing vessel, none the worse for their experience except loss of the little child.

Fremont's party spent a day or two at Sausalito, awaiting the return of its leader from the "gun spiking" episode to the Presidio. The details of the "pursuit" of the De la Torre (Mexican) soldiery to Sausalito are noted in the Marin County notes.

Of the old Sausalito families, Stephen Richardson is in San Francisco, and the Boyle, Deffenbach, Gardner, Rutherford, and Reed family connections still reside in the locality. Perhaps E. H. Shoemaker[169] is now

---

[168] The Pacific Mail Steamer *Tennessee* ran aground March 6, 1853. The engines can still sometimes be seen when the sand is swept away by storms.

[169] Edwin H. Shoemaker (1841-1928) was a water-boy, then conductor, then superintendent of the North Pacific Coast Railway and Town Trustee of Sausalito.

Sausalito's earliest resident and a man whose life history may be said to be the entire history of the North Pacific Coast Railroad Company. Engineering journals of the period note his solution of innumerable difficulties in operating the old Narrow Gauge line as one of the hardest tasks any American Railway Superintendent ever had.

If one were to make a "Feature Survey" of Sausalito, they have but to remember that it is the main gateway to the rich North Bay territories. First a rendezvous for foreign vessels and of seamen of all nations marooned there over the winter months by Spanish law; now a busy maritime and naval outfitting center; then a hopelessly "wrecked" town – Sausalito has emerged from earlier experiences into a thriving residence, manufacturing, and a railroad and ferry terminus city. Lovers of marine views find no choicer suburban residence territory anywhere in the West; and though some people dislike its ever-present fogs and winds, – only the invalid type fails to benefit by its bracing and invigorating climatic conditions. If its ridges were ever reforested as they once were and may be again, this one objection to Sausalito's climate will be largely overcome, according to the testimony of many places along the coast where the matter has been tested out. Houses will then climb higher and higher to the tops of its ridges. One has only to note this tendency of home seekers in all sheltered seaport cities to know that Sausalito's bare hills will not always remain unoccupied. Perhaps if the growing pacifist movement finally reaches its goal, the fair Fort Baker Valley may be abandoned for military purposes and become one of Sausalito's choicest suburban residence suburbs. If such a matter develops it is not beyond reason to believe that its ferry terminal will be there and both vehicle and railroad tunnels will pierce the now forbidding ridge, thus releasing the present constantly increasing congestion along its limited waterfront area.

The Sausalito of today is a thriving community, with its railroad shops, its extensive chemical byproducts manufacturing plant, its boat building yards, and its exceptional suburban residence locations. There are few places anywhere which excel it if one wishes to locate for a wonderful outlook over land and water. Towns have sprung up about it and as the main Marin gateway, it is certain of a definite future development. There may come a time when its waterfront will extend far up in the present neglected Richardson's Bay. Its northern section may become a hive of busy industrial plants, and the slope hillsides in rear of them a continuous line of workingmen's homes. Even now small places are being located here and there almost up to the Mill Valley line. Numerous plans have been made from time to time to develop the Alto Valley and the north shore of Richardson Bay territories as residence sections, and when transportation is available to those places, they too will be thickly populated. If a permanent highway is finally built to Bolinas, Sausalito will largely profit as the staging terminus thereto, for such a drive will be one of the finest scenic routes on the coast.

Just as the Sausalito Land and Ferry Company practically founded and developed the present Sausalito city, other projects for the Homestead and Tennessee Valley sections will add new areas for residence in its environs, which will further extend the distributing facilities of the established center. Practically every industrial survey of the West comments on the assured development of the shore lines all about San Francisco Bay; for if California's central port is to be the New York of the Pacific, and a dominant force in the Pacific maritime activities of the future, then the Marin shore lines will be in demand indeed, – to the ultimate benefit of Sausalito and its furthermost territory.

(End of Sausalito story)

11 January 1923

Bolinas

Going into Bolinas today, one finds a thriving village by the sea bordering an unusually fine ocean beach and situated on a peninsula between bay and ocean shores – altogether an ideally sheltered spot on an otherwise bleak, high-cliffed, rocky sea front of the Pacific. It instantly gives one an impression of rest and quiet charm and of a place where the idle, lazy summer days can be spent far from the restless bayeties [gaieties?] of much easier-reached resorts. But let us go back to 1834, attempting in a review of its subsequent forty years to gain an impression of what it was at first and how it developed into a town at that point. The eastern and northern slopes of Bolinas Bay and the lowlands extending north were then not only heavily forested but possessed trees of the largest size found in Marin County. These must have been beautifully situated forest expanses as viewed from the ridges above, from the ocean front and especially from the present Bolinas town site. What a misfortune to have those grand old redwood trees destroyed for merely temporary uses of the timber concerned! Just imagine the miles and miles of them extending from Bolinas to Inverness, all of greater size than at Muir Woods now; and all available for a great public playground! But such things were not to be.

Naturally, Bolinas Bay then had no mud banks or mud bottom because the ocean tides came in over broad areas of clean sand and the land slopes were covered with perhaps centuries of forest carpetings, both of these usual sources of mud deposits being practically natural filtering methods for all waters admitted to the inlet. In every way the contour of Bolinas Bay indicates that at first only the western estero existed and the long sandspit was afterward formed, leaving a broad, shallow, still waters "pond" at the eastern end. Even when first visited, myriads of the huge Pacific Coast sand clams were found in Bolinas Bay and a small area of clean sandy bottom still harbors them there. We call them very large now but in those days each was a meal in itself. Nowhere along the coast were they found in such size or abundance. In the days of Bolinas' first settlement there was a dozen or more feet of water over the Bar, so that vessels of considerable size or burden could enter and depart at will. In consequence of the busy lumbering period there, Bolinas Bay was filled with many vessels of varying type, and numbers of coasting vessels were built along the eastern end of the Bay.

But careless farming, and especially the reckless clearing of forest lands gave free opportunity for heavy rains to quickly fill up this beautiful inlet with a thick coating of mud and in consequence shallowed the Bar with shifting ocean sands. At the present time one can hardly manipulate a row boat even at high tide in many parts of the Bay. If the Bolinas forests and Bolinas Bay could have been kept as it was in the beginning, few places in the world would have matched its charms for summer homes.

So much for what might have been! Fantastic as the idea may be, it is said that if railroad transportation finally reaches these matchless Bolinas beaches, united action like that at Seattle, the Florida Keys, Galveston, San Pedro, etc., may yet bring Bolinas into its own if all Northern California wants to have such a summering place. Marin County has only three fine beaches in connection with required climatic conditions, which are easily accessible to all Central and Northern California and a time may yet arrive when they will be developed.

Rafael Garcia, of Mission San Rafael Archangel fame in his repulse of an Indian attack thereon, was the first settler near Bolinas, bringing his large family from the San Rafael Mission when receiving the Bolinas land grant in 1834. This was the first inland rancho awarded in Marin territory, and as Garcia in his Mission duties had many times journeyed up and down the coast, his choice was from direct comparison with all the places visited. But his many years spent as a Presidio soldier and Missions guard had developed too strong a spirit of exploration and roving trips. In consequence he soon sold the Bolinas Rancho to Gregorio Briones, a brother-in-law and a Monterey official. Garcia then claimed the adjoining rancho of Tomales y Bolinas, a veritable principality in the Olema Valley and extending to Lagunitas and Point Reyes, where he established an old time Haciendo and organized the territory. Its story is noted elsewhere.

Briones took charge of the Bolinas Rancho in 1838 and thereafter follows the typical story of the development of an early day Spanish Rancho, with all the success, expansion, and open-handed hospitality factors which attended such efforts in many California sections of those times. With about nine thousand acres of the finest grazing land in western territory, his stock soon multiplied into many thousands; and the Garcia home became a timbered adobe structure and the centre for a countryside activity. Briones' record in Marin territory stands outs in bold relief in the early annals as that of a capable, thoroughly-respected and widely-known early pioneer.

Old Spanish families still tell of the far-reaching plans for observance of the first marriages occurring in Marin County. Among all of these tales one of these affairs at Bolinas must take first rank. As stated before, Pablo Briones was a well-known Government official before becoming a rancher in Marin territory. In consequence of the observance of and preparation for the marriage of his daughter[170] to Francisco Sebrean[171] was of more than usual import. Moreover, the Briones' had long been the centre of open-handed hospitality for the countryside and this occasion afforded an opportunity for all to reciprocate. Simple as the event was, it had the setting of romance personified, and in the hand of a qualified writer might easily claim a place on the Coast.

---

[170] Maria de Jesus Briones (1825-1894), born in Santa Clara. They had three children. After Sebrean's death of smallpox in 1852, she married Charles Lauff and had nine more.

[171] Francisco Xavier Sebrean (1823-1852), born at Mission Santa Clara.

Like all adobe homes, the Briones Rancho had no modern floors which could be used for dancing; in fact there were none to be found in the entire territory. But to celebrate the first marriage here without an accompanying dance was not to be thought of, especially on the part of the rapidly-growing shipbuilding town of Bolinas nearby. So Charles Lauff, of later fame in Marin County, gathered the mill hands of Bolinas together and built a dance platform for the occasion, and which was used for similar purpose for many years.

The couple, mounting a single horse in the then style of such trips, started in the early morning hours for San Rafael for the religious service, thence returning the same day to a fitting celebration of the unusual event. A grand barbecue had been in preparation for several days and a feast which for years afterward had no equal in Marin lands was prepared for all. Eating, drinking, and dancing proceeded until daylight hours of the following day, when Bolinas settled down once more to its routine affairs.[172] A forty-four mile horseback ride to the nearest church, a prolonged feast, an all-night celebration, and congratulation of the countryside – is indeed a stretch of the modern imagination when compared with our marriage affairs nowadays.

18 January 1923

About 1849 a number of lumbermen came to Bolinas to get out the huge timbers needed at San Francisco for its wharves and for building the Government forts there. Of these pioneers, the names of Joseph Almy (later county judge), Charles Lauff, Hiram Nott, and others are all closely interwoven in all early day matters of Marin County. Two dollars per running foot was paid for this timber at Bolinas, which then floated down Bolinas Bay and over the bar, where vessels then took it to San Francisco. Joseph Almy tried to improve on these methods by building a huge raft, but it was stranded on the famous "Potato Patch" reef and broken to pieces. A small vessel made regular trips from San Francisco to Bolinas, which town soon became the best-known shipyard and lumber center of the then California.

---

[172] The wedding was May 20, 1850.

One of the relatives of the famous Davy Crockett[173] chose Bolinas for a home and it was in his family that the first American child was born in Marin County. Samuel Clarke, Captain Eskoot, and Captain Peter Bourne were also early Bolinas family heads. The Mahon brothers, of [which] E. B. Mahon was later County judge, started a store at Woodville (later called Dogtown) and afterward removed to San Rafael. Bolinas was practically isolated from all other parts of the county. A trail over the mountain finally reached San Rafael after devious windings and turnings over and around the intervening ridges, and consequently was only used for occasional and necessary horseback trips. Another trail stretched out along the coast to Sausalito. A third, and the usual route, was through Olema to San Rafael, since the lumber roads spread from Bolinas to White's Hill.

In 1851, the first saw mill, a whip saw affair, was erected at Woodville, and the outfit later changed to a circular saw affair. This cut six million feet before the machinery was dismantled and taken to San Francisco. A second mill was started nearby and afterward moved to Pike Gulch and cut three million feet there. In 1853 a third mill was erected on the Ridge and marketed another three million feet. Finally a fourth mill was located toward Olema and its output was about one million feet. In this way about fifteen million feet of marketable timber and lumber was cut from Bolinas' slopes. What an inestimable value it would have now as a part of the Forest Reserve for future generations! Imagine those great logs hauled down by oxen on massive carts whose wheels were circular sections of logs. A small shingle mill was operated toward the north for using up the great stumps left behind by the lumbermen. Several references show that many of the Bolinas territory trees were fifty and more feet in circumference.

Bolinas naturally became a ship-building center because of its bay, the many inlets therein, the nearby timber, the easy distance from San Francisco, and its growing popularity for homes of seafaring men. For example, ten schooners for a total of five hundred tonnage was the output near where the McKinnon homestead is now located. But many other vessels were built there also, one especially being so large that it could not be taken over the bar and had to wait [for] the winter storms before being able to dip into the ocean.

---

[173] John Greenwood, son of Caleb Greenwood, who guided the first wagon train to California. John's child was born March 15, 1852.

This section and its nearby shores have been the scene of a score or more of disastrous wrecks and sea tragedies and many of even the present-day homes possess curious relics of these mishaps. The *S. S. Lewis* from Panama with 400 passengers was the first to come to grief. It struck on treacherous Duxbury reef at three o'clock in the morning[174], but miraculously slid over the rocky ridges on a rising tide and drifted into Bolinas Beach in the dark and particularly foggy morning hours. All hands were saved, but before the baggage and other supplies could be landed, the receding tide took the great ship out again in a few hours and Duxbury took a final revenge in smashing it to pieces. Can anyone say that Providence did not have an especial care for these voyagers? It took several days to get help from [to] Bolinas, and meantime the Bolinas folks had this great number of people to care for. Since then (1853), nearly a score of vessels have been wrecked at or near Bolinas, and at times with considerable loss of life, though the greatest fatalities have been further up on the Point Reyes coast.

Some time later, a fine vessel, the steamer *Continental*, was built in San Francisco for the Bolinas run, but was found to have too much draft for the Bolinas bar, since which time only small boats have continued regular trips. The town has long been the prized residence for retired sea folk and others in search of quiet, peaceful, sunshiny days by the sea. Its early pioneers were nearly all retired sea captains.

Bolinas has had a number of stirring mining excitements, first for copper, then silver, then finally for oil. In fact one copper mine was worked on a small scale for several years and the ore shipped out for reduction. Nothing is known however of the results and the workings were finally abandoned. Nevertheless some exceedingly rich ore specimens exist in various collections, and it is quite possible that future investigators will again float "Bolinas Copper" stock. Similarly with oil. There have been two or three companies organized and actively at work near Bolinas, but since the stock was usually sold as far away from Bolinas as it could be marketed, Marin folks were usually skeptical. Here again, perhaps later methods and more experienced oil men may find out why the Bolinas shore line seeps oil and the Duxbury reef conceals a constant gas fountain. Venturesome fishermen used to light the gas jet out there and only the

---

[174] April 10, 1853.

incoming tides would smother it. Journey down to Long Beach and you will find far less promising prospects fully developed far out in the ocean. The last oil boom to the north of Bolinas took considerable money out of the hidden Marin supplies, but the stockholders have only the still remaining pipe ends to remember the experience by.

In early days Bolinas was well-supplied with religious and temperance organizations. Methodist services were conducted in 1861 until the erection of a church in 1877 made them permanent. The Presbyterians followed in 1874 and the Catholics in 1877. The Good Templars appeared in 1864 and the Druids in 1874. It was only natural that the type of residents coming to Bolinas were later drafted into public service in the county. Among these were County Judge Almy, Surveyor Hiram Austin, Treasurer U. M. Gordon, County Judge Mahon, and others.

Note was made in the Sausalito items of this series of "Marin's Pioneer Buggy Ride," a favorite tale of the patriarch of Bolinas, "Charlie" Lauff[175]. Few of the old California pioneers had such a busy and eventful life as this early Marin resident, and Bolinas notes would be incomplete unless including a brief mention of his activities, if for no other reason than to show the present generation what men of those times could do. How men of his time would scoff at this later generation's difficulties and timidities! Clearly, this Charles Lauff was a man of wide experiences, of infinite adaptability to any difficulty, and unreservedly optimistic under any and all conditions. Moreover, he was especially sternly insistent on right and justice prevailing at all times. He was a native of Strasbourg (then French territory) and lived in New York until nineteen years of age, after which he was a seaman for many years. He successively [successfully] sailed to the Shetland Islands, where he was shipwrecked; thence to Cape Horn; next to Sitka for whaling purposes and then to San Francisco in 1844. Next to southern trading ports and to Callao. Then he began lumbering at the Reed Rancho in Marin County and later floated 80,000 feet of logs to San Francisco, a pioneering feat of its kind in the West. Next he enlisted and served in the Mexican War, safely returning to take up shipping matters at Ross Landing in this county in 1847. The gold excitement hurried him north and he was one of the first arrivals at the Coloma gold fields. But land work

---

[175] Lauff told a humorous tale of how he, Charles Alban and George Brewer in 1849 bought the first buggy in Marin and tried to take a drive in spite of there being no roads that would support a buggy.

did not appeal to him and on return to San Francisco he became a Bay Pilot and took the first ship through to Stockton. He then purchased the boat for $10,000 and cleared its price on the first freight trip to Stockton. In 1850 we find him at Bolinas organizing the work of getting out timbers for the San Francisco wharves. Next he trekked to the Trinity mines but was recalled to Bolinas and from there went to manage the Garcia Rancho in Mendocino County. We next find him at Fort Ross, managing the great B. and M. Rancho there, and afterward with the Kelsey party on a prospecting trip through the Coast Range. He then became manager of the principality known as the Punta de Los Reyes Rancho and finally settled down to ranching near Olema in 1857. It was in 1862 that he purchased the permanent ranch home, where until his death about 1915 he was an energetic, useful guiding citizen and an example – for all – for the younger generation.

Surely Bolinas can cherish the tradition of this early Marin citizen. He is a truly typical example of the western pioneer possessing unlimited capability through breadth of experience of men, of facilities and of possibilities. He seems to have been a soldier of opportunity, rather than the soldier of fortune so often mentioned. His intensive adaptability was wholly due to his implicit self-confidence in any undertaking; and his genial optimism and kindly personality explains why every old-timer has such regard for the Charley Lauff memories of those Bolinas days. Fortunate indeed are those Marinites who knew this white-haired and bewhiskered old gentleman and were favored with his endless reminiscences of early days.

Yet Charles Lauff was but one of scores of other early men at Bolinas who after extensive wanderings found permanent haven at Bolinas and for many years made it the most thriving settlement north of San Francisco Bay. Though Bolinas and Tomales were virtually "Marin County" for a long period in its early history insofar as people, industry, and leadership were concerned, yet each was practically cut off from the county by reason of inadequate roads and their business had to be developed over water routes presenting problems which in these days would prevent development at all. In more recent years the beautiful ridge road over Mount Tamalpais to San Rafael brought Bolinas to the front again, and the daily stage ride was a feature many coast tourists preferred to all others by reason of its comfort and unexampled scenic effects[176]. But the San Rafael folks did not value it enough to hold the mail route to Bolinas, and later the coast road to Sausalito was improved to accommodate the Marin Water District activities – but [both] items combining to divert the Bolinas business to Sausalito.

(End of Bolinas review)

25 January 1923

Nicasio

Nicasio is probably a word of Indian origin, though aside from the local naming of the Indians there, available records do not seem to make special mention of any such early Indian tribe. One item of the "*Alta*" in 1865 states that in 1827 Sonoma and Nicasio tribes under Chiefs Sonoma and Marin, practically destroyed their enemies of the Caymus tribe near Napa, which may or may not indicate the name was extant in 1827[177].

This section began in modern times as a territory extending from the Olompali Rancho to Tomales Bay, and comprised nearly one-sixth of Marin County lands. From earliest accounts of the remains of an old Rancheria, however, its habitation as an Indian settlement must have dated back for generations. This Nicasio Rancho was set aside by the Mexican Government with full and perpetual title to such Mission San Rafael Archangel Indians as would occupy and properly use it. But it was quite another thing to settle a people, long used to roving about as they willed and then for twenty years or more subsisted and wholly cared for by the Mission directors – on restricted land to subsist themselves. This sudden assumption of complete self-responsibility from a state of absolute dependence presented a problem which practically no race of people could solve. Perhaps if these Marin Indians had been assisted somewhat instead of being left as the prey of every form of white man knavery, they might have established themselves in time. But to assume control of this rich and extensive Nicasio domain and to submit and govern themselves thereon was

---

[176] The Bolinas-San Rafael Stage Road was completed in 1879 and the stage line ran until World War II. Much of the road is now under the reservoirs, though the Bolinas-Fairfax Road from Alpine Dam to Bolinas is the original road.

[177] *Daily Alta California*, March 30, 1865.

to them impractical if not impossible. It was a problem for any people, and doubly so for the helpless, childlike Indian to attempt.

Nothing is now to be gained by going over the story of by just what steps these broad lands were taken from the Indians, for the record is filled with such seemingly impossible matters connected therewith that one doubts their authenticity. But it is clearly shown that outside, or rather the white man's, influences so demoralized these natives that their lands became escheat to the Government again because of misuse or rather the non-use, the original Indian Grant was forfeited. This is hinted at in the note of General Vallejo's becoming trustee for all property previously distributed by official decree, much to the dismay of the administrators of the California Mission properties. One comforting item is the record of the stiff fight made by Timothy Murphy, an Indian agent, for retention of the Tinacasio Grant for the remnant of remaining Indian tribes, which application was refused, yet the case was reopened for appeal. But alas! Don Timoteo had spent all he could on the case and no one came forward to take steps for the expensive appeal proceedings to follow, and Murphy's own holdings were attached about the same time. So the appeal was dismissed and a long list of claimants appeared. Every one of our Land Grant confirmations was similarly refused until tried on appeal, and if the unlucky owner – though his title was absolutely guarantee[d] by the Treaty of Guadalupe Hidalgo – then the usurper triumphed, usually sold immediately for what he could realize, and decamped to repeat the same procedure elsewhere.

So with the Indians. Coincident with their legal troubles, the virulent smallpox and measles epidemics noted elsewhere in this series so thinned their ranks that the dispirited remainder cared little what became of either themselves or their lands. One of the saddest stories of early western annals could be written about these early Nicasio Indian matters, yet unless viewed in the spirit of those times, its details interest few people now, and nowise concern the present prosperous and capable farmer folk in possession of this old time Nicasio Grant at the present time.

Let us say then that Nicasio began as an Indian settlement in the long past years, and developed into an Indian Land Grant from Mexico, in the course of time has in turn been divided and subdivided into many smaller farms. Nearly seven thousand acres was granted by Governor Micheltorena to Pablo de le Guerra[178] and John B. Cooper, an act which was undoubtedly one of the many last moment attempts of the Mexican officials – or to be fair, their unscrupulous representatives – to prevent remaining California public lands from falling into the hands of the then hated Americans.

One can find no more interesting record in all early western annals than the biographical accounts of the de la Guerra and Cooper pioneers, both the true type of new country developers, and especially that of John B. Cooper as a typical soldier of fortune. But in this land grant matter in our county, the pair overreached themselves, since the action was plainly not in accord with the existing Mexican law, than which there was never more exacting and definite decrees, even though not always properly enforced. Henry W. Halleck, later Brigadier General Halleck of Civil War fame, evidently found a flaw in the proceedings, for the great Nicasio Rancho wad then divided up among himself and the Frink – Reynolds – Black – Buckelew claimants – he receiving the main portion of nearly forty thousand acres. The Halleck School District name seems to be all that remains in Marin County of the General's connection here.

Black's Mountain, that huge bare "hill" between Nicasio and Tomales Bay – and which Signor Serbaroli[179] has so artistically canvassed – is almost the central point of Marin County. It takes its name from William Black, whose land it was. A volume might be written about this sturdy Scotchman, whose business activities and keen faith in the future of Marin County brought many of the best settlers to our section of the State. He traded a much larger rancho in Sonoma County for the Nicasio lands, because after living in the Sonoma woods and hills, a journey down to a view of beautiful Tomales Bay so clearly reminded him of the Scottish lakes that he considered no sacrifice too great to gain the new possession. His house, the first building in Nicasio Valley, was erected in 1848 from Bodega lumber, and he afterward resided in San Rafael for a time. An amusing incident is told of his Scotch neighbors in Sonoma County, Dawson and McIntosh by name, who were partners and had built a house on their rancho. They then quarreled and agreed to disagree, each insisting upon an exact division of the property. When it came to the matter of the house, with true Scotch

---

[178] Pablo de la Guerra (1819-1874), born in Santa Barbara, was a delegate to the State Constitutional Convention, a state senator, and acting Lieutenant Governor.

[179] Hector Serbaroli (1881-1951) was an Italian portrait and landscape painter who taught at the Marin Academy.

obstinacy they calmly sawed it in half, Dawson taking his portion elsewhere. For many years this "half a house" was a widely-known landmark, since the owner declined to repair or add to the damaged portion.

It was William Black who pointed the way to early Marin fortunes in cattle raising, by scorning the middleman's extortions and himself gathering up cattle from far and wide on a cooperative basis. These great herds were then driven to the mines and sold on the hoof at a handsome profit. Jacob and J. O. B. Short, residing in San Rafael, leased a large grazing tract at Nicasio, and built a log house in the Valley[180]. Thereafter many settlers appeared and the Corey brothers erected the first sawmill there.

1 February 1923

A pathetic story is noted in the early Nicasio annals in connection with these Corey people, duplicated again and again in any pioneer territory. A little child passed away at Nicasio and was buried beneath a great oak tree near the former home. One can picture the tenderly cared for grave and the oft-repeated visits of the bereaved parents thereto. But years afterward the timber supplies were exhausted and the family moved away from Nicasio, the grave being marked by a lovingly modeled wooden slab.

As the years went on this was destroyed and the grave forgotten. Came a final period when the parents returned to remove the remains to a permanent home, only to find that no visible trace remained of the giant tree, the old home, or the grave; and that a large hotel stood on the supposed location of the little one's resting place.

Among the early Nicasio settlers the names of Damphier, Short, Magee, Murray, and Taft recall long-time residents and men who were always active in Marin County affairs. In 1867 a Catholic church was built at Nicasio and still remains, and in 1871 the then best school building in the county was erected to replace an earlier temporary structure. Dixon and Ross built a sawmill in 1862 which ran for three years and was then moved to Fort Ross. Shaver and Michener built another later but soon dismantled it for a planing mill at San Rafael. Shaver then built a shingle mill at White's Ranch and a year later joined with Kiler in a sawmill above San Geronimo. This was later changed to a new place west of the former site

---

[180] At Bulltail Ranch, now Skywalker Ranch.

and ran for several months. Then Scott, Sims, and Parks ran a shingle mill west of Nicasio for a year or more.

It was in 1865 that Shaver and Michener built a road from San Geronimo to Ross Landing at a cost of $800, the work being admirably done by Colwell[181], another well-known old timer in Marin. Doubtless Nelson and Henderson, conducting the then flourishing Olema Hotel, joined in this enterprise and another mention speaks of the Bolinas folk doing likewise, for unless one drove around by Petaluma, there was no road to San Rafael at all. A newspaper item of 1865 states that that week there were ten vessels of from ten to fifty tons capacity daily at the Ross Landing embarcadero loading lumber from the Shaver and Michener sawmill at Lagunitas; and also cord wood from surrounding hills. Further, that at Ross Landing there were then fifteen or twenty houses, two stores, a butcher shop, blacksmith and a shoemaker shop.

It was near Nicasio that the last sad chapter of the Main County Indians was brought to a close. Stripped of all their lands, moved and driven here and there by the new settlers, Chief John Callisto finally gathered up all the remnants of Indian properties and with the proceeds purchased some thirty acres from the Miller Ranch, thereafter making an attempt to uplift his people in a final struggle against the insidious voices of the white man. But this little band was surrounded by every kind of demoralizing influence and the settlers were too busy to banish the vagabonds preying upon them. It was soon very necessary for the county to support these disheartened remnants of a once great race, and one by one they passed on to join the host of their forefathers. It is unlikely that the Nicasios were a separate tribe but probably made up of Lacatuits, Cainimares, or perhaps Tomales Indians.

The Nicasio timber was about exhausted and but for the building of the Lucas Valley Road for transporting Nicasio logs and lumber to the Bay and to Ross Landing for trans-shipment were needed, – practically no trace of its forest wealth now remains except the second growth trees, which are slowly giving way to land and wood clearance in this beautiful valley. One north hillside wealth of trees still remains just above Nicasio village and if the people there could only look on into the next generation period, they would deem even these few remaining redwood trees and second growth of

---

[181] Jesse Colwell (1833-1899) was a guard at San Quentin and a road builder who built the road from San Rafael to Olema (now Sir Francis Drake) and the Bolinas-Fairfax Road.

the old timers as the choicest present possessions of the valley. Some way ought to be found to preserve all of the remaining redwood growths of Marin County for posterity in much the way that Muir Woods and the Mountain Reserve has undertaken to do.

Nicasio was at one time ambitious to become the county seat, as noted elsewhere in this Marin's Old Days review. And viewed in the light of later county development and mismanaged opportunities, it might have been just the plan to have resulted in a permanent county unity so long hoped for. But at that time lack of roads, or county funds, of facilities to provide for county business and markets for county products and most pressing factors elsewhere decided against it, though all Northern Marin approved its claims yet could see no effective results to follow. Nevertheless Nicasio never lost heart, and has always been an active factor in Marin County affairs. Records will again show that the county needs have reached out to Nicasio for properly qualified citizens to assume its governmental responsibilities.

Nicasio's early history is one of lumbering first, then grazing and finally of farms development. Its progress has been orderly and successful and markedly free from disturbing the result-less matters affecting some other sections. Probably this was in part due to its isolation, for the roads into or out of the valley were poor examples of county assistance. Yet it affords still another example of a section whose lands are still in the hands of relatives of early settlers, the surest sign in the West of a solidly started and of a slowly but nevertheless surely developing community.

Any idea of the future of Nicasio's territory must presuppose at least two departures from present matters. First, there must and will be decidedly better roadways and resulting communication factors to any markets and distant transportation routes. Secondly, a variation in its one industry of dairying is certain to come. Nicasio Valley is an exceedingly fertile strip of land, as are all deforested areas where land surfaces were not stripped of the surface soil by floods and improper farming methods. In many respects it closely resembles the well-known valleys of Humboldt County in this respect, but has the priceless addition of a more balmy, equable and wholly pleasant climate. While the details never became entirely public, the writer was given certain details by the parties concerned, of a plan to make Nicasio Valley one of the best known summer camping and outing sections of Central California, but the disaster of 1906 vitally changed this and other closely related plans for Marin County at that time, and Nicasio opportunities await a new attempt in this line.

When a period arrives in which more intensive farming methods are practiced in the Nicasio section, and the silo idea solves the question of an all-the-year-green-food supply for the cattle – the Nicasio hill ranges will again be given up to grazing purposes and herd spaces also, while the rich valley floor will be wholly used for the new crop materials, certain to be tried out, and for the other problems which its population factors and its great future promise will compel. Like Novato sections, Nicasio's future is merely hinted at now with its present development. But meantime it is a thriving, successful and growing dairying center of Marin County, compelled to offer its business, its marketing, [and] its activities to Petaluma business circles, mainly for want of Marin County's recognition of its road transportation difficulties to southern sections.

(New [End] of Nicasio Review)

15 February 1923

San Quentin

From the earliest Spanish days in the West all literature of the period carries frequent mention of "San Quentin." Originally it was designated as "Punta de Quentin" (The Point of Quentin), and changed to "Punta de San Quentin" (the Point of San Quentin) in later writings of English explorers, etc. The original name was derived from the fact that an Indian sub-chief named Quintin resided there with his followers and "Quintin's Point" was a natural designation of the locality in consequence. He it was who so vigorously resisted the Spanish and Mexican interference in the early days, and when Chief Marin was finally driven to a last refuge on the islands out in the bay thereafter called the "Marin Islands," and in imminent danger of capture, Chief Quintin gathered his forces and surrounded the islands with a great fleet of canoes. Since the military then consisted of a few men only, this defiant stand succeeded and the Old Chief Marin was once more able to rule over north of the bay Indians.

Another note states that the Indians and even the Spanish people spoke with the greatest contempt over the change in the name from Quentin's

Point to San Quentin Point, because Quintin persistently declined to have anything to do with the Mission Padres or their work, whereupon they called him "San (meaning 'no saint') Quentin" of which he was inordinately proud. But when the English version of San Quentin, from the European stronghold of St. Quentin times became common, the Indians gleefully noted the original and final names in comparison. This prefix of "san" (the European designation of "St.") was indiscriminately applied to western places by new arrivals in later years and therefore many of the present names of this type are either meaningless or have just the opposite application, thus the original "Quentin's Point," a name intimately related to early history matters is now known as "San Quentin" in honor of a justly celebrated European incident of English history, and originally in derision, is now of religious import.

In the early days Marin County or the territory of Marin's Indians as it was better known then, was only spoken of in terms of the treacherous Lime Point landing from the San Francisco side, and of the even more notorious San Quentin Prison of later years. In the opening years of the great California mining excitement it was quickly realized by all that together with the type of better citizens and citizens to be, arriving from all quarters of the globe, there were included a much too large percentage of the gentry who had either just emerged from prison sojourns or who had just escaped from their home countries just in time to miss retirement at community expense. These individuals were rounded up at the mines in droves and sent back to San Francisco, where sill greater numbers were held in quod and in prospect of being sent to the mines to get away from city troubles. Hence San Quentin was the solution, and an enlargement thereof effected at State expense.

The story of the early years of San Quentin tenure at public expense is a theme which has been written and rewritten again and again and is familiar the world over. Yet nowadays we can hardly place credence in the tales of well-to-do residents of the metropolis, placed in quod for a year or two, moving their entire possessions and servants over to San Quentin, touring the surrounding country with their coach and four, holding open house to their old friends each week-end, and in all respects being considered the gentry type so long as they remained in San Quentin locality. Many of them built small homes there and maintained guards to protect their families from evil doers.

A dead line was drawn as to return to San Francisco, and a still sterner one from venturing to the mines again. Hence since there was not yet any means of subsistence outside of the State support, it was safest to stay in the immediate vicinity until officially invited back to former haunts. Incidentally the privilege of conducting the prison was bid for and the contractor sold labor here and there where needed. Naturally if he made money thereby it was a paradise at San Quentin, for to succeed at one end, there had to be peace and plenty at the other, a fact quickly appreciated by all concerned. Naturally enough the immediate surroundings over which this crowd of "transients" wandered at will was not the most attractive for homes and home makers and in consequence of this fact and that of the closing days of Mission Indian tenure at San Rafael, southern Marin had a hard struggle to gain a proper start, while Northern Marin made steady progress.

San Quentin Point is said to be unequalled anywhere on the American continent for certain peculiar climatic, marine view, geographical, and easy-communication-to-great cities matters. It therefore seems impossible to understand just why Marin County, and especially its southern sections, did not unite on the two occasions when the State Prison was rebuilt, to have it removed elsewhere and have this wonderfully adaptable peninsula come into its own. The return to the county in consequence would be ten-fold and return now or in the future enjoyed from the tenure of the State Institution, while many other sections would clamor for the location of the prison in their territory. Indeed in some places it would be an asset to other activities and resources in a manner quite different than in a section of homes and home makers. Nowadays the San Quentin Prison is so admirably conducted, and the public is so well protected from possible influence therefrom, that stories of the old time troubles to the community may well be forgotten. It stands at the head of the list of most capably conducted state prisons in America and is practically filled to capacity at all times.

1 March 1923

Olema

The word Olema is said to be of Indian origin meaning, "O Beautiful Hills",[182] in itself a charmingly apt description of the exceedingly attractive setting of the Marin County township. Its early Indian residents were called the Olemachoe Tribe. One has but to view the Olema Valley in a morning light from the Tocaloma ridges (meaning "at the foot of the hill"), or from the Bear Valley hills in the afternoon, to instantly understand the distinctive appeal which these Indian names must have made to those Nature lovers of old and which so infinitely outclass such prosaic titles as we in our time apply, as "Bear Valley," "Home Ranch," "Wildcat Gulch," etc.

In a previous note mention was made of San [sic] Rafael Garcia's selling of the Baulinas Rancho, one of the first Marin County Land Grants, to his brother-in-law, Pablo Briones of Monterey – and of his then receiving a grant of the adjoining Tomales y Baulinas Rancho of eight thousand four hundred acres to the north and one of the most fertile sections in all California. Since Garcia distinctively earned the title of "Father of Rancheros" in our county, some facts of his life history ought to be presented if for no other reason that that practically all of Olema's early history centers about the activities of this pioneer. As one reads the facts of this life journey and recalls that Garcia's was the first other-than-Indian family in Marin territory, one cannot fail to better understand the limitless field of the very essence of romance which so fills the period of California's early history and is as yet practically untouched.

Rafael Garcia[183] was a Californio, born at San Diego in 1790 and entered the military service there as a very young boy. He successively served at San Diego, Monterey, San Francisco, and San Rafael Missions as a military guard, and later at Sonoma, San Rafael, and San Jose missions as major domo (general overseer). His tenure at San Rafael is easily recalled from the traditional story heretofore noted of his pausing in plans to repel an expected Indian attack, to place his wife and bambinos in charge of the venerable Mission Padre Amoros, starting them adrift on a frail "bolsa" or tule float on an outgoing tide – then in Garcia style returning to a successful rout of the enemy.

---

[182] Actually, it is a Coast Miwok word meaning "coyote."
[183] Rafael Garcia (1799-1866), a corporal in the guard at Mission San Rafael, was granted Rancho Tomales y Bolinas, and was the first settler at Bolinas. He later moved to Olema to allow his brother-in-law Gregorio Briones to occupy Bolinas.

In 1837 he built a large adobe house at his new rancho in the Olema Valley, which in time came to be known far and wide as the most complete and extensive Hacienda appointment in northern territory, and the typically hospitable center for any wayfarer no matter who he might be. Naturally the Garcia family had a large entourage in consequence and because justly celebrated as indicating the type of the famed Spanish centers of agricultural posts of the West, all of which were mainly copied after the stiffly efficient Mission establishments of earlier days. Garcia soon had several thousand head of cattle and hundreds of horses, and in addition great herds of sheep and hogs roamed over his lands. In fact the Garcia rancho plant and equipment was described again and again by the world travelers as one of the most complete in the West. Garcia had naturally gathered about him the best of the Mission Indian workers who gratefully remembered his direction of them there, and whose only aim in life was now to be domiciled and provisioned in return for constant service.

Nevertheless a long life of roving exploration and expeditions without end had totally unfitted Rafael Garcia for the peaceful happy days of Rancho life after the zest of the development and upbuilding of a complete plant had passed. Therefore, leaving his family in possession of Olema, who refused to take up a new trail, he journeyed to Mendocino where he soon had a new Rancho grant of huge proportions. Yet he was too far along in life, and in particular without the former incentives of providing a family home and subsistence – and later rejoined the home circle at Olema. There his energies were directed toward making his properties entirely self-sustaining. His hides were tanned and converted into foot wear for his people and workers, and even his wool became clothes at the home place, so easy it was to obtain endless Indian labor thoroughly trained in Mission trades. In this way Garcia must be accorded the honor of the first manufacturing plant in Marin, and strangely enough his lands afterward became the location of several pioneering manufacturing industries on the coast. Yet Rafael's open-handed generosity to the countryside in the end became his ruin, for as soon as it became known – and such news traveled fast – that Rafael never allowed any visitor to depart without being loaded down with presents of whatever nature the Garcia plant was possessed, he had plenty of friends and plenty of visitors, and a steadily increasing number of artisans to keep these hungry hordes supplied with remembrances of the Garcia prodigality.

Eight of his sons and daughters grew up in the midst of this unrivaled prosperity, and had little reminder of the long life of hardship and privation of the parents, nor little preparation to note and prevent the ever-growing circle of despoilers which centered on the Garcia properties. So the old couple, utterly unable to retain the wealth of money which came to them through sale of lands and properties, suffered bitter adversity in their closing days, yet in the midst of his dreams of former splendor, old Rafael never lost the old-time unquenchable spirit. Naturally enough in the days when settlers came flocking in, this old timer generously clipped off ranch after ranch from his great estate, eager to welcome and provide for new neighbors, yet unable to himself retain the rewards therefore. Thus it was that when the rush for the famed agricultural lands of Marin County was at its height, and Tomales territory was quickly exhausted, Olema also came into its own and promptly gained its real start. The last sad chapter closing the old Garcia regime is an old newspaper item noting the suit, foreclosure and loss to creditors of the large remaining Garcia holdings for a pitiful few hundred dollars debt. Such endings of pioneer prosperity are inevitable in any new country, mainly caused by an inability to change one's nature and plans as the country itself and the new people develop away from the old practices and old traditions, and this is but a typical tale all through the great West.

15 March 1923

Olema's first known building other than the Garcia home, was the erection of Winslow's[184] "Olema House" in 1857 for a hotel and store, afterward adding a post office in 1859 and a stage center in later years. Gifford's[185] "Point Reyes House" followed in 1860, [Manuel] Levy's store in 1864, and John Nelson[186] completed the first dwelling house about the same time. Both of the hotels noted were destroyed by fires in 1876 and the present Olema Hotel erected later by John Nelson and is still conducted by

---

[184] Benjamin Terry Winslow (1822-1875), born in Freetown, MA. He was the first postmaster of Olema.

[185] John Gifford later built the Flagstaff Inn at Bolinas, the western terminus of the Bolinas-San Rafael stage.

[186] John Nelson built the Olema Hotel in 1876. Largely destroyed when used as troops barracks during World War II, it has now reopened under the same name.

his sons. All of this activity followed the lumbering interests at Bolinas, Olema Valley, and Nicasio points, and especially from the fact that Olema (the wharf was near present Inverness Park) was a port of call for the Tomales-San Francisco steamer line. Olema thereby became the supplies distribution point for all central Marin County. Following the Garcia days of plenty, John Nelson and his pride in the development of the Olema territory became the center of its activities and his widely-known hotel as a popular vacation resort for travelers desiring country life. When the White's Hill road was built, Nelson ran a stage to San Rafael for years and even after the railroad communication was effected, this ride was a very popular week-end undertaking for San Francisco people.

As directly indicative of the new tenure at Olema, a fine new school building was erected as early as 1860, the material being obtained by subscription and citizens donating their labor. Note the typical pioneer structure of "fourteen by eighteen feet, weather-boarded and shaked." Six years later another school district was formed, and a third added in 1878. Under such leadership Olema came to be, next to Tomales, the most busily thriving section of Marin County, and anxiously strove to have the county seat located there, in fact succeeded in having the State Assembly pass a bill therefor. But its difficult access conditions decided otherwise and San Rafael retained the prize by decisive vote of the entire county[187].

In its balmy days, the pioneer paper mill of the Pacific Coast was established five miles east of Olema, on Daniels (now called Papermill) Creek[188] and in 1867 reached an output to the amount of $64,000 worth of paper. In later years a fine modern machinery plant building replaced the first outfit and was burned down some years ago. Some of us have pictures of the great old water wheel there, and of the attractive lake and mill dam, through at present a pile or two and a bit of engine bed masonry are the only mute reminders of past activities. Similarly a masonry pillar above Camp Taylor[189] but slightly reminds us of the tremendous lumbering activities down through the Lagunitas Valley in the old days. The Taylor papermill

---

[187] The fight to retain San Rafael as the county seat was led by Jerome Barney, editor of the *Marin Journal*.

[188] The Pioneer Paper Mill, operated by Samuel Penfield Taylor (1827-1886), who bought a schooner with some friends and sailed around the Horn to San Francisco for the gold rush.

[189] Now Samuel P. Taylor State Park.

had been preceded a few years further up the valley by a powder factory plant, which at one time reached an output of thirty thousand kegs of blasting powder and two thousand packages of the sporting article. But like all early day plants of this nature, it suddenly disappeared in an instant one November day in 1877[190], and though quickly rebuilt, never regained its former output. A third industry had its inception some years later in the attempted development of lime quarries on the Bolinas Road, traces of which are still seen along the roadside there[191]. While rumors still persist that the Russian colony at Ft. Ross, 1825-1841, operated these kilns, the statement has come down to us because some men of Russian nativity operated them years afterward. All that remains of these active Olema days are the Garcia, Taylorville, and Tocaloma names of railroad stations along this once busy Papermill stream.

West of Olema village the Payne Shafter[192] extensive acreage stretches almost to the ocean and is the largest remaining section of the old Garcia rancho of early days, which the widely-known Judge Shafter[193] so highly developed, and in Payne Shafter Senior's time was the best organized ranch in the Olema territory, and a center of old time country gatherings. Across the ridge from this home is one of the most beautiful drives in all California, the Olema-through-Bear-Valley to Bolinas-by-the-Sea trip. It is a practically indescribable and particularly diversified joy of shady woods and giant trees, especial prodigality of western ferns, has all-the-way-along tinkling brooks, inimitable sea views, a charming "three lakes" section, and an open, mesa-like huge table land from which perpendicular cliffs of great height drop off to the sea beach far below, and extend for miles and miles along the coast. Real nature lovers of the hiking fraternity swarm along this route, which is happily as yet closed to automobile trips on account of its narrow, primitive and distinctly dangerous road for ordinary machines.

---

[190] Actually, Taylor's powder mill blew up in 1874.
[191] The kilns, still visible just west of Highway One, were built by James A. Shorb and William F. Mercer in 1850. They were only fired a few times.
[192] Payne Jewett Shafter (ca. 1835-after 1927) arrived by sail in San Rafael with his father James and two brothers in 1856. He became a rancher in Olema and sold some of his land to Neil McIsaac in 1893.
[193] James McMillan Shafter (1816-1892), born in Vermont, became Secretary of State there; then moved to Wisconsin where he was Speaker of the House. In 1856 he came to California and was President Pro Tempore of the Senate and a Judge of the San Francisco Superior Court.

East of Garcia Station[194] resides another old Marin resident, Charles Allen[195] by name, an experienced ornithologist and taxidermist, and an authority on early Marin days and especially on any phases of its past or present wonderful wealth of scenic botanical, hunting, animal, piscatorial or bird life. Acquaintance with this old timer recalls the anonymous lines of:

"I'm glad the sky is painted blue;
I'm glad the earth is painted green;
And such a lot of nice fresh air
All sandwiched in between."

In the same way the welcome one gets at Shafter's bring to mind Foley's[196]:

"Good morning, brother kindness,
Good morning, sister cheer,
I heard you were out calling,
And so I waited here."

No section which has such fertile land as the Olema Valley possesses can be long held back from full development, and the wide areas still untouched there, as well as the certain to come new types of farmers and farm crops assure a glowing future for this beautiful section. Coupling its scenic beauty [and] definite climatic superiority over all surrounding territory, with this natural and abundant wealth of soil, the Olema Valley has as glowing a future now as it once had as the distributing center for Central Marin County in the early days.

(End of Olema's early history)

---

[194] A former settlement and station on the train line two miles east of Point Reyes Station.

[195] Charles Dennison Allen (1843-1921) came to Marin at the age of eleven with his father Oliver on the *Mayflower*, which his father and sixty other men purchased and sailed around the Horn.

[196] James W. Foley (1874-1939), American poet from North Dakota.

22 March 1923

Point Reyes

Point Reyes and vicinity is as little known to a majority of Marin County people as it is to other California folk up and down the coast and by Americans in general. Yet all the foreign histories virtually make it a starting point of western American History from the time of Cortez in the sixteenth century to the nineteenth in our time. Marin county school children will invariably tell you that "it is a railroad station up on Tomales Bay," and others more distant recall it as "a north coast point of many shipwrecks." Indeed, our people usually think of it as a place of perpetual fog, endless sandhills and an especially rocky coast. We seldom hear of it except when a smuggler's crew is apprehended there or an occasional vessel comes to grief on its shores. Also some wag now and then finds a "relic" of Drake's visit and we then have the story in all varieties.

Nothing could be further from the truth than these ideas about the Point Reyes country, and few places on the coast have a more certain future in development when proper roads are constructed and a century old industry is intensified or diversified into several other lines adaptable to the territory. Historically there is said to be no other point on the Western Hemisphere whose discovery by Old World explorers had such an immediate, continuous and lasting effect upon the Old World affairs and around which can be centered the great World changes which brought about the intensive development of North America. The main facts of the early history of Point Reyes were briefly noted in an earlier chapter of this series, and if properly presented by skillful instruction would vividly interest any school child.

But Chapman's recent translation of old Spanish records shows that the wreck of Rodriguez Cermenho's[197] vessel in 1595, the "*San Augustin,*" was perhaps more directly accountable for the establishment of Spanish Missions from Mexico to San Francisco than any previously mentioned cause. We owe this version to the Native Sons' History Scholarship Fund, and this latest contribution is of especial interest in that it more clearly and definitely gives an account of as long a stay as Drake and a decidedly more

---

[197] Sebastião Rodrigues Soromenho (c. 1560–1602) (in Spanish, Sebastián Rodríguez Cermeño), born in Sesimbra Portugal.

definite account of the early Indians, inland country, animals, etc., than the fantastical tales of Chaplain Fletcher of the Drake party. While this note belongs to an earlier chapter that this series, it is now added a year late as the *Journal* goes to press on the Point Reyes article.

It seems that Drake's party, probably with hidden purpose, had return[ed] through the famed Straits of Anian (Northwest Passage). Then the Spanish ambassador in London learned of preparations for a second Drake expedition and hurried plans were made in Spain to circumvent him. About the same time[198] Francisco de Gali gave hint of a great California coast line, as occasionally viewed on a Manila-Acapulco trip via the northern current route. He it was who first advised a northern port of call on the Orient route for vitally needed health and supplies purposes. Then the English raider Cavendish[199] demolished the New Spain Pacific commerce plans, spreading alarm to all quarters but, like Drake, escaping via India back to England with the spoils from the richly-laden galleon "*Santa Ana*." Hawkins came to grief on the third English attempt of the same kind, but as a result of this raiding the King of Spain ordered a survey of the California coast for an available port.

Rodrigues Cermenho left Manila in the "*San Augustin*" for this purpose and eventually arrived at Drake's Bay. There he was careful to send his vessel far off shore each night as a protection from unknown shores, and held his crew on shore to build a smaller boat for survey purposes. But within a few days [of the] completion of this small sailboat, the "*San Augustin*" was mysteriously wrecked[200] and the party marooned on shore. Thus the slight accident of the vessel's wreck at this time and place completely changed the history and subsequent international division of the whole world, because Cermenho's previous carefully carried-out survey plans along the coast would have undoubtedly discovered the great western bay to the south and made it a thoroughly protected Spanish base for the Pacific extensions, besides effecting an immediate overland junction with the Spanish territory on the southwest Atlantic coast and in the West Indies.

It is this wreck incident that directly concerns Point Reyes. Cermenho completed the launch, made two expeditions inland for food supplies, and with seventy men set sail in the frail craft for far away Acapulco, which he

---

[198] 1584.
[199] Sir Thomas Cavendish (1560-1592), English explorer and privateer.
[200] Late November 1595.

reached with only a few men two months later. Truly a remarkable journey from Manila and one worthy of an intimate story when the Spanish Archives are thrown open to complete historical research. Cermenho had remained on Point Reyes shores for about thirty-two days. Some of his men returned to Drake's Bay in 1610 with the Cabrillo[201] party and it was primarily due to the previous enthusiastic descriptions of our northern Marin territory by the *"San Agustin"* survivors that Spanish preparations were hurriedly completed for a start on the long overland Missions conquest of northern Mexico and California as a shield for the military advancement. Further, it is noted that from that time all diaries of exploring parties traveling north had Point Reyes as its objective and had any one of these been able to cross or encircle San Francisco Bay, then Drake's Bay would of a certainty, have been the fortified northern outpost of Spanish conquest, if not a new base for still further northern advances.

Therefore, in Point Reyes and the great territory we now include under that general name, Marin County has a priceless heritage which some day will be a Mecca for all world travelers. Upon its shores was celebrated the first Christian Church service on Pacific shores, and eventually some great memorial in commemoration thereof will be located where it rightfully belongs instead of at San Francisco where it was placed mainly because there were no proper leaders in Marin County to claim it, as well as practically no communicating roads for outside people to so consider it.

The Point Reyes territory is a principality in itself. As early as 1838 the Pierce dairy[202] on Tomales Point was the first up to date modern dairy in all California and almost until recent years was the premier producer and a center of the thriving Marin dairying interests. There appears to be no record of the earlier Point Reyes settlers, other than the fact that returned sea-folk were living there as far back as 1834. They were probably deserting sailors who were satisfied with the abundant wild game, sea food, and Nature's bounty in berries and other wild products which abound out there – and so were content to live amid such peace and plenty for their remaining years. Some of them, however, were retired sea captains and others, who had probably landed at Drake's Bay at some time or other for

---

[201] Juan Rodríguez Cabrillo (Portuguese: João Rodrigues Cabrilho (1499-1543) was a Portuguese navigator in the service of Spain. He discovered San Diego, the Channel Islands, Santa Barbara, and Monterey.

[202] Built by Solomon Pierce in 1858.

fuel or water, and in later years hied away there to enjoy remembered charms of its territory and simple life of peaceful retirement.

29 March 1923

Lieutenant Joseph Warren Revere of the *U. S. S. Cyane*, gives an interesting, exciting, or pitiful (as the reader may decide) account of elk hunting on this peninsula in 1846.

There were so many elk in Marin County in those days that it is surprising to find so little literature thereon and stories of elk hunting trips to tell us more accurately about such early Marin matters. The writer has heard several old timers tell of elk hunts here, and as late as 1865 occasional mention of Marin elk is found here and there in papers of the period. Every few years elk horns show up on Corte Madera and San Rafael ridges when it happens that some landslide or surface disturbance uncovers them. Lieutenant Revere was an American Navy officer who was sent to Sonoma to officially raise the American Flag when the California Bear Flag was lowered there. It was when he was sent with a small party into Marin County to disperse a rumored crowd of organized Mexican sympathizers that the episode of his Marin elk hunt occurred. In late years he returned to claim the San Geronimo Rancho occupied by Rafael Cacho, a mission Indian product[203], but although Revere was in possession for some time his claim was disallowed. He was a descendant of Paul Revere of Revolutionary War days.

Concerning the Marin elk hunt, on learning that the supposed hostile party of Mexicans was only an assemblage of hunters gathering at the San [sic] Rafael Garcia Rancho, he sent his armed party home and joined the expedition. He at once noticed that the Spaniards were mainly armed with the so-called "rancherios rifle" or riata, and that some vaqueros prepared a "lima" weapon enroute. This would correspond to our taking an old-fashioned cycle blade and fastening it on a long pole, and when horsemen rushed upon the fleeing elk, the man behind this murderous weapon would reach out and ham-string the poor animals, leaving them here and there as the chase proceeded and the[n] returning for leisurely knife work.

---

[203] Rafael Cacho was actually a Mexican military officer. He was granted the rancho in 1844 by Governor Manuel Micheltorena.

The hunting party pursued a band of several hundred elk, driving them on toward the present lighthouse point, where the peninsula grew constantly narrower. Finally the slaughter began, and a typical slaughter it must have been between the wicked "lima" weapon, the ready riatas, Revere's buckshot outpourings, and the crashing of maddened animals over the precipices there. It is comforting to note that the Lieutenant did not approve of the methods used. He speaks of the sufferings of the poor hamstrung animals, of the wounded elk struggling at the bottom of steep declivities over which they had been driven, and of one noble old buck strenuously resisting the efforts of several riata throwers to bring him down. This one incident may serve to offer a cause for the speedy extermination of Marin County elk. Note is made of one vaquero coolly sitting upon his horse which was holding a lassoed elk, the rider "addressing the struggling animal by the familiar title of 'cunado' (brother-in-law), pleasantly assuring him that 'we only want a little of your lard wherewith to cook some tortillas (meal cakes)'," which joke the resisting animal seemed to be in no humor to relish.

Another Point Reyes elk hunt shows that an elk drive was occasionally made toward Tomales Point, a still worse trap for the huge animals. When corralled there they had no possible chance of doubling back, because the land narrows to a "V" point. A few escaped across Tomales Bay, but as a party of hunters on the far distant shore awaited their arrival, they were quickly despatched there. Surely such accounts as these show the need for our great state to now maintain a Fish and Game Commission to control equally repugnant methods of market hunters, hide and horn collectors, game hogs in general and poachers in particular – all of our own day and time.

Point Reyes Township includes the largest undivided original land grant holdings of our county, and because renters merely come and go, no definite improvements are made there, and no new homes developed. On the other hand, however, the leases are explicit and so specified that conditions of the properties and such matters remain unchanged as the lessees arrive and depart. Snook's[204] grant of the Punta de los Reyes Rancho numbers 8872

---

[204] Joseph E. Snook (1798-1848) was born in Weymouth, England and became a ship master, making numerous trips between Peru and California. He settled in San Diego and in 1833 converted to Catholicism and became a Mexican citizen. He married Maria Antonia Alvarado in 1837. He bought the land on Point Reyes in 1838.

acres, and Osio's of the Punta de los Reyes Sobrante Rancho of 48,089 acres, were the original holdings and made up an isolated peninsula of excellent grazing territory. One has but to think of the wonderful development which would take place on this great section if a colony of hardy coast people of Europe settled there under ownership terms. Some experiments are now being made concerning new crop possibilities, but while the elderly owners of this vast domain retain control, but little changes will result. For pure sea air, filled with fog at times and plenty of wind at others, the climate is always cool yet vigorously stimulating. It is no territory for an invalid but the healthy folk out there and their sturdy children tell the real story of Point Reyes climatic conditions.

A. M. Osio, one of Gov. Micheltorena's retainers, was given this large grant in the closing days of Mexican control in the period of scramble to get all land grant territories out of danger of American ownership. Being so isolated, no one else cared to contest the award. Both Snook's and Osio's titles were proved up by Randall, probably by agreement, and the holdings thus thrown together. Osio lived at San Rafael as a country estate owner. He built the first adobe structure far out on the peninsula in 1843. Numbers of small shacks appeared and disappeared from time to time on the several inlets of Tomales Bay as tenants drifted here and there. The first boat built on Tomales Bay was launched from Keatley's Gulch on Tomales Point in 1856. The Steele brothers[205] were the pioneer dairymen and conducted a large business at the head of Limantour Bay, and other settlers followed soon afterward.

Two School Districts were formed as settlers began to come in, one at Point Reyes and the other on Tomales Point (the Pierce District).

5 April 1923

In 1870 Uncle Sam finally erected a lighthouse on the extreme land's end, after numbers of vessels had come to grief up and down the coast for want of a guiding light. As indicative of the trend of swirling currents in the vicinity of this dangerous coast, there is no record of any vessel ever getting off again once grounded there. This Point Reyes light is one of the

---

[205] George, Isaac, and Edgar Steele and their cousin Rensselaer came from Ohio in the 1850's and established dairies on Point Reyes.

most powerful made, and in later years the safeguard to mariners was supplemented by a fog siren station and more recently by a Life Saving Coast Patrol station. Point Reyes [line missing] point of land, and all over the world mariners know of it a graveyard of many ships. By reason of its nearness to San Francisco Bay, and of the trend of currents apparently toward its shore and reefs, many navigators have lost their vessels there for lack of precaution rather than from unescapable dangers. Before 1870 a major portion of the many disastrous wrecks were caused by inexperienced captains steering into its forbidding shore in heavy fogs thinking that they were enroute through the Golden Gate.

For example, the English merchantman *"Cambridge"* calmly sailed up the narrow Tomales Bay entrance one perfectly clear day in 1856 – stranded of course – and then sent a boat ashore to ask whether that were San Francisco Bay. Needless to say, the *"Cambridge"* sill lies in Tomales Bay sands and will forevermore. Then the "Sea Nymph" struck on Point Reyes in 1861[206] with all sails set and was slowly destroyed. The "Sea Nymph" carried a cargo valued at $60,000 and consigned to William T. Coleman who later resided in San Rafael. It was sold "as is" on board for $6000 only, and the salvagers made a fortune therefrom.

This shipwreck uncovered a hero well worthy of the present system of Carnegie Medals for such unselfish acts. The captain and several men were capsized in the breakers when attempting to land and helplessly battled for their lives. C. S. Abbott[207], a spectator, promptly loosened several riatas from nearby saddles, knotted them together and with one end about his waist and the other held by bystanders, rushed into the breakers and with a free riata recovered the men one after another.

Then the *"Warrior Queen"* from Auckland, drove ashore[208] but managed to drop her anchors in holding ground. Unable to land thru the surf, the small boats proceeded to San Francisco. When the *"Warrior Queen"* was deserted in the night, shoremen could see no sign of life on

---

[206] Saturday, May 4, 1861.
[207] Carlisle S. Abbott (1828-1920) was born in Ontario and came overland to California in 1850 and settled at the H Ranch on Point Reyes in 1858. He moved to Monterey in 1865.
[208] July 20, 1874.

board next morning. Thereupon, Henry Claussen[209], an ex-sea captain and nearby rancher, took a line and swam out to the vessel to render possible aid. On arrival he inferred that the crew had put to sea because all papers and instruments were gone. The vessel was later wrecked for its copper bottom, for in those days there were no towing vessels to pull ships free.

Three years later a Russian man-of-war[210] stranded at almost the same spot. It was being sailed by an English chart showing a lighthouse on Point Reyes – six years before any lighthouse was placed there. From this vessel a crew of 150 people were all saved, but the vessel broke to pieces. A schooner capsized off the point and all were lost.

Some time later a cord-wood schooner came to grief on Point Reyes also.

Few San Franciscans know that practically all the early day granite used in San Francisco came from a quarry near Drake's Bay. Since there were no railroads then, the rock was quarried and floated down to San Francisco on huge barges. Finally, as communications developed and other deposits became known, vigorous and successful protests were made to Uncle Sam against further allowance of granite quarrying from the lighthouse reservation. This granite was dark in color but perfectly adapted for street flagging, curbs and foundation walls. A second nearby find of the best gray granite was never thoroughly developed.

Naturally the eastern edge of Point Reyes township has developed the most rapidly on account of the railroad, lumbering and wood industries and a more adaptable agricultural and other industries locality. Some years ago Inverness narrowly "escaped" having a great country hotel erected to the west on the mesa above the present village, a site somewhat reminding one of the pictured "Banff" hotel in Canada, since the narrow entrance of Tomales Bay and its enclosing high ridges give that sheet of water every appearance of a mountain lake. Only a few years ago Inverness was merely known by a dairy ranch there. Clearly showing what possibilities are in store for such beautiful settings on Marin's bridges, is the fact that this dairy section of a few years ago is now a congested summer resort and contiguous to many others with similar intent. For years Inverness had a fine sand beach but now the best bathing is half a mile west of the village.

---

[209] Hinrik Nicholaus Johan Claussen (1819-1872) was born in Sweden and settled at the G Ranch in 1871.

[210] The Russian screw corvette *Norvick*, on September 26, 1863.

For years more or less desultory efforts have been made to build a road out to Point Reyes, since the three U. S. stations there are difficult to reach over slipping sands. When that is done a certain-to-be-placed Drake's memorial will be located where it should be – on the shores where Drake really landed – and the great undeveloped sections of present Pt. Reyes will be broken up into small holdings and many new home circles result. And further, once the proper transportation is provided, and marine artists discern this one place on the coast where real waves crash on the shore – a series of pioneer shacks will again appear in the gulches just as they did in the early period. Perhaps they will be [for] different purposes, yet their denizens will be similarly bound to the shore lines by love of the sea and its mildest moods; – and Point Reyes can provide angry waves to any degree of perfection desired, probably offering the wildest water at short notice of any point on the Pacific Coast.

(End of Point Reyes early history)

19 April 1923

Marin's Educational Development

It is indeed a simple matter to make up a history of education of a community by compiling a consecutive record from its beginning as noted in existing files or previous reviews. But when we find that available records deal only with matters of the past fifty years, and at the same time one knows that prior to this there was a period of about three hundred and twenty years of no definite record – then the task becomes more difficult. To accomplish this, we must either intimately study the conditions governing in pioneer times and from knowledge of method in many places arrive at probable conditions here also – or we must, if we wish to make a consecutive account, read many volumes concerning early day affairs and supplement them with notes gathered from here and there.

Marin county records of an official nature concerning school matters exist from about 1870. Yet we have a fairly accurate account of Marin county educative matters in a broader sense since 1817, and more vaguely since 1542. If one were to intimately cover the "History of Education in Marin County" it would result in a voluminous treatise. Such review would include almost every art and practice known to man, as well as the later text book instruction. The earliest inhabitants here knew nothing of lasting methods or ideas, hence instruction followed by precept and example of the invaders to the western coast. Being unable to know which was of benefit or which was fatal to his tenure here, the early Indian was inevitably attracted to that time of impression and emulation which in the end denied his very existence.

While we are more interested in an account of the direct development of our schools and school buildings, there were nevertheless some earlier items which should be noted, the real foundations upon which later additions were builded. A school's development is usually considered as a phase of development after pioneering is completed. In a broader sense, Marin's educative history might be termed "From Savagism to Civilization," if mention is made of matter prior to 1832, when definite schools instructions began for the children of Spanish families.

We have no direct or even legendary evidence that Cabrillo's visit to Drake's Bay in 1542 left any imprint on Marin's then children or their elders. We can well believe that these simple Indians thought of it as a visit from the heavens, but since seen from a distance the educative value may have been only a keener interest in the possibility of developing some way to themselves glide over the surface of the inland waters here. But all historians agree that early western Indians knew little and cared less about their ancestors, therefore did not hand down traditions to their children. We must therefore assume that the visit of Sir Francis Drake in 1579 afforded the first direct educative factors for Marin's aborigines, since through direct contact with these voyagers the early Indians first became aware that there were ideas, customs, habits, foods, and people differing from their own. Therefore in reviewing Marin's Educational Development, we can discuss the Aboriginal Period (to about the Mission Days of 1830), then the Pioneer Period (about 1865), and the organized Period (to the early eighties of this review).

Let us therefore begin with Drake's visit to Point Reyes on June 17th, 1579, when he sought a haven there for repairing his ships. Since his party remained for thirty-six days, primitive exchanges of educative value resulted. Attempts were made by both his party and the Indians who gathered from far and wide – to impart and receive instruction in respective languages. Also, the Reverend Fletcher, Drake's Chronicler, strenuously endeavored to afford the natives some idea of, or at least the forms of, the white man's religion. Fletcher's chronicles are so filled with fantastic descriptions that there seems to have been no space left for these more intimate and definitely historical items. An old tradition is said to have noted Drake's gifts of seeds, beads, and ship's biscuits – doubtless failing to have the simple children understand the difference between articles for adornment, for feasting and for agricultural purposes – as all the articles were gravely planted for later results! The sum total of Marin's educative processes in 1579 were therefor, only quiescent, and in the order of merely fleeting memories of a new faith, of new words or of a language which became mere sounds only – and regrets at only partial success with agricultural attempts. One must add that the use of metal edged tools must also have then become known to the natives, since theretofore trees were "bruised" down by persistent splintering with sharp stones whirled at the end of a long thong. Perhaps also, we can infer that the Indians learned new ways of preparing food and or storing supplies because before this they had roamed about for summer supplies, and virtually hibernated in winter, even in our equable climate. It is possible that in the operations of careening Drake's vessels and caulking the seams thereof, many articles strange to Indian knowledge were removed from the ship to their wondering gaze, yet after accounts thereof to more distant tribes no doubt were heavily derided in the then Indian way.

26 April 1923

In 1595 the natives gained much from the white man, because the Cermenon party only spent a forty-five day period at Drake's Bay, but its richly laden galleon was wrecked there, an extended inland survey party was conducted, and a smaller vessel built of the rescued timbers. The desperate attempts of this shipwrecked party to cultivate the Indians, learn their language, have them assist in gathering supplies, etc., etc., and finally to directly assist in building a ship – must have left some lasting traces of the white man's ways. Yet it is [a] far-fetched claim to date Marin's first instruction in the manual training arts from this Cermenon visit in 1595. Early in the seventeenth century the Viscaino visit to Pt. Reyes made no mention of a landing or of contact with Indians, hence no further education of the aborigines.

One would consider that these four visits of a strange people here – almost in one generation – would have left a generous tradition yet such is not the case. So we then pass over a period of nearly two hundred years, regarding which the mind of man knoweth not concerning this country. On August 6th, 1775, came the next, and in fact the "first" definite record of educative instruction in Marin territory. This was when Fray Vincente Santa Maria and party from the survey ship "*San Carlos*," landed with a party at Tiburon and were hospitably received and entertained by the natives there. The Spanish Father especially mentions his satisfaction on finding that patient instruction enabled the simple natives to repeat many Spanish words. Further, that the Indians instructed the seamen in the mysteries of making tamales, and acorn bread. From this record our claim can be made to definite languages and domestic science instruction for the first time in Marin County. Since the *San Carlos* was beached and dismantled at Angel Island for several weeks, one can infer that Fray Vincente continued his educational work with the natives, and directly paved the way for easy communication with the Spanish forces arriving the following year at San Francisco.

We next find that in 1776 a Spanish party under Captain Quiros, instructing the Indians at the Olompali Rancho in the art of making adobe bricks and constructing buildings thereof, while at the same time each people endeavored to learn the other's language over a period of several weeks. Thus again, languages instruction gained new progress, and when partially effected, resulted in valuable instruction to the Spanish explorers concerning geographical matters of the surrounding country. So Olompali claims to have instituted architectural matters in Marin. It still possesses one of these adobe walls, the earliest existing evidence of manual arts instruction in any north of the bay territory.

What an opportunity exists for our teachers to connect the activities in Marin County in this period with the strenuous days of 1776 on the Atlantic coast! How it would stimulate the interest and quicken the imagination of the average child to think of what pioneers of some of our present day families were doing in western lands for us – when most of our own ancestors were fighting back to back on the Atlantic Coast to establish a future for America.

3 May 1923

Next comes the real foundation of education in Marin county in the founding of the Mission San Rafael Archangel on December 4th, 1817 – because organized instruction then began and has continued consecutively to our own day here. Previous articles of the "Marin's Old Days" review have told the story of its work in detail, and from it we gain the facts of there having been organized, definite and fruitful results of a curriculum equally or perhaps more comprehensive than any of ours of the present period. At least it will compare as to being of a more intimately practical and disciplinary nature than that of a later period. Padre Gil taught the Indians how to prepare material for the distressed neophytes sent from the sick-ridden Presidio over the bay. Later, Padre Amoros arrived from Santa Clara, a scholarly, kindly, capable director whose success in Mission work was for fourteen years unexcelled anywhere in the West for comprehensive, definite results. His was the first "library" in the county, and his was the first completely organized instruction of mental, religious, productive arts, and future aim direction more nearly approaching all well-organized educative matters.

So we must rank the old Marin Mission as the first educational institution of the county. Religion, sanitation, agriculture, carpentry and construction, animal husbandry, rancho direction and simple accounting, domestic science and home making, weaving, pottery, basket making, music, dancing, games and equestrian feats, a program far beyond the range of any one man's ability in these times – were features of Padres Amoros' wise and efficient teaching. Prior to this the Indians had no horses, and riding became their chief diversion and employment. So also the natives learned how to catch fish, to capture small animals, to lure water fowl, etc., etc. The older people were merely "controlled" and used as laborers, while the young people were started on a twelve-year course of instruction intended to afford a thorough preparation for managing or owning a rancho. Two generations of a family at Olompali Rancho are all that are recorded as having finally been ceded lands in full ownership, while the terrible epidemic of measles and small pox in 1828 and 1835 doubtless broke up all previous endeavors because of the great loss of Indian lives everywhere.

There is a record that as far back as 1818, one Ramos de la Vegas probably had the direct scholastic work at the Mission, because from 1795 he had been schoolmaster at San Jose Mission, (at the munificent salary of $25 a year), and came to San Rafael with Padre Amoros.

In 1824 Don Timoteo Murphy donated lands for the St. Vincent's Seminary (now St. Vincent's School) which was opened January 7th, 1825, "for the maintenance and instruction of children in neighboring districts," in charge of Sister Francis McEnnis of the Sisters of Charity of San Franciscso. Doubtless the "gente de razon" children of the community were also instructed there because of the difficulties resulting from association with Indian children about the Mission properties. From the fact that school was held in the old adobe home of James Miller at Gallinas in 1849, near the St. Vincent School, there must have been some subsequent change in the plans regarding the purpose of the larger institution.

In 1849, James Miller erected the first frame building in San Rafael at the present Fourth and A Street corner, which was planned for school purposes and used therefor until 1871. The community then determined to erect a new structure and James T. Stocker proceeded to build "a structure 64 by 36 and two stories high," which is the present "B Street" building. Father Dobette, a missionary, first taught the school, though probably not a free school at that time, as it was customary for families with children to raise a fund for instruction purposes. In 1850, one Walter Skidmore is mentioned as taking charge of this instruction, and while teaching there, he studied law and later passed the Bar. In 1860 the Gilbert Institute was opened as a private school and flourished for many years.

In 1864, the San Rafael School census showed one hundred and thirty children between the ages of four and eighteen, and one under twenty-one. Of those, sixty-three attending public schools, and thirty did not attend any school. There were then only four Indian children of school age – a pitiful reminder of the once 1200 neophytes "studying" at the Mission. A Marin county census of January 22, 1862 gives 37 children in Novato; San Rafael, 174; Corte Madera, 74; Bolinas No. 1, 57; No. 2, 59; Tomales No. 1, 32; No. 2, 30; American Valley, 41; Chileno Valley, 51; San Antonio, 52 – a total of 607. The county census now gives the approximate total of 5345 school children.

10 May 1923

Marin territory became a county on April 25, 1851. Then the New Constitution of September 4, 1879 afforded the County Government Bill, whence the first public money for schools was authorized. Yet it was several years before any attempt was make [made] to organize the County Education matters. John Sims was Superintendent for three terms, 1857-60. Then Thomas J. Ables of Tomales, one term 1860-61; James Miller two terms, 1861-63; J. M. Zurer two terms 1863-65; Samuel Saunders one term 1875-76, and S. M. Augustine, 1877-80 for three terms.

It is interesting to note that several of Marin's pioneers were former school teachers in the East. William J. Dickson of San Geronimo Rancho; Ai Barney, founder of the *Marin Journal* and afterward County Judge; E. B. Mahon, a Bolinas merchant then attorney and for years the County Judge; and Thomas J. Ables of Tomales, were some of these gentlemen through whose efforts the county system of education was fostered and finally effected. Thomas J. Ables was the only Republican elected in 1860 and as Superintendent of Schools organized the county system on the promise of a salary when money was available. After a year's painstaking effort and definite completion of his labors, the then Board of Supervisors allowed him the sum of $300 for the year. Dr. George W. Dutton of Tomales was another ex-school teacher, who, after coming to the coast found that the greatest need was for physicians and straightaway prepared himself for that work. Every school child in Marin county ought to be told of the struggles made by these pioneers for proper educational facilities here and for the final foundation of progressive methods thereon.

Tomales' first school was built in 1857. There seems to be no record of the date of instituting public schools at Bolinas, but a second school there, the Bay View institution, was built in 1863 when the lumber industry began there. It was not used until 1876 and had two teachers up to 1880. Olema had the Olema and Garcia Schools in 1866. The first named was erected in 1860 by subscription and was built by the citizens themselves. It was a 14x18 room, weatherboarded and with a shake roof. An Englishman, James Band, was the first teacher, and boarded around among the various patrons in turn as part of his salary and held school for three months, or as long as the subscription provided for him. The Garcia School followed in 1866 as a 30x40, two story building. In 1878 the Garcia district was divided and a school built north of the station. Olema town was then in the district. In 1866 the Nicasio-San Geronimo folks built a small school and in 1871 erected a 35-45 building at an expense of $3000, which was for many years the most substantial and pretentious school structure in the county. Novato erected a small building in 1858, and a much better one in 1875. A recent substitution there, now places Novato in the front ranks of modern school equipment. The Pt. Reyes-Pierce Districts held a grand Fourth of July Clam Bake, on which occasion ample funds were raised for their school buildings. Naturally, since San Antonio, Chileno Valley, Laguna, Richardson's, Sausalito, and Reed's were all on very large land grants, the schools were small and conducted for a few months only among a few families. On March 11, 1871, J. A. Richards, a local teacher, donated his books for a public library for Marin county, which was in those days of unusual assistance in educational work, since books had to be read to a number, and passed about, because of so few copies being available.

In these days of modern schools, complete and varied equipment, small classes, and specialist teachers, full year tenure, playgrounds, etc., etc., is it any wonder that the youth of today has little knowledge of the earlier struggles or ambitious students or patience with the ideas of the older generation who had to make the most of the meagre opportunities before them. The recent newspaper articles of James Wilkens on pioneer schools afford an account of further Marin county educative matters subsequent to 1870.

(End of Educational)

(Continued next week)

[The Marin's Old Days column ended at this point.]

CPSIA information can be obtained
at www.ICGtesting.com
Printed in the USA
FSHW02n1253101018
52908FS